# On the Way
# to the Wedding

ALSO BY LINDA SCHIERSE LEONARD

*The Wounded Woman: Healing the Father-Daughter Relationship*

# ON THE Way TO THE Wedding

## Transforming the Love Relationship

Linda Schierse Leonard

SHAMBHALA
BOSTON & LONDON
1987

Shambhala Publications, Inc.
314 Dartmouth Street
Boston, Massachusetts 02116

9  8  7  6  5  4  3  2  1

FIRST PAPERBACK EDITION
Printed in the United States of America
Distributed in the United States by Random House
and in Canada by Random House of Canada Ltd.

*The Library of Congress catalogues the original
edition of this work as follows:*

Leonard, Linda Schierse.
   On the way to the wedding.

   Bibliography: p.
   1. Marriage.  2. Love.  3. Interpersonal relations.
I. Title.
HQ734.L392   1986        646.7'8        85-27888
ISBN 0-87773-349-x
      0-394-55250-4 (Random House)
      0-87773-402-x (pbk.)

Design/Joyce C. Weston, Boston
Typesetting/Graphic Composition, Athens, Georgia
in Linotron Garamond #3

Front cover: *Mädchen mit Pfingstrosen* (*Girl with Peonies*), by
Alexej von Jawlensky. Oil painting, 101 × 75 cm., 1909,
courtesy the Von der Heydt-Museum der Stadt Wuppertal.
© 1987 by Cosmopress, Geneva.

# CONTENTS

ACKNOWLEDGMENTS ix

PREFACE: THE SEARCH FOR A SOULMATE I

*Part One: The Wandering* 13
  1. Through the Woods 17
  2. Prince Charming and the Special Princess 25
  3. The Ghostly Lover 39
  4. The Bewitchment 63
  5. The Demon Lover 77
  6. The Ring of Power 111

*Part Two: The Loving* 131
  7. Into the Clearing 135
  8. The Missing Bridegroom and the Woman
    in Black 149
  9. Beauty and the Beast 165

*Part Three: The Wondering* 187
  10. The Divine Wedding 191
  11. The Veil 205
  12. The Vow 221
  13. The Ring of Love 245

NOTES 253
CREDITS 261

*For Keith,*
*who inspired this book*

# ACKNOWLEDGMENTS

The process of writing this book has been graced with help from many people. I would like to thank everyone and especially the clients, workshop participants, and friends who so generously shared their dreams, visions, and stories. I am especially grateful to Keith Chapman, the soulmate who inspired and encouraged the writing of this book with his love, creative insights, dialogue, and help with revision; to Emily Hilburn Sell, editor of Shambhala Publications, my editorial midwife and "analyst," who helped me give birth to this book through her finely tuned intuitive eros and her ideas and editorial suggestions; to Stephanie Silva for the typing of the manuscript and for her loyalty to the process and her valuable insights; to the friends and colleagues who read the manuscript and gave me suggestions: Marjorie Foster, Donald Sandner, Harold Booth, Janine and Steve Hunter, Cindy Verson, Phyllis Kenevan, and Lara Newton-Ruddy; to Helmut Barz, who introduced me to Rilke's world; and to Marjorie and Gordon Foster, whose forty-five-year soul marriage has given me hope and inspiration.

# The Search for a Soulmate

Ever since I can remember I've longed for a soulmate. I was never particularly interested in marriage itself since my parents' marriage was so terrible. And when I was young I looked down on weddings. To me they were bourgeois, materialistic, nothing but "show." But a soulmate, that "other half," as Plato called it, that one who would make me whole, who would lead me to the divine mystery—was this not the very purpose of existence toward which life strives?

I grew up as an only child in a house full of anger and chaos. I had three parents who loved me—my mother, my father, and my grandmother—but because they were unhappy in their own lives and relationships they fought constantly, and each projected their idea of meaning in life onto me, not allowing me a life of my own. Shy and introverted by nature, I retreated into an imaginal world to find my own space. And in this world there was always one Other—a friend and companion with whom I explored and learned in various adventures and with whom I grew in soul. Together we fought witches, braved giants and dragons, ventured into enchanted forests, crossed oceans, climbed mountains, found new and adventurous lands. This was my secret, exciting world, safe and inviolable from the curious, possessive eyes of my parents.

With my imaginal companion in my secret world I could share my feelings, dreams, hopes, and fears and finally be myself. These secret companions, these soulmates, varied—sometimes a girl, sometimes a boy, sometimes an animal. When I read *The Black Stallion* by Walter Farley, my soulmate image took a new form as a couple, "the boy and the horse." Sometimes I was the boy in my fantasy and sometimes the horse, but this was a pair who loved each other faithfully in depth and explored the world adventurously together, a couple who loved each other so much they were willing to die for each other. In their relationship I saw through my child's eyes a wedding with the divine, a mysterious union that reached beyond the everyday world in which I lived and which embodied noble qualities: courage, questing, faith, loyalty, trust, sacrifice, confrontation with death. This was an ecstatic, transcendent, mysterious relationship of two beings who loved each other in a complete creative fidelity.

Another pair of soulmates with whom I lived were Heidi and her grandfather in the Swiss Alps. Heidi brought life and love to her isolated grandfather, who in his old age had become cynical and had lost a human relationship to love. Although she was an orphan with a difficult past, Heidi's élan vital and exuberant, adventurous spirit, and her relation to the mystery of the mountains and nature, infused all whom she met with new zest for life and a belief in new beginnings. This, too, was a divine wedding—of the spontaneity of youth and the wisdom of old age within the healing presence of nature.

Hansel and Gretel were another couple in my life. This romance with a soul-brother compensated for the brother I did not have, and it was sexually safe. In my adolescence, a period when I was cut off from men because of my revulsion and hatred toward my father, which I projected onto men and marriage, I wrote a number of short stories about my brother, "Bob." Together we struggled to get away from home to a better life. Like Hansel and Gretel, we outwitted the negative mother in her witch form, the one who was trying to keep us from growing. We ventured forth into the enchanted forest, daring the unknown to break the chains of our past.

Finally, a foursome became very important in my soul-world— Dorothy, the Scarecrow, the Tin Man, and the Cowardly Lion in the Land of Oz. Dorothy was a feminine self figure with whom I identified. She loved her foster parents, her aunt and uncle, and when she was unexpectedly whisked away to a strange new world by a tornado (as we are so often in dreams), she was receptive to her fate and went on the journey that was required to return to her home in a new way. She related to the new figures she met, appreciating the intelligence of the Scarecrow, the heart of the Tin Man, and the courage of the Cowardly Lion. She learned to accept their positive qualities in herself and to know the dangers of those who would obstruct her path: she learned the difference between the good witch Glinda, who could help her with her magical powers, and the Wicked Witch of the West, whom she had to kill.

When I look back now, these early soulmates seem to be a natural prelude on my way to the wedding. The boy and horse brought together the forces of human and animal power; Heidi and her grandfather united the young girl and the wise old man; Hansel and Gretel joined together the growing masculine and feminine within me; and Dorothy and her friends symbolized the integration of the feminine self with intellect, heart, and courage in a magical cosmos.

While all this discovery was happening inwardly, my outer life was chaotic and frightening. My father was drinking to the point of violence or stupor every night, my mother was anxiously working to support us and substituting me for her companion, and my grandmother was trying to protect me from the brutalities at home by encouraging me to develop my mind. Intellectually I was leaps ahead of myself, but physically I was years behind and emotionally I was very confused. In high school and college I was not part of the dating scene—I looked too young, and inside I was very frightened. My soul projection at this time went mainly to women teachers, as I needed some guidance from the feminine. My major concern was to get away from home, and all my energy went into study and professional preparation that could free me from the suffocating parental home. My mother wanted me to stay with her, and put pressure on me emotionally to do so, but I knew to save myself I must leave. Just at this time I read *The Fountainhead* by Ayn Rand. The architect Howard Roark, creative and independent, became my first erotic male soulmate, a symbol of the man for whom I was searching.

When I left home for my first job far away I fell in love for the first time. Like Howard Roark, this man was an architect, a creative man who dared to actualize his vision of organic architecture, of the wedding between human home and nature's transcendence. To me this man symbolized the searching creative spirit who refused to remain a slave to the status quo of the collective. And so I gave my heart and soul to him, hardly able to believe that such a man existed, ecstatic that such a relationship was possible. In my naiveté, it never occurred to me that such a man might be married. When I finally learned this fact, my heart was torn asunder. With my intense idealism I could not continue the relationship and so began my soul's search on a more conscious level to find meaning in this broken world.

In despair I turned to philosophy to try to understand. My experience with men and the childhood experience with my father had been devastating. But my soul's hope had broken through this devastation and with compensatory idealism I had envisioned a grand possibility for relationship—creative and without limitation, a vision surpassing the bonds of human finitude. Now, conscious in my despair of this broken vision, I had to try to understand what was humanly possible—if anything was possible at all. My first disillusionment in love had brought me before myself in a way that even my wounded childhood had not. And it brought me before all human suffering, before "human fate."

Down deep in depression I searched. I read the philosophers, trying to find a way to reconcile my heart's hope and my soul's despair. Was there an explanation of life's paradox? The existentialists alone spoke to me, for they spoke of the human condition, the wounds of mortality, the sickness in the soul, the alienation of the individual, the necessity to face death consciously, and, most important, the "courage to be." I spent my twenties in this way reading, studying, questioning, searching. I wrote my master's thesis on the notion of friendship, trying to understand the nature of human relationship. What was love all about? During this time I married a man who was searching, too. His search was for God, to reconcile the findings of theoretical physics with the divine mystery he experienced in the world about him. But his way was through Logos alone. I believe our marriage was a "wedding," a meeting of two souls on the same path, but it was only a partial wedding, more a meeting of minds than of whole people. Our wedding lacked the fullness of earth. We were both very wounded from our parental origins, and neither of us had yet dared the descent to face our suffering within. Instead we looked at the suffering of the world in the abstract and formed a united front against the travesties of the times. But we isolated ourselves in this way, finally turning away from each other. In isolating ourselves from the world, we ceased to grow and thus we grew apart.

After this marriage ended, it took many years of solitude and suffering to work through the pain of separation and the resentments I had harbored over those "unlived" years in my twenties (devoted so intensely to study and to Apollonian reason that the Dionysian zest for life had been excluded); nevertheless, my life's course was influenced creatively by this first committed soulmate. With him I learned the devotion and discipline necessary to follow a creative vision to its completion. And I learned to leap in the realm of knowledge, to take on the creative challenge no matter how difficult and dangerous the flight into the mind's outer reaches might seem. It was he who encouraged me to continue my studies in philosophy, to make the commitment to work for a Ph.D. degree. Together we discovered the philosophy of Martin Heidegger, a way of thought we found exciting in its dialogue with the great philosophers and poets of the past and its daring venture into the mysteries of Being and Time.

The philosophy of Heidegger gave my thought and experience a creative ground and offered a way for me to explore the great questions of life and love and death on my own quest for meaning. I wrote my doctoral dissertation on Heidegger, drawing out from his thought a way to re-vision the notion of detachment. For in my personal life I found myself so attached to people, places, and things that finally I was cut off, in a despair that detached me from life's vitality. The brothers in Dostoyevski's novel *The Brothers Karamazov* symbolized the figures battling in this great tension in my psyche: Dmitri, consumed by impulsive passion, and Ivan, the cynical, controlling rationalist—both hating the drunkard father who abused them. It was the younger brother, Alyosha, born of the same father but of a different and mystical mother, who loved them both and showed a different way, the path of loyal and faithful heart. And it was Alyosha whom I was seeking in myself, who twenty years later emerged for me as the inner "man of heart." As I struggled with these opposites in myself, the opposites of desire and fear, attachment and detachment, Heidegger showed me a way of thought that acknowledged that experience yet went beyond it to the greater mysterious rhythm of existence.

But as essential as philosophy was for me to give the Logos my father had been unable to provide, my emotional life was in crisis. I needed help to integrate these battling forces in my soul. I had found an existential ground for understanding. Now I needed the psychological way to guide me through the labyrinth of my confusing feelings. Around this time I discovered a deep, inspiring book—*Memories, Dreams, Reflections,* the autobiography of a pioneer of depth psychology, Carl Gustav Jung. From Jung I learned there was a new exciting world to explore—the world of dreams and symbols. I discovered that if I listened to the creative voice which spoke to me at night I could find my way through the labyrinth of my life into the open clearing where I might meet my soulmate. And so I went to Zurich to experience what a Jungian analysis might uncover. My first session of analysis, in which I was invited to open up my feelings, frightened me, and I left deciding not to return to this irrational realm. But my dream that night woke me up in terror, revealing a truth of my being. And so I made a vow to follow this path wherever it might take me.

In Zurich a new life began. Alone after the breakup of my marriage, committed to follow the path of my destiny, I knew the work to be done was within myself to transform the terrors of my traumatic childhood so that I could lead a creative life. This required of me a descent into the depths, into the uncontrollable regions of my psyche. Down there I met many of the figures that populate this book—the Ghostly Lover, the Demon Lover, the masculine muse. And, as is the nature of my path through life, I encountered some of these figures in my outer travels as well—the expressionist artists and German romantic poets who set my creative soul afire all over

Europe; the dark African Berber tribesman, who, like Pluto, took the pure Persephone one dark night in London; the guiding muses, my analysts who accompanied me through the dark and helped me through my "night sea journey"; the men of soul and heart personified in the poet Rilke, who helped me to my inner "man of heart"; and, most important, the manly mountain muse who broke through the ring of fire that encircled me to become my outer soulmate fourteen years later.

I have discovered in the course of my journey that life and psychic growth move in cycling spiral rings of descent and ascent. Every new growth in myself has been preceded by a descent of the seed into the dark ground. I began my first major conscious descent when I started analysis, and it culminated when I wrote *The Wounded Woman,* an effort to heal the father-daughter wound within me. For I knew that the redemption of the inner father was necessary to free me for a healthy and creative soul relationship with a mature man. Writing *The Wounded Woman* was the journey of my descent, and it was during that period when I encountered the obstacles of the bewitchment and the Demon Lover most intensely. But I did not effectively deal with these figures until the writing of this book. Writing *On the Way to the Wedding* has been my ascent from the depths.

Two major images emerged in my dreams during the writing of this book and transformed, changing my life, the man of heart and the feminine spirit. To find my way to the wedding I needed to develop both of these within myself. Both images had first appeared toward the close of writing *The Wounded Woman.* In that book the feminine spirit came toward me as a necessary future, but it was still vague, while the man of heart was still in the form of a young man in his twenties. As I started writing the present book, the man of heart appeared in my dreams as a mature, accomplished, and famous flute player. He was gentle and loving and looked at me with his large green eyes. As our eyes met we fell deeply in love, and a single tear glistened at his right eye. Then, to my dismay, I realized he was married. Here was the man of heart developed, but he was still unavailable. In another dream about this time, the feminine spirit appeared as a woman who lived in an artist's garret, with a hidden back room that was a museum containing ancient art works that were only to be seen there. She had a daytime dress of rich red wool which mysteriously changed to a long, elegant dress of luminous silver fur at night. She invited me to dinner, but she did not have enough food on hand to invite my lover, too. Here was the numinous feminine spirit, but she was unrelated to my lover. As I wrote *On the Way to the Wedding* and encountered the archetypal figures which spontaneously appeared, I underwent a change within myself. No longer, I realized, could I be the high-flying "eternal girl." This identity was no longer appropriate to the strength and consciousness I had achieved, nor to my current age, nor to the new committed relationship with my soulmate. I needed to sacrifice this old, constricting identity. Somehow the writing of this new book was a centering process for me, enabling me to move on to transform my energies. Finally I was graced with a wedding dream, which gave me a new image of the feminine spirit who opens up to love.

> I was at an open-air operatic performance of *The Ring* in a city that reminded me of Zurich. I had come in time for the last two operas. It was intermission, so I stepped onstage, an open clearing at the edge of a forest. To my right in the forest was a wedding couple dressed colorfully to sing in the opera. There was a drawing for two grand prizes to be awarded, one for each opera. I looked at my tickets, and I had both winning numbers.

I had this dream a few weeks before attending a performance of *The Ring,* Wagner's cycle of four operas. After seeing *The Ring,* I understood the meaning of my dream. *The Ring* is, in part, about the father-daughter wound and the struggle between love and power. The last two operas focus on the freeing of the daughter, *Brünnhilde,* a feminine warrior spirit whose divinity has been taken away by her father because she dared to defy him by trying to save the divine love of two human lovers. Brünnhilde, who embodies heart, courage, and wisdom, is freed by the hero Siegfried and falls in love with him, experiencing human passion. She feels the ecstasy of human love but also its suffering and the power of revenge when she thinks Siegfried has betrayed her. Ultimately she realizes she has to sacrifice her possessive love for the greater love of compassion.

Brünnhilde, was an image of the feminine spirit that I needed to integrate within to be on my way to the wedding.

Ten years earlier, when I started to write *The Wounded Woman,* my first woman analyst had suggested Brünnhilde as a feminine image that might help with healing the father-daughter wound. But I needed first to experience the descent into the rage and tears of my wound, into its humiliation and horrors before I could relate to an affirmative, powerful feminine figure. In my descent, through my own humiliation, I came to have compassion for my father and his suffering and to discover that the redemption could not come from the outside but only from finding the feminine spirit in myself. Only by allowing myself to fully experience the wound in all its horrific depth could I emerge with the courage, compassion, and wisdom I needed to enter a relationship with a soulmate.

To acknowledge my wounds in relationship in all their depth took faith that the wound could be transformed, that growth could come from suffering. I had spent many years alone after my marriage ended in despair, wondering if I would ever meet the soulmate for whom I longed. It was Rilke who helped me through this period. Reading about his struggle to find meaning and faith helped me transform my despair into affirmation. Rilke was my soulmate for many years and helped me find my inner man of heart. I had associated the flute player of my dreams with him, for Rilke, a musician of the word, valued the tear in the eye. He knew that sorrow was the ground for growth and that, like the seasons, our interior life grows in a cycle of transformation. His cycle of poems, the *Duino Elegies,* were his heart-work.

Over and over again I return to the wisdom in Rilke's poems. They inspire me and give me hope; they give me depth of feeling together with objectivity. I wanted to share my understanding of Rilke in this book because for me he is an example of the transformation process on the way to the wedding; he shows a way to make the vow. After I had finally finished writing about Rilke, I dreamed about a creative man who was a muse for me, the man who first introduced me to Rilke. And then I knew there was a wedding of the feminine spirit with the man of heart.

The outer relationship, with my soulmate has been an important part of the way to the wedding within myself. I have had to develop the inner feminine warrior spirit to hold my own in our dialogue and to learn when to give and when to receive. My soul partner has inspired me and challenged me to grow and transcend the artificial limits I had set for myself. At the same time, I have had to learn to accept the limits that a relationship requires. In the course of this relationship I have had to confront the inner obstacles that emerge in the first part of this book: the Ghostly Lover, Prince Charming and the Special Princess, the Bewitchment, the Demon Lover, and the Ring of Power. I have had to learn the lessons shown in the relationship of Beauty and the Beast. And finally I have come to see that the transformation process expressed in the last chapters—The Veil, The Vow, and The Ring of Love—are necessary for a creative relationship as well as for the creativity of an individual life.

The soul wedding is not always with a concrete outer soul partner. Rilke is an example. His wedding was with the inner creative muse, and his poems are the child of that relationship. Whether one lives the wedding in an outer relationship, in work in the world, or in a meditative life, it is the transformation within that provides the transcendent ground of the wedding.

"The Wandering," Part One of this book, explores some major archetypal obstacles in our psyche—obstacles that relate to parental and cultural influences, yet form as interior figures within our psyche. These are not the only psychological obstacles, but they are formidable figures to be confronted. The fairy tales and legends, the dreams and the stories I tell of my friends and my clients and of my own life struggles, all helped me to find a thread of meaning and a way through the dark woods of our mysterious journey through life. I present them as they came to me, as a spring wells up here and there, as the stars shine out differently during the night, lighting possible paths.

"The Loving," Part Two, explores some of the challenges to lovers when they meet—the fear of the unknown, possessiveness, power, anger, jealousy, learning how to separate and to come together. These, too, are stories of living individuals and stories that have been passed down through the ages—stories that have helped me in my search for love and in my learning to love.

"The Wondering," Part Three, explores the soul's wedding, the existential encounter with the divine, the search for meaning in human existence. The story of Rilke's search, expressed in his writings, mirrors the way to the wedding for all of us, whether we seek a wedding with a lover, with our creative work in the world, or with the divine. For it expresses the universal quest to affirm life in our divided human existence, an affirmation that provides the transcendent ground for any authentic wedding.

# PART ONE

# The Wandering

*The minute I heard my first love story*
*I started looking for you, not knowing*
*how blind that was.*

*Lovers don't finally meet somewhere.*
*They're in each other all along.*

RUMI

*For one human being to love another: that is perhaps the most
difficult of all our tasks, the ultimate, the last test and proof,
the work for which all other work is but preparation.*

RAINER MARIA RILKE
*Letters to a Young Poet*

# 1
# *Through the Woods*

The wedding is an image in which we humans delight. We long for the wedding day, dream about it, plan for its arrival. We hold elaborate ceremonies with wine, food, dress, song, and dance. Our mothers and fathers participate and often project their own unlived lives onto this event. And for many of us it embodies a spiritual union blessed by the divine. But paradoxically, just as we envision the wedding as a culminating point in our lives, we often dread it. Unconsciously we sabotage its actualization. The following dream images this paradox: the anticipation and readiness, yet the inability to commit because we don't know who our partner is and hesitate to ask or fear to risk a choice.

> The day of my wedding had arrived. I was excited and went to the door to greet the groom. But as I was about to open the door I blushed because I realized I didn't know who was the groom. I was in a quandary and unable to greet anyone because I didn't want to make a mistake. Everyone else at the wedding knew who the groom was, but I was afraid (ashamed) to ask.

When the wedding possibility approached me recently, I was overjoyed. My whole life seemed to be a journey to this end. I had studied philosophy, become a Jungian psychoanalyst, even written a book about fathers and daughters to try to free myself to meet a partner. Now I had met the man and he had proposed. A new book about this was forming in my mind. A title appeared: *On the Way to the Wedding*. And numinous dreams of bridal couples, real and mystical, illuminated my nights. But then came a series of events, inner and outer, which blocked my path. We consulted the *I Ching* for its oracular wisdom. The hexagram received was Obstruction, with moving lines which changed to The Well. For me the wedding was not only an outer event. To be sure, it had always meant a committed soul relationship with a man I loved, a relationship in which we would both grow creatively in the challenge of each other's mystery. But it also meant a union with the inner lover, with that man of heart who appeared so often in my dreams. As inner event, it meant nothing less than a spiritual transformation which would lead me to a new relationship with the cosmos. It meant within me a marriage of heaven and earth.

The way to the wedding was present, but like Dorothy's gold brick road in Oz, it wound through many landscapes, and I would encounter many strange and frightening figures as I traveled on it. But there would be helpful figures as well. On the way to the wedding were many obstacles which I had to meet. And I was not alone in this, for as a psychoanalyst I had discussed, encountered, discovered many of those same obstacles with my clients. Frequently a proposal of marriage would bring to the fore a neurotic pattern which had dominated their lives, reflecting a bondage to the parents and a barrier to commitment to the lover. Or, perhaps more frequently, the obstacles would be felt most intensely in the lack of relationship—either to another human being or to life itself.

One woman, who had been professionally independent for years but longed for a partner, was afraid to disappoint her parents when she fell in love with a man of another religion. Even though she had confronted her parents by moving far away from home and pursuing a "man's" profession, she became anxious when the wedding possibility arose. Her mother had taught her that life was work and duty and that she had no right to pleasure or to what she really wanted. As a result, she had internalized a negative martyr voice. Another client, a man, was consumed by a jealousy which seemed to repeat his father's jealous rages. He was suspicious and wanted the woman he loved to cut off relationships with her male friends, and unconsciously provoked fights with her whenever a jealous fantasy overtook him. She, in turn, was continually in flight from a possessive mother and tended to flee from any situation in which she felt dominated. So to escape his accusations she sought relief in drugs, but this flight led to her lack of presence in the relationship. And he, in his fight to possess her, was continually driving her away.

Sometimes the way to the wedding is blocked by an inability to get into a relationship, or even to meet a suitable partner. Over and over I hear the complaint "There are no mature men" or "Where are the women who really want a relationship?" This complaint often covers up an inner image of the lover so idealized that no human could compare. Such a person may have had a parent who was idealized in childhood because of a bond that was too close, or an inner idealized parental image formed to compensate for the parent's absence or rejection. Some of the men and women caught up in this syndrome find themselves in love with married partners, wonderful but inevitably unavailable.

Another obstacle on the way to the wedding is the inability to go through hard times. So when the glow of infatuation begins to dim, people look for a brighter light elsewhere. And sometimes the obstacles have cultural roots. As one woman expressed it, "Who wants a lifetime of servitude?" Many women refuse to be trapped in a role which requires them to sacrifice their personal and professional growth to be a domestic housemaid or a beautiful manikin. And many men are tired of bearing all the financial responsibility and decision making for a relationship.

A common central factor in all of these examples is a fear of change. A marriage means change, and people don't want to take the risk. At the bottom of all these obstacles is fear of death, of letting the old pattern die so that a new, creative relationship can be born. Ultimately, the greatest challenge to the wedding is death. For to wed is to die to the Other, to give up one's ego wishes, fantasies, illusions, and obsessions and to honor the greater mystery of the relationship. "Death and the Wedding" is a frequent theme in dreams. One woman dreamed she was at her own wedding in a beautiful white dress. The atmosphere was full of sparkle and warmth. Suddenly the wedding became a funeral. Now the dress was black and the atmosphere bleak. At the time of the dream she was eighteen and had just refused a wedding proposal.

A woman at a different stage in life, approaching fifty, also dreamed of a wedding of death.

I was at my wedding when suddenly I noticed a woman dressed in black. When I looked at the groom I noticed there were chains around his chest. Suddenly the groom had a heart attack. I wondered what I could do to help him.

When asked what she could do for the groom, the dreamer, who in reality was a nurse, said the best cure would be rest. She herself needed a resting of the heart, for at the time of the dream she was overworked, not experiencing joy in her life. Her first marriage had been to a controlling, rigid man, and she had lived as an eternal girl, but later she had married a second time to a boyish man and she had assumed an "armored amazon" role of work and control.[1] When she had the dream she was seeking an inner prince to wed within herself, but this figure was still bound up in chains with a weak heart. She had to suffer a death of her tendency to control and allow herself a heart rest before she could wed.

When the way to the wedding is blocked by an obstacle, the psyche often shows us a new way. This dream of a woman who was rejected by her father and suffered from a negative self-image as a result illustrates how the psyche was trying to show her a way through her obstacles.

I was approaching an old New England–style wooden church with someone I knew. Inside, a colorful Mardi Gras–like procession was taking place. Music, lights, colors, candles, and gaiety abounded. Along the side of the church were religious booths, formalized and somber, like the Catholicism I grew up in. I knew these booths were obstacles, so I chose to go in the colorful procession. Up front was a black minister. He was colorful, musical, and exuberant, and he performed the wedding ceremony, marrying me to the man I was with. The people in the procession sang as he tied a huge rainbow-colored bow around me at the end of the ceremony. I turned to look at the man I had married, and it was my father. I was surprised, but it felt fine.

An obstacle to the wedding for this woman was her fear that she was like her father, distant, rejecting, perfectionistic. Her father had been absent because of divorce, and she felt she could never get close to him. He seemed uninterested in her, except insofar as he judged her for not coming up to his ideals. She tended to be attracted to this type of man, always fearing she'd be rejected. And if the man became attracted to her, she'd lose the attraction to him. Then she'd feel guilty and afraid that she was like her father.

The dream gave her a positive image of the inner father, for to her the marriage symbolized overcoming the rejecting father. The gloomy religious booths were the obstacles of moralistic judgment with which she constantly criticized herself. In the dream she had chosen to go past these booths of gloom and join the colorful singing and joyous procession instead. The black minister, a warm, instinctual man with heart, blessed this wedding, and the rainbow bow he tied around her symbolized a bright, optimistic view of herself. She had this dream at the beginning of her analysis. The psyche was showing her a way to the wedding.

A wedding requires no less than a personal transformation, and that brings up another issue. Many of us have had formal weddings and marriages which lacked the mystery of transformation. We have had the illusion of a wedding, the physical, external ceremony, but not the inner spiritual uniting with the mysterious Other. Some of us have given up on the wedding ritual for this very reason—it seems to have trivialized the most meaningful of events. We have mistaken the external ceremony for the inner event.

At the deepest level, the wedding we seek is really a wedding within ourselves. To have a whole, healthy relationship with another person requires me to be whole and healthy myself. When people come into analysis they often present an outer problem: "I can't find a lover." "My relationships don't last." "My partner inhibits my freedom and creativity." "I can't find meaning in life." At bottom, all of these outer problems reflect a conflict within. And that is where the work of love begins—the work of looking within to identify the obstacles to one's development as a whole and healthy person. Some of the obstacles have come from outside—from the culture or from the way we were brought up in our families. And these obstacles must be looked at and identified. But once this difficult task is under way, we must look within to see how those obstacles have been internalized. For it is within that we have the power to change them. And then we must look at the human condition itself—at the universal conflicts we all share, each in our own unique way. For there will be no authentic wedding if we are out of tune with the fundamentals of human existence.

*Seldom or never does a marriage develop into an individual relationship smoothly and without crises. There is no birth of consciousness without pain.*

C. G. JUNG
*"Marriage as a Psychological Relationship"*

# 2

# Prince Charming and the Special Princess

One couple we meet on the way to the wedding is Prince Charming, and the Special Princess. Prince Charming is that magical figure who rescues the Special Princess from her imprisonment and supports and takes care of her forever after. Many women in our culture, particularly those prone to the "darling doll" pattern, have been enchanted by this figure and have married men who they hoped would rescue them from a difficult situation in their lives, thus never looking within to deal with their inner conflicts or looking without to see who was that man they married. Others, with this ideal in mind, remain alone and isolated, unable to find their Prince Charming. As in the fairy tale of Rapunzel, there is often an enchantment by the mother, who provides a developmental influence, and sometimes the daughter is locked away in a tower of fantasy.

Rapunzel was given at birth by her parents to an enchantress who demanded the newborn child as payment for the theft of a plant called Rapunzel from the enchantress's private garden. Rapunzel's parents had longed for a special child, but the mother could not give birth, and both grieved over this lack. One day the wife looked from her house over a high fence which guarded a forbidden garden and saw a Rapunzel plant and had an insatiable craving to devour it. To please his wife, the husband entered the forbidden garden, which belonged to an enchantress, and took some of the plant. But the enchantress caught him, saying he could save his life only in exchange for their first child. In terror, the father consented.

Rapunzel grew up to be very beautiful, and when she was twelve years old the enchantress locked her away high in a tower which no one but she could enter. There were no doors in the tower, only a window very high up from which Rapunzel looked out at the world. When the enchantress gave a secret signal, Rapunzel would let down her long golden tresses for this witch to climb up and enter the tower.

One day a handsome young prince came along and, hearing singing, looked up and saw the beautiful girl in the tower window. He wondered how to reach her, and when he heard the witch give her signal and saw her climb up Rapunzel's long blond tresses, he decided to try this, too. Rapunzel was surprised when, instead of the witch, a handsome prince entered her tower window one day. She looked at him in wonder, for she had never seen a man other than her father. Seeing that he was young and handsome, she agreed to be his wife when he asked her, for she thought he would love her more than the enchantress. The prince would come often, using the enchantress's signal, but one day Rapunzel let her secret out and told her captress about the strange visitor. Angry at this intrusion into her private domain and Rapunzel's deception, the enchantress cut off Rapunzel's golden tresses. Then she dressed up like Rapunzel and at the prince's signal let down some long tresses for the prince to climb up. When the prince climbed up and found the enchantress, he leaped in despair from the tower and fell into a bush of thorns, which pierced his eyes and blinded him. The enchantress punished Rapunzel by sending her into a desert to suffer alone, where she gave birth to twins, a boy and a girl, and lived in wretchedness. Meanwhile, the prince wandered blindly for many years searching for Rapunzel. Finally he wandered into the desert, where the weeping Rapunzel saw him. In their embrace two of her tears touched his eyes and healed his vision. After many years of suffering, the two were reunited.

Rapunzel is the story of many women who are locked away in a tower, cut off from relationship by a devouring, possessive enchantresslike mother. Although they may long for relationship, like Rapunzel they often give their chances away by speaking of the man to the mother, who then attempts to destroy the relationship. And like Rapunzel, often they must leave the mother and go off on their own journey, consciously suffering through life's experience, entering the desert of emptiness and wounds, the dark night of the soul, before they are independent and ready for the hard work of relationship.

One young woman I worked with was blocked on her way to the wedding by such a constellation. Her father, whom she loved dearly, had died prematurely and unexpectedly when she was eleven years old. She was the youngest daughter, and the widowed mother became very possessive of her, wanting her to be the new companion to replace her father. On the one hand the mother made this daughter very special, but on the other she constantly undermined her appearance, focusing on her adolescent acne condition, and criticized all her boyfriends. Nancy looked like her mother and had even been named after her. Since she was so special to her mother, Nancy felt they had a good relationship. But she was tormented by her inability to be in a good relationship with a man. Her pattern was always to choose as partners eternal boys who became dependent upon her, emotionally and financially, and to the point of invasiveness. They were not men upon whom she could rely for security. Secretly, Nancy also felt she was unattractive because of her acne and was afraid there was something so defective in her personality that there was no hope for her cure.

When she first entered therapy she was suffering from a deep wound to her feelings of self-worth. Her first therapist suspected something amiss in Nancy's adulation of her mother and insistence that theirs was such a wonderful relationship. As their dialogue in therapy unfolded and Nancy's dreams emerged, it became apparent that the mother had been shaping Nancy to her own needs and not acknowledging that Nancy was a very different person who could not live out her life in the mother's image. The mother had unconsciously been locking Nancy away from men in an ugly tower of appearance so she could have her all to herself. This situation was so extreme that for her own survival Nancy at first took distance from her mother to the extent that she had to cut off all contact. For as Nancy's natural interests, talents, and beauty emerged, the mother would try to undermine this new daughter she couldn't control by making her feel guilty and ugly for being herself. For a long time Nancy could not shake off her mother's power over her, and much of her initial work in therapy was to find her own power and feelings of self-confidence.

In Nancy's development there had been no father to counteract this dominant, possessive mother and to give her positive feelings of her feminine beauty and worth. Luckily her first therapist was a sensitive and warm man who was able to affirm Nancy and to help effect a necessary separation from the undermining, invasive mother, who by this time had become a strong inner figure in Nancy's psyche. Nancy was becoming independent and feeling her own power, but she still wanted to be a special princess, and part of her special princess fantasy was to meet a Prince Charming who would support her. Her older sister had such a Prince Charming relationship of which her mother approved, and Nancy was very envious. At the same time she was terribly afraid of abandonment by men since she had experienced abandonment at her father's death. Her Prince Charming fantasy was like a Ghostly Lover binding her to the dead, idealized father—the one who would take care of her but also could abandon her at any moment. And she was still binding herself to her mother unconsciously since this was the type of relationship her mother had approved for her older sister.

To loosen the grips of her Special Princess fantasy, Nancy wrote a fairy tale. In the fairy tale, to compensate for the loss of her father, the king, the littlest princess loved her mother and brothers and sister even more. They were a special royal family, set apart from the world by the king's death, which bound them all the more closely together, and the littlest princess felt safe and secure. But when the others grew older and married, the littlest princess felt left out. "The littlest princess mourned, and when they married she pounded her ears in rage." She did not want to hear about change, for in the littlest princess's paradise there was no room for growing older. There was no room for partings. And there was certainly no room for spouses, not even one of her own. Then she had a dream. (This dream was one that Nancy had in reality when she was thirty-two years old.) In the dream she was in a cemetery with her mother. A brick wall sequestered a family plot with six grave sites. In one the king was already buried. The mother said the other grave sites were for herself and her children. In this family plot there was no room for spouses or anyone else. After thinking about the dream, the princess realized she had to say goodbye to her dream childhood with her dream family, for to keep this dream meant a living death, as the image of the enclosed family plot showed. It didn't matter that the princess was thirty-two years old when she stepped out of her storybook tale and became a real person, a nonroyal woman. It didn't matter because, as she said, "one day of life as a real person is more than an eternity as a fantasy queen." Now she was free to lead a genuine life and love others, unhindered by the attachments of her childhood. And so she found new people to love, including a very special man who loved her just for being who she was.

Nancy wrote this fairy tale over a year before she actually met the man she was to marry. But writing it helped to loosen up the tight hold of the Special Princess complex that was blocking her way to the wedding. Writing her own fairy tale also led the way to another dream in which she cracked open coffins in her grandmother's attic. She had been afraid to open the coffins for fear they might contain stinking corpses. Instead, when she cracked the coffins open, two little feminine figures came forth, alive and magical and wearing jewellike emerald garments. The two tiny women had a common name—Joy. For Nancy this dream symbolized her separation from her family and the liberation of her feminine self—the joyous possibility of her womanhood. It seemed as if the emergence of her feminine spirit was a prerequisite to the wedding.

As Nancy began to separate herself from her mother, develop her own unique feminine selfhood, feel her own power, and value herself, she became more independent. She risked a career in a field her mother scorned. Still she longed for an intimate relationship and worried that her new growth would make that harder to find. Finally she met an interesting man who wanted a committed relationship. But immediately came her fears of abandonment together with her disappointment that this man would not be able and willing to support her financially. In the course of her therapy she had a series of money dreams which reflected her wish not to have to pay her own way. One dream in particular revealed that her desire for monetary security was connected to unavailable men. She dreamed she had a lover who was an insurance man, but he was married to someone else. During this time she also dreamed that she was moving into the house of her fiancé (a mixture of a former puer boyfriend, who was financially dependent, and her present boyfriend) and had brought her father's piano with her. In the dream the man she was to marry already had a piano, but it was much inferior to her father's. Nancy associated her father's special piano with her Prince Charming ideal and saw how in comparison it made her see her fiancé as not special enough. This enabled her to look at some of the obstacles to the relationship, for example, a fear that her creativity and being in a relationship were incompatible. She realized that unconsciously she still associated being the Special Princess, the special creative one, with being her father's daughter. But this made her creativity dependent on her father, and it also made relationship with other men seem inferior.

In outer life, as the date to move into her fiancé's house approached, Nancy had a flurry of dreams in which she found fault with him. Frequently his lack of financial abundance was a focus. In one of these not only did he have no money; he also had different religious values. In the dream he was a "Jesus freak," something Nancy abhorred. That was the last straw, she thought in the dream, and at that point she saw her brother-in-law and fell in love with him. In actual life her brother-in-law was well-to-do and she envied her sister, who could stay home and didn't have to support herself. Nancy felt as though fate had dealt her a bad hand. Her sister seemed to have everything—a handsome and rich husband, unblemished skin, a secure home life, and the approval of her mother. Her sister never seemed to suffer and always said she was happy, although nervousness about traveling suggested otherwise. Nancy, whose life had been directed by the search for inner riches, by the quest for wholeness and creativity, was taunted by the voice of an inner demon asking, "Do you need inner riches if your life is not wounded and if externally you have money and success?" Despite her personal growth in the last eight years—the beginning of her own successful career in the healing professions, an incisive intellect and a gift of intuitive vision, a charming personality, and now finally a proposal of marriage from a mature, interesting, and unique man whom she loved—the old fears and doubts were invading her life.

Personified in the dream by her brother-in-law, the collective image
of the Prince Charming who would rescue her from all suffering,
who would give her a secure and happy life forever, emerged as an
obstacle to the real possibility for a creative inner and outer
wedding.

As if to counter this obstacle, her dreams revealed another picture—the creative possibilities for love. In one dream she and her
fiancé were cuddling on a love seat. In another, her fiancé emerged
as a helper, but one who demanded consciousness and strength from
her. In this dream she was lost in a reverie about her father when
from a hidden closet out reached the hand and arm of her fiancé,
drawing her away from her fantasy. In actuality the relationship with
her fiancé required her to be a mature woman with her own power,
a woman free from the infantile dependence on father, mother, sister, or brother. This relationship was requiring her to face the obstacles to the wedding as an adult—to deal with each fear and each
limitation she found in her lover, to accept that neither he nor she
was perfect, to begin to dialogue with him, and to take the risk
to actualize the creative possibilities they did have in their relationship.

In her analysis we were looking at each of these obstacles and projections, trying to differentiate which were the projections and desires she had to give up because they compensated for the wounds
from her childhood and adolescence and from a collective image of
marriage that did not suit her individuality, and which were the
genuine needs of her personality and the changes that could make
the relationship better. By this time Nancy had many years of analysis behind her and had gained the inner confidence necessary to
confront her lover. Instead of falling into her fears and anxieties and
acting them out hysterically with her lover, she saved them to dis-
cuss in her therapy sessions. She was developing a sense of timing
and an objectivity that enabled her to dialogue with him in a conscious and constructive way.

The process of therapy takes time, and its course is not linear and
direct. Rather, it is like a stream that flows around rocky obstacles,
winding this way and that, running off into various rivulets, circling
around and back to its source, and flowing on with renewed force in

new directions. In the same way Nancy kept coming back to her original conflicts, but each time the effort and consciousness, the courage and receptivity she brought to her wounds gave her depth and new direction in her life. Now she was able to value her own unique mystery as a human being and dialogue with a mysterious Other.

The story of Prince Charming and the Special Princess can reflect an obstacle to relationship for men as well as women. Many men are caught in the Prince Charming role, searching for the Special Princess and continually feeling that they must rescue women. This pattern may be the most prevalent in our culture, and men are beginning to be aware of the trap it holds for them. They are tiring of all the responsibility, the expectation that they will provide everything for women, from financial security and important decisions to "making" their partner happy. Like the prince in "Rapunzel," these men often have an internalized devouring mother to deal with. They need to recognize the enchantress behind the golden tresses and to realize that they have been blinded by their naive perception of the feminine. They need to accept the long period of suffering and conscious search and work required to withdraw their projections from outer women and work to redeem the feminine within and to strengthen their sense of masculine selfhood.

One Prince Charming who came into analysis to find himself and to improve his relationship to work and marriage was immobilized by his inability to say no to women's requests or to disappoint them. Instead of standing up to his wife, who wanted his protection and fathering, his tendency was either to withdraw into himself or to adapt too much and come to her aid. His mother had fluctuated between cold withdrawal and hysterical outburst, which left her dependent. His father had been responsible and hard-working but emotionally unavailable to his son. Paul was brought up to be a good, dutiful son, to hide his feelings, and to do what his parents expected, which corresponded to the collective American image of the male and of marital happiness.

In his efforts to please everyone and to do what was expected, Paul sacrificed his assertiveness, and this often made him feel paralyzed in his ability to act and make decisions. Unconsciously this took the form of a passive aggressiveness in his moods of withdrawal. His Special Princess fantasy was projected onto a woman with whom he was in love. He loved his wife, too, and he could not decide between the two women. Paul did not want to hurt either woman, so he did not act and remained in a perpetual state of guilt, which made him feel constantly bad about himself and depleted his energy for life and work. This indecision tortured him and left both women hanging and angry at him. Paul lived in this vicious circle of agony for many years.

The Prince Charming image was the one he lived out consciously—the handsome, golden-haired rescuer who was neither vulnerable nor brutal. But his dreams revealed another side to him, an underworld full of figures who threatened all the order and responsibility that Prince Charming represented. First there was a wild, unruly adolescent boy who was disturbing an old man by making a lot of noise and clamor in the house. Then there was a series of gangsters who threatened and mugged him and his wife in one dream and who stole the briefcase which contained all his creative artwork. In another dream one of these men tried to damage his musical instrument case. Next he was confronted not only with male gangsters, but with a misfit teenage girl who tried to seduce him and then kill him, quite the opposite of his pure, romantic image of the feminine. She was in league with an even more dangerous figure, a Mafia leader who tried to kill Paul by injecting poison in his veins. Paul fought back in a battle of life and death. His dreams were showing him that he had a wild, aggressive side and that unless he acknowledged this it would steal his creative powers and kill him. This meant confronting his wife instead of withdrawing—taking the risk of battle and conflict, the risk of hurting and suffering. Paul and his wife were already suffering anyway, for their relationship lacked the intimacy and depth of conscious confrontation of two mature, independent adults growing together and working out their differences. And this possibility of depth was what drew him to the other woman. But, of course, since there was no daily work of living their lives together, the depth was like Rapunzel, locked away in a tower of fantasy.

Along with the wild gangster images, Paul had two important

dreams about the transformation of his "prince." In one he had traveled far away to a mysterious kingdom hidden high on a mountain ledge where he encountered a mystical, wise guru who taught him many things and told him he was moving to a new stage of development—to maturity. At this point he was lowered in a gourd from the high mountaintop to the ground, where he was to actualize what he had learned. In another dream he was a prince and was told by his guardian mentor that he must prepare himself to become king. To be king meant to give up the Prince Charming image, to own his dark side and reap that manly strength that would give him depth. His dreams seemed to indicate that before he could be ready for the wedding with the feminine, he had to feel and express the strength of his manhood. In the course of therapy Paul was beginning to experience this transformation. He left his job as a rescuer in the helping professions, a job with which he was not engaged, and started his own business in an artistic profession, something he had been wanting to do. He confronted his wife and insisted they needed to face and work out their marital conflicts in therapy. Instead of remaining in passive withdrawal and symbiotic dependency, he said he needed a period of separation to become conscious of himself as a man and his wife as a woman. This time of reflection enabled him to make a conscious commitment to work on the marriage, a vow based on the mature strength of his developing manhood.

The philosopher Martin Buber has described the dilemma in human relationship in his book *I and Thou*. As humans we have two conflicting ways of looking at ourselves and others. One attitude is that of I–It, the other I–Thou. The I–It attitude belongs to and is necessary in the practical world. It separates, takes distance, organizes, uses, makes life comfortable and secure. We cannot do without it. But the I–It attitude never speaks with the whole being. The I–Thou attitude, in contrast, can only speak from the whole being, for "When Thou is spoken, the speaker has no *thing;* he has indeed nothing. But he takes his stand in relation."[1]

The relation to the Thou is direct and cannot be controlled. Neither aim nor lust, neither anticipation nor fancy, no system of ideas, no foreknowledge, can intervene between I and Thou, according to Buber. The Thou cannot be found by seeking; rather we meet the

Thou only through grace. Every means we use to find or obtain the Thou is an obstacle. The meeting of I–Thou occurs in a mysterious moment which cannot be fixed, for were the moment of meeting to stand still it would already be objectifiable and thus an "It." Thus we live in the paradox between the two worlds of I–It and I–Thou— seeking the I–Thou relation which cannot be sought, trying to hold fast to this meeting which cannot be held. As soon as the I–Thou relationship has been worked out, this relationship takes the form of I–It. Thus every Thou is fated to become an It, or to reenter the state of being a thing. From the Thou we obtain nothing; it is only via the I–It attitude that we find certainty and security, the attainment of identity, or that of which we can make use.

> In this chronicle of solid benefits the moments of the *Thou* appear as strange lyric and dramatic episodes, seductive and magical, but tearing us away to dangerous extremes, loosening the well-tried context, leaving more questions than satisfaction behind them, shattering security—in short uncanny moments we can well dispense with.[2]

Prince Charming and the Special Princess are identities that reduce the whole person to an It, to a controllable object, a "thing" which can be dealt with in the practical world. While this sort of identity makes life easier to handle, even makes us feel secure and comfortable, the price we pay is loss of mystery. We lose the mystery of the Other, of the Thou. The irony is that both Prince Charming and the Special Princess seek the unique mystery of relation. They seek each other as a Thou, but in wanting to be secure and settled, to be in control, they give themselves away as objects of possession and restrict themselves to only parts of a whole being.

The conflicts of Nancy and Paul are akin to that of many of us in the Western world today, both men and women, who have been brought up with external collective ideas of who we should be and what our marriages should be like. These collective images often fail to reflect our "specialness" as the unique persons we are. We confuse being special with approval from the outside and forget that our specialness is that mystery of growth, the unique *way* we are from within. In trying to control our identities and to adapt to an image from outside projected by parents or society, we become reduced to an object, to an It. Our lives become mundane and banal, we become fascinated with trivial matters, and mystery is lost—the mystery of our unique selves, the mystery of the Other, the mystery of the cosmos. We forget to go deep into ourselves, forget that suffering is a source of creativity and that life is a work of love and creative effort. As Rilke expressed it:

> To love is good, too: love being difficult. For one human being to love another: that is perhaps the most difficult of all our tasks, the ultimate, the last test and proof, the work for which all other work is but preparation.[3]

. . . because he's more myself than I am. Whatever our souls are made of, his and mine are the same. . . . I cannot express it; but surely you and everybody have a notion that there is or should be an existence of yours beyond you. What were the use of my creation, if I were entirely contained here? My great miseries in this world have been Heathcliff's miseries, and I watched and felt each from the beginning: my great thought in living is himself. If all else perished, and he remained, I should still continue to be; and if all else remained, and he were annihilated, the universe would turn to a mighty stranger. I should not seem part of it. . . . Nelly, I am Heathcliff! He's always, always in my mind; not as a pleasure to myself, but as my own being.

EMILY BRONTË
*Wuthering Heights*

# 3

# *The Ghostly Lover*

The Ghostly Lover can be a powerful obstacle on the way to the wedding. This idealized image of an imaginary lover, with its haunting hints of the divine, has a fascination which can make mere mortal lovers seem dull and ordinary. The Ghostly Lover is a figure in the psyche, a part of the psychic reality of all men and women, the one who promises us divinity, an experience of infinity, of magical union with the sublime. As such, the Ghostly Lover can lead us toward our inner creativity and spirituality and bless our outer wedding relationships. But until this figure can be understood and experienced as part of ourselves, it can keep us in the realm of "impossible possibility."[1] This inner image can be projected outward on an external lover or in the form of an inner drama expressed in a work of art. Whichever the case, for transformation it needs to be consciously integrated in the personality so the relationship or inner vision may be realized concretely.

Some men and women fall hopelessly in love with their teachers or therapists or with public figures who symbolize for them a relationship with the creative process and the mysteries of the spiritual life. Since these "love objects" are usually unobtainable, they are like Ghostly Lovers since a daily relationship with them is impossible. Others fall in love with married men or women, which restricts the chances for a working relationship. Still others fall in love with one person after another, and when they finally look at their pattern of infatuation and disillusionment in relationship, they realize they were in love with an ideal which changed from person to person as each lover fell short of this ideal. And then there are many who are unable to fall in love at all. No one, it seems, has that special mystery that can hold their attention. It is as though there is a "lover" inside, drawing all the energy. Many people who dwell in fantasy and do not dare to actualize their visions or creative ideas in a work of art or action in the world are also under the spell of the Ghostly Lover.

Although the Ghostly Lover asks attention from every human being, the way a particular individual relates to it is often influenced by developmental factors. Women who have had a father they loved and idealized as a young child, but whose father could not allow the idealization to grow into human proportions, are prone to seduction by the Ghostly Lover. The father may have died early, been absent owing to sickness or divorce, or been overattached to his daughter, so that she remains bound in fascination to a ghostly love for him. The same holds true for men who remain fascinated or repelled by their mothers. For example, consider the artist Edvard Munch, whose mother died when he was a child and who later fell in love with an unobtainable married woman. His paintings express the anguish and despair of this loss. Brother-and-sister relationships, too, when an unconscious identification has formed, can be a developmental origin of Ghostly Lover seduction.

The Ghostly Lover figure abounds in legend and literature and is a favorite motif in opera and ballet. The legend of the Flying Dutchman, for example, has enchanted us for centuries. It dates at least from the seventeenth century and was very popular in the nineteenth century, particularly through Wagner's operatic version. The Flying Dutchman is a ship captain whose fate it is to sail forever on the seas, shunned by everyone, because he dared to round the Cape of Good Hope (the edge of the world), defying what seem to be the natural limits of space and time, defying the limitless power of the ocean. But the devil has heard his defiant curse to the ocean and condemns him to sail on and on without rest. His only redemption is to find a woman who will be faithful and love him unto death, who will sacrifice herself for him. But he is allowed to land only once every seven years to find a woman with such sublime love. The Dutchman is weary of life, disappointed in his futile search for the love that could redeem him, and angry that others have the joy which is denied to him, and now finds meaningless even his former lust for adventure. What challenged and thrilled him before is now his curse.

On land there is a woman, Senta, daughter of a Norwegian ship captain, enchanted by this legend—so enchanted that a picture of such a man hangs on the back wall in her house. Dreamily she sinks in contemplation of this picture and sings the ballad of the Dutchman's story, which she has often heard:

> The storm wind blew with bitter force
> as once he fought the rising sea.
> He shouted then that reckless curse:
> "I'll fight you till eternity!"
> Hui! And Satan heard,
> Yohohoe!
> Hui! And took his word,
> Yohohoe!
> Hui! So condemned he must sail
> on and on, without rest, without hope!
> One chance remains to gain this poor man
> his peace and salvation,
> only a woman true unto death can bring
> him redemption.
> Oh, wretched man, who can tell when
> you'll find her!
> May God in Heaven grant you
> a wife faithful and true!
> Each seven years he lands again,
> to seek that true and faithful bride:
> each seven years he seeks again,
> but sails alone upon the tide.
> Hui! "So hoist the sail!"
> Yohohoe!
> Hui! "Love is false, so is faith!
> To the sea, without rest, without hope!"[2]

Senta dreamily imagines herself as the deep-souled woman who can save the Dutchman, but at the same time she has received a marriage proposal from a young huntsman, Eric, who loves her faithfully. The girls of the town, hard at work at their spinning wheels, chide Senta for wasting her youth and beauty on this fantasy of the Dutchman, but Senta is overwhelmed by his suffering soul and longs to save him. At the same time, when Eric worries about her infatuation with the man in the picture and ballad, Senta replies: "I am a child, I don't know what I'm singing! Now look really! Are you afraid of a song or a picture?"[3]

Just offshore Senta's father, Daland, has cast anchor to wait out a violent storm, just where the Dutchman is about to land, for once again the seven years have run their course. The Dutchman sings his fate—"Nowhere to lie! Never to die!"[4]—wishing only for death. But when Daland approaches and asks who he is, the Dutchman tells part of his strange story and offers a chest of treasures if he can be Daland's guest for the night and all he possesses if he can marry Daland's daughter. Daland replies, "Yes, stranger, I possess a lovely daughter. Her childish heart is full of love for me. She is my pride, the best of my possessions, she soothes my troubles and inspires my joy."[5] Daland gives his consent, for, as he says, the aim of every father is to find a wealthy husband with an honest soul for his daughter. And hope rises in the Dutchman's heart, for he believes a daughter who loves her father will also be true to her husband and so be able to redeem him.

> She'll be my wife . . .
> Will she redeem my life?
> If I should crave my soul's salvation
> from black despair and mortal pain,
> am I allowed this aspiration
> the only hope that can remain?[6]

When Daland arrives at home with the stranger, Senta and the Dutchman fall in love immediately, their eyes transfixed upon each other. Senta sees the tormented face and yearns to save this agonized soul, fulfilling her childhood dreams. The Dutchman sees the look of a woman full of sublime sadness and heavenly compassion for his suffering, the face of his deepest reverie, the image of his soul's salvation. When Daland asks his daughter to accept the Dutchman's proposal and she consents, all three, father, daughter, and lover, are overjoyed. But this joy is short-lived, for the Dutchman doubts any woman is capable of such a sacrifice and at the same time is horrified by the dangers in which she places herself by sharing his fate. So, upon hearing Eric's human plea for Senta's love, the Dutchman's faith is broken and, fearing she will betray him, he reveals that he is the Flying Dutchman, condemned to eternity, and leaves to sail away forever. Desperate, Senta breaks free from Eric, Daland, and the town girls who try to hold her back, runs to the edge of the cliff above the sea, and, calling to the Dutchman, pledges her love unto death and throws herself into the ocean. Immediately the Dutchman's ship sinks and the two are seen transfigured in close embrace, soaring upward in the waves from the wrecked vessel at the bottom of the sea. The opera ends with "Liebestod," a culmination of love in death.

In this legend, which many of us reenact daily, we see an obstacle to relationship. From the woman's side is the grandiose image of a doomed lover, a suffering soul whom only she can save. And she is pledged to this image by her father's wish for wealth and his extreme love for his daughter. The legend also shows an obstacle from the masculine side—a life of perpetual daring and adventure which shuns ordinary limits and security to the point where there is no stable place from which to commit or lead a human life. The only union possible between these two ends in *Liebestod,* a love in death, a love possible only in the supernatural world.

Sometimes both sides of this legend are lived out by one person, and this was true for me. I have always been prone to the seduction of the Ghostly Lover and lived both sides of this legend for many years, always in despair and longing for a relationship. On the one hand I was Senta longing to find the extraordinary in another. This seemed to be a legacy from or for my father, for I was always searching for the creative, sensitive, exciting man I imagined my father could have been if only he hadn't succumbed to drink. The artist and the poet fascinated me, and I lived out this fantasy by immersing myself in German romanticism and expressionism. The romantic rebel became my Ghostly Lover. At first I sought him from afar by reading, but when I moved to Europe I wanted to find out about him as directly as I could. I traveled all over Europe to the homes and graves and haunts of the creative men I admired—to Crete to experience the spirit of Kazantzakis and to the hill towns of Tuscany that he loved so much; to Norway, where in awe I saw the magnificent paintings of Munch; to Duino in Italy, just north of Trieste, where Rilke was given his first vision of the *Duino Elegies;* to the castle of Muzot in the Raron Valley of Switzerland, where he had his final outburst of creativity and where he wished to be buried; and then to Prague, where Rilke was born and where Kafka wrote and wandered. I went to Tübingen and sat in the little round tower on the river where Hölderlin lived and ended his life in madness. Seeing his writing desk, which looked out at eye level with the line by which the water flowed, I felt I understood his life on the border between the conscious and unconscious and the draw to submerge in the depths. I went to Paris to see the French Impressionists and to retrace the steps of Victor Hugo, then south to Provence, where Chagall and Matisse and Picasso painted. In Ireland I went to Innisfree, the beloved place of Yeats, and to the Aran Islands, which had haunted J. M. Synge so much. I went to Berlin to see where Käthe Kollwitz had lived and worked and where my father's father was born. And, of course, I went to Heidegger's writing hut at Todnauberg in the Schwarzwald and to Jung's tower at Böllingen. In the course of these travels I lived out the side of the Dutchman, searching and daring, forever flying from place to place, but always longing in loneliness for a soulmate. Finally, I started to enter the world of my own dreams, traveling to the places my dreams took me—to the Himalayas following my dreams of Tibetan temples, to Peru on the path of the Incas to Machu Picchu, and to Africa to climb Mount Kilimanjaro, a living dream from my childhood. These travels gave me meaning, and I touched parts of my soul never before encountered. They were tasks of transformation on the way of Psyche's search for Eros. But they kept me on the move in my "high flyer" pattern of existence. When did I stop long enough to meet the man for whom I was searching? Between this romantic image of my Ghostly Lover and my own enactment of his creative search, was there space and time for a real relation to come into being? The burden of loneliness and longing seemed to be the retribution required for following the path of my dreams.

Those who have read my first book know that writing eventually became my own road to redemption. I learned I must wander and wonder on my own way with writing, and not just merely follow the words of others. And so I wrote *The Wounded Woman* to work out the wounded relationship with my father and with the world of men. The writing required me to settle down, to commit, to write from a place "standing by words," as the poet Wendell Berry expresses it. Writing allowed me to explore the possibilities of my imagination while throwing me before the limits of my abilities. I was not Rilke, but I could write something meaningful for others within my own limitations. And like Rilke, the writing brought me down to a deep river of sorrow within. I don't really understand what happened to me during that time of tears while I wrote *The Wounded Woman,* but two unexpected things occurred. My dreams and the writing process revealed that I must return to the feminine spirit as my center, and to do so I must withdraw my projections of creativity from outer men. I suppose the very writing itself required the withdrawal of these projections. The second unexpected event was that several days after the book was published and in hand, I met the man with whom I now live. This relationship has required me to accept the limits inherent to it—limits which the Flying Dutchman did not accept. And I am learning to transform the energy of this archetypal figure for creativity and love in life rather than a romanticized love possible only in the supernatural realm. Elizabeth Barrett Browning, after she met her husband, Robert Browning, expressed it this way:

> I lived with visions for my company
> Instead of men and women, years ago,
> And found them gentle mates, nor thought to know
> A sweeter music than they played to me.
> But soon their trailing purple was not free
> Of this world's dust, their lutes did silent grow,
> And I myself grew faint and blind below
> Their vanishing eyes. Then *thou* didst come—to be,
> Belovéd, what they seemed. Their shining fronts,
> Their songs, their splendours (better, yet the same,
> As river-water hallowed into fonts),
> Met in thee, and from out thee overcame

My soul with satisfaction of all wants:
Because God's gifts put man's best dreams to shame.[7]

The brother-sister relationship is also a frequent source of Ghostly Lover fixations which can block creative relationship on the inner or outer level. The French film *Invitation to the Voyage* shows the story of a pair of twins, brother and sister, whose relationship is so close that their identities become confused. The story is told from the point of view of the brother, who idolizes his twin, a rock star who has become a celebrity. He follows her around as she records and performs, and is jealous of her relationship with men. One night he prepares a bath of milk for her, before a trip for one of her tours. As she lounges in this milk bath she electrocutes herself when the wire from a light in the ceiling accidentally falls into the bath. The brother is horrified, and after he recovers from the shock of her death, he goes on the journey himself, taking her corpse in a bass case with him. As if she were alive, he distributes publicity posters for her performances in the towns through which he passes. All the while we hear over and over one of the songs she had recorded, including the lyrics "I'm suffering—don't follow me." When he reaches his destination, the place where she was to board ship, he builds a funeral pyre on a hill and gives her a burial by fire. Then he boards the ship and puts on her clothes. The film ends as he goes off on this voyage dressed as his sister; finally he has become one with her.

In this film story the sister has become an irresistible Ghostly Lover, so powerful that the brother loses his own sense of identity in his love for her. This often happens in reverse to sisters who idolize their brothers. The way to the wedding was blocked for one woman who had been searching for a twin soulmate for most of her life. Finally she found him—he even had the same name as the brother soulmate of her dreams, and they seemed to be at one with each other in all facets of their life, from the most important value to the smallest details. It was when they started to live together that she received the shocking realization that the differences were much greater than the similarities. This confirmed the fear which she had always carried with her hopes—that there really was no such twin soulmate in existence. Previously she had chosen distant men so that she did not have to deal with her deepest longing, and now that she had finally allowed herself to love a man who she thought was her secret soulmate, she had to deal with her disappointment. In looking at her past, she understood how the intensity of this ghostly love had developed. She was the first child of parents who had wanted a son so much that they did not even consider the possibility that they might have a daughter. They had chosen a boy's name for the baby, but had given no thought to a name for a girl child. When she was born, the parents were so shocked that they did not even select a name for several weeks. As many daughters who are first-born children often do, she felt her parents' intense disappointment that she was not a son. Later she learned of the name originally chosen for her and took it for the name of her imaginary twin brother. This happened to be the name of the man with whom she later fell so much in love. When this relationship finally ended, she realized she had been seduced by her own Ghostly Lover ideal, and she had to let this ideal twin lover image die, and mourn this death. After she freed herself from him, she met a man whom she is now about to wed.

Frequently the older brother is idolized, particularly when the father is absent, passive, or wounded himself. If the idolized brother plays a positive paternal role toward the sister, her choice of mate or inability to find a suitable one may be a direct result of his influence. One woman from a Jewish background had this sort of Ghostly Lover formation. She could never meet a man who could compare to her talented, princely brother. She was in continual despair that she did not meet men to whom she was attracted. And when she finally did fall in love, the man was not Jewish and her brother disapproved of the relationship. To wed, she needed to separate her identity from her brother's and realize he was a finite human being. In this case the brother had a Prince Charming allure, and she herself had to grow from wanting to be that special "Jewish American Princess" who should be supported in the right style to finding her womanly dignity in her own right.

If the idolized brother suddenly turns on his sister, this can be very confusing and can tie her to the suffering, wounded Heathcliff type of Ghostly Lover. One woman told me she had idolized her brother, who was nine years older. When she was near puberty he had sexually fondled her and stared at her. Because she had idolized him, she was unable to tell anyone about this traumatic event. Like most incest victims, she felt shame, guilt, and anger at this betrayal. She was identified with him, and now this identity had become shameful. As the brother grew older he did little with his life and was unsuccessful professionally. The sister, who was identified with him, was unable to surpass her brother and felt guilty if she did. One day her therapist said to her, "You are not your brother!" These words suddenly broke through her ghostly attachment to him, and she began the process of separating herself from him. Breaking the ghostly identification with her brother freed her to pursue her own professional development and her life.

The angry, suffering man became a Ghostly Lover image for another woman, whose father and brothers were deeply wounded. She internalized this wounded man as a figure in her own psyche. She was a very attractive and charismatic woman and had no trouble attracting men. But an outer wedding was not possible until the inner wedding of trusting, spontaneous bride and bridegroom could be celebrated. Her father was a volatile and sensitive eternal adolescent, dominated by a powerful, witchlike Old World mother and married to a naive, nurturing wife to whom he wanted to remain like a son. When his eldest son was about nine, the father initiated an incestuous relationship with him. Gina, the only daughter and middle child, was at this time about five or six. The father plagued the older son with his advances for some years, and later, when the younger son neared puberty, the father began plaguing the younger son, too. Gina remained untouched in a sexually explicit way by her father, but the fearful aura of emotional incest pervaded the entire family constellation like a ghostly specter. While as a child she wanted to love her father, he was quite emotionally unavailable, and so she turned to her older, handsome, popular, athletic brother, whom she idolized. But the young boy slowly withdrew from the family, living in an inner agony of anger, fear, shame, and confusion. He mysteriously seemed to avoid both his naive mother, who "should have known," and his brother eight years younger, the obvious next victim. And he tried to avoid his "adoring" sister, whom he alternately suspected and distrusted for "knowing," and held in contempt for "*not* knowing," yet over whom he felt torn, as it was the "innocence" of her love in which he sought refuge and hope.

Gina was twenty-nine and had been in therapy for a year before she learned of these deep wounds in her family. Her initial reason for beginning therapy was to deal with an intense, free-floating anxiety which was paralyzing her life. From the start her older brother was a prominent figure in her dreams. Since he was such a positive outer figure for her, we tended to look at his dream presence in this way, too. When, in an early dream, she defended him when he announced to the family that he was "bisexual," we wondered what this could mean in her psyche, and, taking it on a purely symbolic level, we interpreted this as the announcement of an inner androgynous figure, a symbol of integration of masculine and feminine qualities. Now, several years later and after having struggled together through the depth of the shock, we can look back in humility and tempered humor at this dream revelation that her brothers had been molested by her father in actuality. The sudden and violent disclosure of the family secret plunged Gina into a dark descent. She was encased in the deep, depressive belly of the whale, on what seemed to be an interminable night sea journey. It was almost as if she had taken on her brother's identity—this naturally exuberant, passionate, and almost naively trusting woman withdrew and became distrustful of her family, especially of her older brother, her friends, at times of the therapeutic process, and even of the mystery of life itself. Several years later, writing of her experiences, she said:

> The appearance of harmony and "normalcy" in the family becomes an obsession with a victim of incest and the appearance is maintained by learning to deny and censor all genuine feeling true to self at all costs. The incest victim is constantly censoring, avoiding confrontation, and on guard against the next assault on his psyche. As the unknowing sister finding her place in such a family constellation, I

internalized the incest victim as an inner figure in *my* psyche. There now lives within *me* the figure of a wounded woman tensely armed and ready to shoot the next "assault" on her psyche.

Her wounds felt as deep as though *she* had been the incest victim herself! This in part was the profound identification with her brother(s), yet emotionally she *was* an incest victim of the volatile family constellation which seemed to keep her symbiotically at its center; as the middle child and the "untouched" one, she became the mediator—the one who had to save everyone. As she has put it, "Everyone is suffering something from which they must be saved. I must find out what it is and save them." She was a feeling, intuitively oriented person and very medial, and, as medial children often do, she intuited that something was very wrong in her family, that her father and brothers were in pain—particularly the older brother, who was himself a feeling, medial person. She slowly became a fearful, adapting person, trying desperately to win this brother's approval and bring harmony to the family, but she did not know just what it was that was so wrong, and sometimes she felt contemptible for not knowing. Yet she felt responsible for all this pain in her family. Gina consciously carried the anxiety, the panic, and the burden of shame and guilt for her family. And it was Gina who went into therapy to try to understand what was wrong in her life.

Throughout the process of therapy her dreams kept pointing to her brothers—both before and after the incest secret was revealed. In one dream her older brother had "the key" to understanding. In another dream her husband told her that there was still another secret even more devastating than the secret of incest that had recently been revealed. Still another dream provided a profound image of the horror, shame, guilt, and utter devastation she was feeling as a result of her brother's control over the direction of her life force.

I am on horseback with my brother on the down side of a long mountain journey. My brother has control of the horse. He has the reins and I am sitting behind him. I love the horse we are riding very much. All is well until I become panic-stricken as suddenly my brother turns the horse off the path. I know he is deliberately leading us to some disaster and don't want him to turn off the path, but he has complete control of the horse! He directs the horse into a large fan with very sharp blades that are turning counterclockwise. I somehow get off the horse, crying and begging him not to do this, asking why he is doing such a horrible thing to this horse. He is unreachable and does not respond. I am horrified, as I know the horse's flesh and blood will soon start flying. Then I am back on the path but the blood is flooding in torrents, washing me down the path. I am drowning and vomiting from the stench. Then I am at the bottom of the mountain and all I can think of is washing the blood off my body, wondering if the smell of this horror will ever go away.

What was it about this brother who knew so much, who was her childhood hero, yet who distrusted and showed contempt for her, who both loved and hated her and seemed to lead her into such devastation? This is one way she expressed it after the hard work of remembering and trying to understand in the context of her whole life.

I became deeply addicted to my brothers and their approval, overjoyed when the softness and poignant love appeared (they wrote music for me, brought me little gifts), confused and frightened when the sudden and unpredictable rejection and contempt appeared. . . . My "ghostly lover," that inner man no mortal man can live up to, became . . . the Flying Dutchman, the eternally suffering, condemned man who could only be saved from his fate by the faithful love of a pure woman. And so, though I married, I remained the Unravished Bride, saving myself emotionally for "my brothers," the suffering man, my "ghostly lover."

For Gina one of the major revelations came through consulting the *I Ching* when she was in turmoil over her older brother, shortly after she had learned of the incestuous abuse. The hexagram she received was The Marrying Maiden, one of four marriage hexagrams in this Taoist oracular book of wisdom. She felt thunderstruck as she read, "The picture is that of the entrance of the girl into her husband's house. . . . The Marrying Maiden . . . shows the elder brother leading his younger sister to her husband."[8] Literally translated, the title of the hexagram means "the maiden who passes into ownership."[9] Gina could suddenly clearly see her "marriage" to her brother, and his to her in the demands he was making on her. The hexagram provides this image of the entrance of a girl who is not the primary wife into her husband's home and comments on the conditions necessary to transform this transitory situation. She sadly knew that she had to cut off contact with her brother until she felt capable of facing him without losing herself to him, without feeling she had to "save" him, and without competing with his "primary wife" for his approval and affection. This effort to separate and distinguish herself from this deeply loved brother with whom she had previously identified lasted over a year.

But Gina could also see the double, larger meaning intended for her in the hexagram. With the disclosure of the incest secret, her brothers had given her a gift that started her on the path to finding her own identity—they had released her and given her the possibility of the marriage of the bride and bridegroom within. She could see, as the hexagram reads, that it is necessary to "understand the transitory in the light of the eternity of the end," and as the commentary says, "The Marrying Maiden describes the great meaning of heaven and earth. If heaven and earth do not unite, all creatures fail to prosper." [10] So this hexagram gave Gina a picture of her wounded condition, the subordination to her brother, and miraculously it showed the way to healing for her which lay in understanding the facts of her developmental past (the transitory) in the light of the eternal perspective. This was the task of her transformation.

Blessed with the gift of vision and awe before the mystery of the divine, Gina had always found hope in meaning in the revelations from her dreams, from the *I Ching,* and from synchronous events. But she tended to live in an "all or nothing" mode. Either she reduced her life to the facts of her concrete existence, which seemed to her intolerable because of the incest wounds, or she wanted to escape to the eternal realm where finally she would be free of the pain of human wounds. At one point she expressed it this way: "Unfortunately, I know only too painfully that I still have not 'chosen to be on this planet,' and have not embraced my humanness. I continue to defy the order of the universe by fending off human experience while living in the sacred space of fantasy. When will I give up my fantasy and enter human life?" Gina's task of transformation was to live in the tension of human suffering and the divine mystery. She was graced with the following dream which gave her a vision of this task.

I'm in a Southeast Asian country where a coup has taken place. . . . Throngs of desperate people are trying to get out, "every man for himself." It's chaos, it's impossible, and I'm doomed—even our own police are drunken and murderously unpredictable. . . . I stand paralyzed with nowhere to turn and know this will be the end for me. At this crucial moment I see an Australian worker digging a ditch on the road. He catches my eye, conveying that he fears for me but also that there is a way to safety revealed to few. Across the road appears a passageway down, and his voice guides me to the proper place. I now have with me a wounded little girl and a woman. Just stepping down is like stepping into peace and salvation. The building is on the left, and a blind nun, expecting us, is waiting at the door. She hurriedly ushers the wounded child in first, and I know she will be taken care of. The nun glances to her right to indicate where I should go: there is a simple table as an altar with a doll and flowers in a vase on it. I am immediately drawn to it, and my woman friend follows me to kneel at this humble symbol of the Holy Mother. I am in a convent containing only the bare essentials, yet it is filled with a sense of God, and I know others are being, have been, and will be sheltered here in preparation for a new life. After this I will be sent to a room at the left of this table to see the Mother Superior for my instruction. I am sobbing, fervently praying, pouring out all the sufferings of my life and my family. I tell the Holy Mother I have left everything behind, I am completely alone now, how do I go on from here, I have nothing to live for, I don't want to go on living . . . all essentially through "telepathy" . . . and I grow frightened and in awe as this figure comes to life and speaks to me in the most wise and wonderful voice, laughing gently, saying, "Yes, Gina, you have had a hard life, I 'know' all about what you *and* all your loved ones have been through, but *you* are safe now . . . and I want you to know that *I envy you your physical life.* The way has been cleared for you now to continue on a new path and you must, as my divineness depends on your humanness, on your living out the human life intended for you to its fullest. We cannot do our work without you doing yours. You must go on. There is work intended for you." I awake and it is as though there is a glow in the room, a divine presence, and I stay awake for quite a while, unable to move from the power of this "vision."

The first part of the dream dramatically showed the anxiety and chaos in which she was living, the way in which her world had been violated so that she seemed to have no way to turn. She *was* a woman "without a home," and indeed felt doomed, as do many children of incestuous and/or alcoholic families. But there was a way out known only to the Australian ditch digger. Here was an inner masculine figure who could empathize with Gina and also point the way to safety. This worker from "the land down under" symbolized the hard work this would take, the necessity to dig down into the psyche and descent, and the productive working relationship to the earth which she needed to honor. He was the working figure she needed to follow in herself to reach the holy realm of safety, the sacred space of the Holy Mother, an image of feminine spirit. Indeed, as she later realized, she felt as though she had "descended to the depths of pain, depression, and chaos where the powerful goddess Ereshkigal resides, where the possibility of feminine transformation still lives to empower women to face the masculine as an equal." And in her dreams this sacred space was not above, but deep in the heart of the earth; not apart from finite physical existence, but in the very reality of her mortal human life. The heart of healing was not in escaping from her human woundedness but in *living* out her human life, an image of the Wounded Healer, and she was told that the divine needed her *being* for this task. Her journey was not to end in conscious suicidal images or a dream image of being "released from human suffering into the white light of peace and salvation." Here, in this other magical, wonderful dream, was an image of the way to the wedding for Gina—the cosmic wedding of the human and the divine! And she has courageously taken on the difficult work to that end, trying to remain "actively receptive" to both human relationship and an experience of the divine.

The Ghostly Lover can also be a potent force in a man's psyche, dancing before his eyes like an ephemeral vision, dazzling him so that he cannot relate to the real women before him. Many a man has been entranced by this inner sylphlike image, which calls him away

from the wedding. The ballet *La Sylphide,* a romantic story of old
Scotland, is such a dance of the Ghostly Lover. A young Scots peas-
ant, James Reuben, is about to leave his mother's home to get married. It is just before the wedding and he has fallen asleep, already
dressed for the ceremony. He is lost in the world of dreams when a
beautiful winged sylphid in a long, diaphanous white dress appears
and dances around his chair. In his dream James follows this graceful
creature from another world and sees on her face a smile of love that
he feels can live on in the ordinary world. Suddenly he awakes and
reaches out for the sylphid, but, frightened by the transition to reality, she eludes his grasp and disappears. The vision has been so
powerful that James cannot believe it was just a dream. Just then his
mother enters with his bride-to-be, Effie, and James is shocked to
realize he has forgotten all about her. He kisses her and tells her he
has long awaited this wedding day. James's mother embraces the
couple, and James, now in the presence of his lover, forgets his
dream. The bridesmaids arrive, and preparations for the wedding
ceremony are begun. But James, catching sight of the dancing
flames in the fireplace, is distracted by a fleeting memory of the
sylphid. He sees something move into a dark corner where he last
saw the dancing sylph, but instead of the beautiful sylphid, a frightening figure comes forth—Old Madge, the village sorceress. Now
looking at this ragged, filthy, ghostlike face, James tells her to leave
and angrily walks away. Old Madge is a fortuneteller, and Effie,
holding out her hand, asks if her marriage will be happy and if James
loves her. Old Madge says yes to the first question but no to the
second. Indignant, James chases Old Madge away, and Effie, reassured by his reaction, believes in his love. And when James looks
into Effie's eyes, he believes it too. James's mother comes to take Effie
to dress for the wedding.

Once he is alone again, James's doubts about the forthcoming
wedding rise up. The sylphid was so enchanting. And just then
there she is again, now sweetly sad because she knows James will be
married. She loves him, she says, and since she feels there can be no
more beauty in her life, she must die. James confesses his love for
her, and the sylphid dances around the room as he watches, enrap-
tured. But he is also anxious. What about the wedding? The sylphid

vanishes again, and the bride and wedding guests come in. The couple is toasted, the music plays, and James and Effie begin to dance. But the sylphid returns, seen only by James, who looks away from his bride to the astonishment of all. The couple's dance now becomes a pas de trois, for the sylphid imitates every movement of Effie, who does not notice James's frantic efforts to follow the sylphid in her dance. The wedding ceremony begins, and just as the rings are to be exchanged, the sylphid takes the ring from his hand. The guests are aghast and Effie is in tears. The sylphid whispers to James that she will die if he marries anyone else. James is appalled and makes his choice: he will save the sylphid. The strange-acting bridegroom vanishes, and the wedding veil is removed. James's mother and his friend, Gurn, who secretly loves Effie, comfort the abandoned bride-to-be.

Leaving the wedding scene to follow his sylphid, James enters a forest. He has been carrying a delicate bird's nest with colorful eggs and is now dressed for a wedding with the sylphid. He comes upon a small, dark cave where just before Old Madge and her sister witches had been stirring a brew in a black cauldron, from which they pulled a lovely magical scarf. As James approaches the cave the sylphid suddenly appears, silently dancing in and about the trees. Enchanted by her charm, he gives her the gift of the nest with its eggs. But the sylphid is afraid of the nest, for the living birds of the forest are governed by a different power than she is. So she dances away with the nest, then returns with other sylphs, who surround the lovers, honoring them. James bids the sylphid to dance, but mysteriously she is gone every time he is about to take her in his arms. This happens many times—now she is there, now not, and James again becomes frantic. Why in the forest, where they are free to love, does she appear and disappear so mysteriously? Is his love an illusion? he asks himself in confusion. Just then he hears the rustle of branches coming from the place where the sylphid last vanished, and out from the cave comes Old Madge. In despair he says to the sorceress, ". . . the sylphide is never with me: I search for her, and she is not to be found; I reach out to touch her beside me, and she eludes my embrace." [11]

Offering to help him with her occult powers, Old Madge gives him the magic scarf and tells James that if he places it around the sylphid's shoulders, she will never be able to elude him again. James bows before Old Madge in gratitude as her eyes glaze in triumph. She retreats into the cave as the sylphid approaches. Aglow, James embraces her and places the shimmering scarf around her shoulders. But the sylphid cries out in agony, her wings flutter to the ground, and, with a look of horror, she pushes him away as she falls to the ground dead.

The sylphs tenderly take their dead sister in their winged arms and bear her away. Amid the cackles of the gloating sorceress echoing from inside the dark cavern walls and the joyous music of the wedding bagpipes in the distance, James weeps, aghast with grief, overwhelmed by the ruin of romance. The wedding, home, and happiness he might have had with Effie are now lost to him forever, for she is marrying his friend, Gurn.

The man who wants the magic of the sylphid really wants it in himself. James is a mother-bound man who has lived with his mother up to his wedding day, and there is no father mentioned in the story. He is also a romantic, close to the world of dreams and visions—so close they intermingle in his life to the point where distinguishing the two becomes vague and confusing. The bride-to-be, Effie, is beautiful and appealing. James truly loves her. But compared with the enchantment of the sylph, her everyday loveliness is pale and undramatic. The sylph, of course, is connected with the witch sorceress—they appear and disappear from the same dark places. And the witch knows the secret of the sylph—her wondrous wings are free to fly *only* when she is not possessed. Although she whispers to James that she will die if he loves another, the truth is she will die if he loves her too much. She is truly a wedding mate for him, but not one of the material world. And this is where he errs. He literalizes his love for her on the earthly plane—hearth, home, and happiness—whereas hers is the realm of spiritual space, of the free flight of creative imagination. Had he dealt adequately with Old Madge, the witch sorceress, he might have been able to integrate these two realms and the two weddings, inner and outer. It is Madge who understands the split in James, and she uses it to destroy him. His first reaction to her was repulsion and anger, and he orders her away. But when in the forest he realizes she has powers that might help him, he cajoles her, willing to do anything to bind his sylphid to him. In neither case does he respect the witch or her knowledge—he merely condemns or cajoles. His life with his positive mother has not given him an understanding of the power of the feminine. And he has had no father to guide him to a masculine instinctual wisdom that might provide a counterpoint.

The modern prototype of James is very confused about what he wants. A man often meets a woman who outwardly seems to be either sylph or Effie, yet he discovers that she is both of them, plus the witch. Were he to look within, he would also find this trio in himself, a trio that needs to be integrated. In a certain way the witch is a key to the integration. She knows the dark caves one must enter in both weddings—the wedding of creativity and the wedding of the hearth. Were he to honor her, she might even join the hands of the three—the sylph, James, and Effie—and perform the wedding ceremony.

If the Ghostly Lover is honored as the mysterious one who draws us into the secrets of the psyche, then there can be a wedding with the muse. But just as the sylphid dies and loses her wings, the flight of fantasy, if she is possessed or captured, so is the soul lost when we literalize and project it on a person or anything concrete.

The struggle to honor the Ghostly Lover on an inner level as the creative muse was the task of transformation for one man who had the following dream.

> I am with a mysterious, beautiful young woman. She is a concert pianist. I am trying to persuade her to play, to perform for an audience, but she is reluctant. I also talk with an older female figure (a wise old woman?) who may be a leader of an orchestra or head of a music school. I'm trying to gain her support to influence the young woman, who protests, "But you don't love music!" And it's true—the desire, the appreciation is there, but the knowledge, the understanding, the love or the faith is lacking.

The dream came at a time in his life when he was faced directly with the issue of commitment to his own soul's growth. For many years he had been in love with a woman who embodied soul for him.

It was she who first inspired him to go into analysis to see where his own soul's journey led him. But he was already married, and although he was very much in love with this woman he also loved his wife and family. For years he lived in indecision—he could not commit himself fully to either woman. Nor could he commit himself fully to his own creativity and its external expression. In many ways his life was like James's on the day before the wedding with Effie. Most of the time he was lost in his dream of the mystical sylphid, which he projected onto the "other woman." Yet he would awaken to see the lovely and practical wife to whom he was married but not wholly committed in the depths of his being. By profession he was an architect, and this same conflict was present in his work. He was afraid to venture forth with the full expression of his heart's artistic vision for fear of failure on the practical level.

Inwardly he was tortured by self-doubt, guilt, and shame over his inability to make a choice. As with James, there was an inner witch undermining his capacity for commitment. He had grown up with a mother who had functioned like a witch in her despairing and bitter feelings toward love and faith, mystery, and all things mystical. The split he experienced between the practical world and the world of art, between his practical wife and the woman who carried soul for him, reflected a split within himself. Before he could really commit to either woman or to his artistic work he had to heal this inner dichotomy. And this required that he face the witch figure in himself, who now functioned as a trickster like the witch in *La Sylphide,* leading James to think he could humanly possess what is supernatural and can only be honored in awesome appreciation. To deal effectively with this inner witch, he had first to acknowledge her existence in his psyche and confront her. In the course of analysis he was able to find his own strength to confront her, a necessary step in transforming the inner feminine. For him this meant expressing his angry feelings toward women, feelings which he tended to hide and consequently turned inward against himself, leaving him in the despair of inactivity. As this came up in therapy, with women in his work, and with his wife, communication improved. In the process his wife entered therapy, embarking on her own soul work. He also had to confront the reality of the other woman, who decided to marry after many years of waiting for him. Her marriage made him angry, but that reality also loosened the concrete woman from the meaning of life which he had been projecting upon her.

This outcome freed him to encounter his inner soul woman, who appeared for the first time in the above dream. (Previously she had always appeared in the figure of the other woman.) In the dream his mysterious muse was present but did not want to perform. He knew he must call upon the experienced wisdom of the feminine and gain that support to influence his muse to express her creativity. But the muse confronted him, saying, "You don't love music!" Upon awakening, he realized his task of transformation: to honor the mystery of the creative muse within himself so he could commit himself fully to her in love and faith and be able to express this inner creativity in his life.

*The moon is no door. It is a face in its own right,*
*White as a knuckle and terribly upset.*
*It drags the sea after it like a dark crime; it is quiet*
*With the O-gape of complete despair. I live here.*
  . . .
*The yew tree points up. It has a Gothic shape.*
*The eyes lift after it and find the moon.*
*The moon is my mother. She is not sweet like Mary.*
*Her blue garments unloose small bats and owls.*
*How I would like to believe in tenderness—*

SYLVIA PLATH
"The Moon and the Yew Tree"

# 4

# *The Bewitchment*

Many couples find their way to the wedding blocked by a paralysis of the power to act, to decide, to commit. This paralysis, which is usually experienced in the side of oneself that is boyish or girlish, can keep a person trapped in an enchanted spell of melancholy or wishful thinking. When this state of indecision and the inability to make a final commitment in one's life or in a soul relationship occur, it is as though one's creative energies have been bewitched.

The ballet *Swan Lake* is a romantic but tragic story about a wedding that is blocked on the human level by bewitchment. In the background are a powerful mother, an evil sorcerer, and a dark but enchanting creature of imagination. The ballet begins on the twenty-first birthday of Prince Sigfried, who is enjoying his youth and freedom with wine and dance at a hunting party to celebrate his coming of age. His levity is interrupted when his mother arrives to remind him that he is now a man and that it is his duty to choose a bride at the formal celebration of his birthday, a court ball to be held the following evening. Although the prince is upset, he responds dutifully to his mother's command, but as soon as she leaves the party he continues to dance and play, trying to dispel his apprehension about losing his carefree youth. When a flight of swans passes overhead, a friend suggests a hunting party to Sigfried, hoping to distract him from the morrow.

While Sigfried is hunting he sees a magnificent queen swan leading the swans, which have settled on a great lake. Entranced, he sights the swan more closely, and to his amazement, she transforms into the most beautiful woman he has ever seen, a magical creature who appears to be both swan and woman. Immediately the prince falls in love, and as he steps closer he startles her. But when she sees how gentle he is, she reveals that she is Odette, Queen of the Swans, and tells him her story. She is a princess of high birth who fell under the spell of an evil sorcerer. The sorcerer changed her into a swan during the day. Only between midnight and dawn can she return to her human form, and she must remain this way unless a man loves her, marries her, and swears eternal fidelity. Only then will she be saved and be a human woman again. But if her mate should be untrue, she must be a swan forever. Indeed, Odette tells him that the lake where they are was made from her mother's tears at this bewitchment. Sigfried pledges his love and faithfulness to her. Just then the sorcerer appears, and in anger Sigfried takes up his bow and arrow to kill him. But Odette intervenes, for if the sorcerer is killed before the spell is broken, she will die with him. When the sorcerer disappears, the prince embraces Odette, telling her she must come to the court ball the next evening, for there, at the command of his mother, he must choose his bride. Odette replies that she cannot appear at the ball until she is married and the sorcerer no longer has power over her. She also warns Sigfried that the sorcerer will use any means to keep her in his power and will try to trick Sigfried to break his promise of love and fidelity to her. If this happens, Odette's fate is death. Once more Sigfried swears eternal love. As dawn approaches, Odette, changing back to her swan form, disappears and Sigfried is left distraught.

The next evening the guests assemble for the court ball, presided over by Prince Sigfried's Queen Mother. The Queen Mother has selected six princesses as eligible brides for her son, but Sigfried is preoccupied with his vow to Odette and is uninterested in the princesses. Angry and jealous over her son's inattention, the Queen Mother criticizes him for his strange behavior. Just then a fanfare announces the arrival of two new guests, the mysterious Baron von Rothbart and his daughter, Odile. Sigfried stares in bewitchment at Odile, for although she is dressed entirely in black, she is the image of his beloved Odette. Odile returns his stare with cold but passionate interest and holds out her hands to him. In the distance is a vision of Odette the Swan Queen, beckoning to Sigfried, but he does not see it, for he is too enchanted with the dark Odile, whom he has mistaken for Odette. The Baron, seeing Sigfried's involvement with Odile, smiles triumphantly, for he is really the evil sorcerer and has transformed himself and his cunning daughter to deceive Sigfried into breaking his promise never to love anyone but Odette. He turns and smiles at the Queen Mother, who is taken with the Baron's flattery and his daughter's appearance, and hopes her son will marry Odile. Infatuated with Odile, Prince Sigfried dances with her—not a dance of tenderness as he had danced with Odette, but one that is dazzling, cold, and arrogant. Seduced by Odile's beauty and her resemblance to Odette, Prince Sigfried is no longer the lead in this dance. Rather, Odile displays her power over him with breathtaking precision, and as the prince supports her she takes her hand away and stands on point alone, masterfully self-sufficient. The vision of Odette appears again in the distance, but Odile flirtatiously steps between Sigfried and the vision, so he does not see it. Odile, in triumph, dances a series of quick circles around him, summing up her power over him. Now totally bewitched, Sigfried asks the baron for Odile's hand in marriage. The Baron consents to the marriage and asks Sigfried to swear an oath that he will never love another. Sigfried feels uneasy at these words, for they ring familiar, but his love for Odile is so great he takes the oath. As the image of Odette reappears, the music screams her despair while the Baron and Odile laugh cruelly and triumphantly reveal the deception. Sigfried is horrified and now sees in the distance the weeping Odette reaching out to him in helplessness. In the guilt and horror that he has fallen victim to the sorcerer's evil plot, Sigfried swoons to the floor.

At the lakeside the swan maidens grieve over the fate of their queen. When Odette returns she tells them she has been betrayed by Sigfried, who was tricked by the Baron-sorcerer, and that she must die. The swan maidens advise her to wait and listen to Sigfried, who is a mere mortal and could not have known the power of the Baron's sorcery. In desperation, Sigfried searches for Odette, and when he finds her pledges his love, begging for forgiveness. Odette forgives him and tenderly expresses her love for the prince in dance, but reminds him that she must die, for only in death can she be released from the Baron's power. The Baron appears, Sigfried defies him, and for a moment the lovers embrace. But then Odette throws herself into the lake to die and Sigfried follows her, drowning himself. Sigfried's sacrifice for love breaks the power of the Baron, who is struck dead. The swan maidens bow in grief at the loss of their queen and in gratitude to Sigfried, whose sacrifice has liberated them from the sorcerer. In the distance of the great lake glides a jeweled and magical bark in which Odette and Sigfried embrace, united in love after death. The swan maidens wave farewell to the tragic couple.

In the Swan Lake legend we have a picture of a young prince (an eternal boy, or puer) with a dominant mother who wants to control his life. In the ballet she is connected with an evil sorcerer (symbolic of her unintegrated ambitious masculine power drive) who has bewitched the feminine in the form of the swan queen, a symbol of the divine feminine cut off from human life. There is no father in this story to confront the witchlike mother and be a positive masculine model for the son, so the challenge for the prince is to free himself of this witchlike mother and the evil power which bewitches the feminine, to assert himself, and to make his own choices. This requires constant consciousness of the power of the witch and the evil sorcerer, a prerequisite for the wedding to the feminine.

Men who come from this developmental background usually have a weak self-image since their masculine strength has been undermined by the dominant mother and the lack of a strong masculine role model. When a man's mother has been witchlike—either cold and rejecting or possessive and devouring—frequently he is attracted to seductive but cold women, as Prince Sigfried was attracted to the beautiful black swanlike Odile. Because he has not had warmth and nurturing from his mother, he often feels he does not deserve to be loved. And having heard the hard, cackling voice of the critical mother at every movement of independence and freedom he has made, he is often paralyzed in his ability to act far into adulthood. For even though the mother may be dead or far away, her cackling voice has lodged in his inner ear. This prevents him from relating to the divine feminine within and without.

Richard, a handsome man in his fifties, came into analysis to work on his relationship to the feminine. He had read *The Wounded Woman* and felt the torturous trap of the "darling doll" pattern in his own life. Richard was in the process of divorcing a woman very much like Odile. He had been attracted to her youth, beauty, and intelligence and tried to please her in every way, even to the point of trying a new career in a profession which interested her but was inappropriate for his very introverted, sensitive, reflective temperament. When he was not very successful in this field of her choice, she was condescending, he felt, and withdrew her attention from him. She had a son by a former marriage, and the boy superseded Richard as a focus for her energies. Richard became an addendum in the relationship, someone to take care of the son, but not worthy to be treated like a husband. At the end of the relationship he felt he had been used, taken for his money, but never valued for himself.

Richard had grown up an only child in a wealthy family. His mother was a matriarch, queen of power and money, and dominated everyone around her, including her husband and son. The husband retreated into his own world, while Richard became the focus of his mother's attention. She coddled him, dressed him like Little Lord Fauntleroy, and wouldn't allow him to play with the group of children his age. Every night she read him the story of Ferdinand the Bull, who wore flowers and didn't like to fight. She made him into her little male doll, an object of her possession. And when he tried to do what he wanted, to be different from her, she criticized him unmercifully, calling him selfish. On the one hand she discouraged him from developing skills and strengths while on the other she berated him for being incompetent and not successful like the son of her dreams. He was extremely intelligent, and on this she could not fault him. But wherever she could she undermined his confidence and masculine strength, trying to keep him dependent on her for love and money. And so, though he was brilliant and talented, he did not trust his own instincts, either in the area of work or love. He grew up afraid that he was a rich playboy who would never be successful in the world, and he felt that all his relatives looked down on him. Whenever he tried to accomplish something, the internal voice of his mother undermined him. Although in his first marriage he had been a good father and his children were interesting individuals with meaningful lives, and although he had played a productive role in organizing a nationwide movement seeking to curb excesses of corporate power, Richard still heard the witch voice that negated his existence as a man. And now, in this second marriage, he heard the same voice from his wife. It was as though fate had driven him into this marriage to confront the dominating witch once more— externally in the projected form of his wife and internally in the voice which constantly denigrated him.

In our sessions he frequently wept at the way he felt humiliated and used, and just beneath the tears was his rage. Once, when he was alone in the desert, he let the rage out in an imaginal dialogue with his mother. He said all that he had wanted to say to her and asked her the question he had never dared to ask: had she substituted him as her lover when her husband proved inadequate? It was in this active imagination that the connection between his mother and his wife became clear. Although the divorce was in process, although the external separation was being made, Richard was still bewitched by the rage and resentment at the humiliation he had experienced. In part he was angry at his own naiveté, at being seduced by the external beauty of his wife and failing to see the ice witch underneath it. About this time his wife had tried to seduce an old friend of his, and the friend naively responded. Richard was enraged at his wife for taking her revenge in this way, in effect trying to separate him from his best male friend, and he was enraged at the friend for being duped by her. This outer event reflected the inner pattern that was enslaving him—the revengeful witch separating him from his masculine strength, and the naive boy within who allowed this to continue. When Richard saw this connection between outer event and inner pattern in his life, he felt freed. The energy which this outer event was consuming in the form of resentment and rage was released for more creative ventures and for commitment to another kind of woman, a nurturing woman who loved him.

Like Sigfried, Richard needed to see the treachery of the black Odile and to make the sacrifice of commitment to the pure Odette side of himself. The Odette of *Swan Lake* was not a naive girl. She recognized the deception and wickedness of the sorcerer who had bewitched her, and she knew it took no less than an ultimate vow of fidelity to be free of this evil power. This conscious vow of fidelity was what Richard needed to make to himself. The new woman in his life understood this. She had also fallen prey to a witch mother and had suffered from the resulting self-betrayal. She supported Richard in his search for his authentic self and in the actualization of his creative efforts. And she had her own creative avenues of expression she wanted to explore in the relationship. This new couple moved in together. Outwardly they found an apartment by the sea where each could write. Inwardly Richard found his feminine muse and wed her to his newfound masculine strength and consciousness. The psyche seemed to approve of this wedding. The first night in their home by the sea Richard dreamed that Albert Einstein was guiding him. Now he had within a wonderful masculine image of wisdom and creativity—the wise old man—as his inner friend and guide, an inner father blessing this wedding.

A woman who identified with the Swan Lake legend felt herself cast in the role of the dark swan. She was very beautiful and had had a powerful, sorcererlike father who encouraged her to play the dark beauty who could seduce men and have power over them. It was as though her dark beauty were an extension of his power. This worked for her in her twenties, as it does for many young women, but when she reached her thirties and the midlife crisis that required her to look at her life, she realized she was destroying her soul. She learned that although men might project the dark swan beauty on her, she did not have to accept the projections. So she started saying no to these bewitching projections and showing who she was. Through the process of rejecting the enchantress projections that did not correspond to her real self, she began to free herself from the evil sorcerer influence and connect with the white divine swan, the feminine spirit within.

The enchanted swan motif came up for Diane, a woman caught in the despair of never choosing to develop her own potential. She had a pattern of giving herself to depressive, dependent men, whom she would finally have to leave. She was extremely intelligent and could easily have gotten a Ph.D. in her early twenties, but the men she chose were always in the way. She was always living through others. Her father was an eternal boy who had gambled his way through life and was away from the family much of the time. Her mother, unhappy in her marriage and chronically depressed, warned her not to expect much out of life and also predicted that Diane would be unsuccessful in marriage. Thus she dominated her daughter through her inertia, depression, and cynical pessimism. When Diane was still a child she had the following dream, which she later wrote into the form of a fairy tale.

I was on a trip with my family sitting in the back seat of our Buick with boxes and a bird cage beside me. In my fantasy I was in the sky looking down at myself, so I could see what was coming. The car came up to a huge canyon, and the only way to cross was over a narrow swaying bridge. We made it across to the other side, but as soon as we did, we were in a village marketplace and our car and its contents were gone. Before we had time to orient ourselves, a strange dark lady came up to us. She was small and hunched with a shawl that covered most of her face, and I knew she was a fortuneteller. As this dark lady approached, my mother grew distant until finally my mother disappeared with a strange look on her face. It was almost as though the fortune lady had replaced her. I was left with my father and brother, and we saw some beautiful white feathers in the fortune-teller's hands. The dark lady threw the feathers at us and said, By nightfall you will be turned into swans. Suddenly the villagers turned away from us, and we realized we had to leave. In the confusion we couldn't find our father, so it was just my brother and me alone, and we were very lonely and frightened. A voice spoke suddenly and warned us there was a wizard who had the power to restore us to our human form but who instead searched for enchanted swans to torture them. We were afraid for our lives and knew the fear of being hunted, so we hid, and all the while I could not forget my mother's face as she disappeared. Then the voice who had told us about the wizard told us to fly as our father had. We had seen the wizard once in his dark blue robes with moons and stars all over, but though he looked gentle, we knew he was as fierce and dangerous as were the men who were with him. So when it was dark we tried our wings and flew up in the sky. The wizard saw us but we were too high for him to catch us. And we flew so high we landed on a cloud where our daddy was eating. We joined him for breakfast, smiled at the other swans nearby, and were all very comfortable living in the clouds.

Diane felt that the disappearance of her mother was linked with the appearance of the dark fortune-telling lady who turned her into a swan. The cruel wizard seemed to be in their service. On the surface, Diane's mother had wanted her to be a princess, to have the life she never had. She had even linked Diane with Princess Grace, who eventually became mistress of Monaco, the royal capital of gambling. In some ways Diane was a fantasy figure for her mother, like a beautiful white-feathered swan. This image, of course, complemented that of the father—that high-flyer side of life which the mother had married. But then there was the grim, boring reality and the inertia and pessimism and depression that went with it. This, too, was projected on Diane—the cruel-wizard view that life offered no real beauty or flight of fancy and that Diane would fail in relationship as the mother had. This conflict was internalized in Diane. A creative writer with a rich imagination, she had the gift of words to go with the flight of her images. She could easily live in the clouds, but then she would not be on earth actualizing her talents. But the evil wizard–dark fortune-teller was in her psyche, too, and this combination pulled her down, away from her creative talent and from creative relationships, away from the development of herself and toward the care and service of her mother or men like her. She couldn't stay floating on the clouds with her father, but neither could she sink into the inertial existence of her mother. One wedding dream warned of this. In the dream she was riding in a car on the way to her wedding. When she looked over to see who the groom was, she realized it was her mother. She woke up from this dream in great dismay. The dream showed the pattern of her relationships to date—the series of dependent men to whom she gave her energy, men who tended to oppose her creative development and devour her as her mother had. She had to learn to separate from these men, to give time and space and energy to herself.

An obstacle to the wedding for many women and men is this tendency to give themselves away. Instead of choosing to be their own authentic self, they serve another. Although men usually get the blame from women, and women get the blame from men, I have found that developmentally this pattern often results from a difficult marriage—the demanding mother and the passive, absent, or wounded father. Sometimes the mother is demanding by virtue of direct power and control, like the mother in *Swan Lake*. But sometimes she asks for servitude out of her weakness, like the mother who remains an eternal girl. There are many images from fairy tales that tell this story: the stepmother figure in "Cinderella" and in "Snow White and the Seven Dwarfs," the mother in "Red Riding Hood," and, again, the powerful mother in *Swan Lake*.

At the beginning of my Jungian analysis I had an awesome swan dream in which the bewitchment of the swan seemed directly connected with the mother. In the dream I was walking with my mother along a lake that was near my analyst's house. As we turned to go back, the lake was on our left and suddenly in the glow of the setting sun I saw a giant swan whose stately neck and head reached far upward into the heavens. Silhouetted in the grand disk of the setting sun was a sailboat, floating freely on the water. In awe I turned to my mother to show her this marvelous sight, but she could not see it.

For many years I lived with the mysterious image of the swan, always wondering exactly what it meant but knowing it was God-given, a revelation of a divine reality that someday I would experience. It is only now, fourteen years later, while writing this chapter and musing upon the mystery of the swan maidens, that its meaning as a sacred symbol of the hermaphroditic wedding in my soul has shown itself to me. My mother had been disappointed in her marriage to my alcoholic father and had been pessimistic and depressed about relationships. She could not see the divine sight of the swan. It took many years for me to work through this inner hopelessness about life and relationships and allow myself to receive the reality of the swan.

In *Swan Lake* the swan maidens (both white and black) are under the domination of the evil sorcerer, the power-bound masculine. The prince is under the domination of the Queen Mother, the power-bound feminine. This reflects a cultural situation which prevents the sacred wedding within and without. It is not just the power-bound patriarchy which prevents the wedding, but the controlling, power-hungry matriarchy, too, as the legend and the cases I present show. And usually these two are in a secret collusion. Their arrogant, often veiled claims to dominance must be seen clearly to redeem the bewitched swans, be they male or female.

The motif of the bewitched swan is universal; in *Swan Lake* it is the maidens who are bewitched, but in the fairy tale "The Six Swans" and in the legend of Lohengrin, it is the male. But what is it that is enchanted, inaccessible to human relationship? In legend and story the swan is connected to the supernatural realm. It is a graceful, stately, beautiful creature that feeds our fantasy and our fanciful eye. In Greek legend it is a bird of Apollo, a bird of music, a swan that is said to sing before its death (the swan song) and hence has knowledge of the future. In Hinduism the swan is a symbol of the divine spirit, of the Atman. Perhaps the swan is the beauty of the creative soul, the divine spirit which is hermaphroditic (its shape is both phallic and womblike), the essence of the sacred wedding within us. Our task, then, would be to free this holy creature from the power aims of the possessive ego to enter human life and relationship and to honor the sacred swan within us.

*When men are gone,*
*ignorance of this union*
*where no alive man sits,*
*gives vent to a deep red demon*
*who lives in an empty corner of night,*
*better than complete oblivion,*
*he holds down the curtain on morning,*
*an image,*
*beautiful and deadly,*
*growing out of dry bones ad bitter dirt,*
*shaped by forced labor in a stone country without trees or run-*
*    ning water.*

*He devours the gentle sweet thoughts that caress the softest*
*    folds,*
*blooming flowers wither and faith turns in on itself*
*my being, crawling on its belly away from the identifying*
*    light,*
*believing itself a grey worm,*
*it is reluctant to come out at all.*

*The air begins to stink of decay*
*propping up corpses, all in a row,*
*the eyes glaze over*
*I forget to light a candle,*
*enslaved, not in love, with a dream demon,*
*smiling down on me from a cemetery plot.*

M. MERCEDES GIRÓN-CERNA
*Dracula*

# 5

# *The Demon Lover*

On our journey to the wedding we may confront the frightening figure of the Demon Lover, who halts our progress by possessing us. The state of possession can be experienced in many different ways—for example, through obsessive jealousy, any form of addiction, the state of being a perpetual willing victim, feeding off the blood of others, or offering up one's own lifeblood or creativity to another. Whenever we come under the power of the Demon Lover, we experience a loss of soul.

The story of Dracula expresses this archetypal obstacle. It is a tale of diabolic craving, of those who feed off the blood of others by seducing them and of those who willingly give up their blood to this process. Though preceded by legend, the story was first presented in novel form in 1897 by Bram Stoker. Since then there have been many adaptations and elaborations of it, particularly on the screen, from the early silent movie *Nosferatu* to more recent versions such as the well-known film starring Bela Lugosi, the film based on the stage play, starring Lawrence Olivier and Frank Langella, and the version by Andy Warhol. The popularity of this story in our culture and century suggests to me that it expresses an archetypal message for our time.

Dracula is a count from the land of Transylvania, a mysterious man from a mysterious country in the midst of the Carpathian Mountains, one of the wildest and least-known areas of Europe, a land containing most of the world's superstitions, an imaginative whirlpool in which werewolves, witches, vampires, and other satanic beings of the night dwell. He lives in a ruined castle of ancient origins, high on a cold, windy hill, dark and shadowy, with tall black windows, a fearsome sight to behold when its jagged line of broken battlements shines on a moonlit night. As if to reflect the image of his habitat, Dracula himself is a tall, thin man dressed in black, with a strong, aquiline face, sharp white teeth, arched nostrils, a high lofty forehead, pointed ears, and long pointed fingernails. An atmosphere of pallor hangs over him, despite the blood-red color of his lips. In the Stoker novel he is an old man with white bushy hair and massive eyebrows and mustache, but in the later film version with Frank Langella he is young with dark hair and glistening eyes and a face both romantic and aesthetic.

The encounter with Dracula begins when a young novice real estate solicitor journeys from London to Transylvania to transact a business deal with Count Dracula, who has just bought a large old estate outside London. The solicitor, Jonathan Harker, soon finds out that Dracula is no ordinary man. After a long, frightening train journey through a dark and ominous stormy night to reach his destination, Harker is met by a carriage drawn by four coal-black horses and driven by a tall, grim coachman clad in large black hat and garb. Nervous as he is from his harrowing ride and the forewarnings of the superstitious fellow travelers on the train, Harker's original curious anticipation of this trip becomes more and more anxious and increases to terror when from nowhere in the darkness a ring of howling wolves surrounds the coach. But the coachman disperses the wolves with a gesture of imperious command, and the carriage moves on in uncanny silence. When Harker arrives at the castle and first meets Dracula, he awakens as if from a horrible nightmare.

It is nighttime, Dracula's time, and Harker is welcomed to a late supper before going to bed. He finds Dracula to be courteous, alert, and curious about affairs in London and the details of his journey. But he cannot shake off a vague feeling of dread. As Harker's stay in the castle continues, his doubts increase. He finds that the doors and windows do not open, and that he seems to be the only human being in this castle aside from the Count, whose habits are peculiar: Dracula never seems to eat or drink, and his reflection is not visible in the mirror. He meets with Harker only at night, confessing his love of the shade and the shadow, and says of himself, "I have been so long master that I would be master still. . . . "[1] Even the coachman who resembled the count so much and could control the wolves by a mere gesture is none other than Dracula himself. When Harker sees Dracula emerge from a window face down, his black cape spreading around him like the wings of a giant bat, his terror becomes the awful realization that Dracula is no mere mortal but a horrible creature in the semblance of man. Finally Harker realizes that he is a prisoner in Dracula's castle.

To avoid going mad, Harker writes down all that he sees in shorthand to send to his fiancée, Mina. During the day, when Dracula is absent, he desperately searches the castle for a way to escape. During one of these ventures he falls asleep and wakes up in the moonlight to see three young women. Two are dark, like the Count; the other is fair with wavy masses of golden hair and pale sapphire eyes. As Harker notes:

> I seemed somehow to know her face, and to know it in connection with some dreamy fear, but I could not recollect at the moment how or where. All three had brilliant white teeth that shone like pearls against the ruby of their voluptuous lips. There was something about them that made me uneasy, some longing and at the same time some deadly fear. I felt in my heart a wicked, burning desire that they would kiss me with those red lips. . . . I was afraid to raise my eyelids, but looked out and saw perfectly under the lashes. The [fair] girl went on her knees, and bent over me, simply gloating. There was a deliberate voluptuousness which was both thrilling and repulsive, and as she arched her neck she actually licked her lips like an animal, till I could see in the moonlight the moisture shining on the scarlet lips and on the red tongue as it lapped the sharp white teeth. Lower and lower went her head as the lips went below the range of my mouth and chin and seemed about to fasten on my throat. Then she paused, and I could hear the churning sound of her tongue as it licked her teeth and lips, and could feel the hot breath on my neck. Then the skin of my throat began to tingle as one's flesh does when the hand that is to tickle it approaches nearer—nearer. I could feel the soft, shivering touch of the lips on the supersensitive

skin of my throat, and the hard dents of two sharp teeth, just touching and pausing there. I closed my eyes in a languorous ecstasy and
waited—waited with beating heart.[2]

Just as Harker is about to give himself over to this swoon of seduction, Dracula enters in a fury, hurls the woman away, and, with
his eyes red and blazing and in a voice lurid with rage, says, "This
man belongs to me." The women laugh soullessly at him but obey
his command, jeering at him that he never loves. Dracula alludes to
former nights of love with them, promises Harker to them when he
is done with him, and for the meantime throws for their devouring
a bag from which emerges the wail of a half-smothered child. Harker, who has observed all this while pretending to be asleep, now
faints in horror.

Upon awakening Harker finds himself in his room. Not sure
whether he has dreamed this horror or Dracula carried him back
there, he determines to escape from the castle in any way he can. He
tries to get letters to his fiancée and his employer, but Dracula clev-
erly foils this attempt and manipulates him into writing short notes
that say he is all right and will soon be home. Believing that Dracula
plans to leave him to the blood-sucking vampire women, Harker is
driven to any lengths in his desperation to escape. Realizing that it
is only at night that he has been threatened or molested, he enters
Dracula's bedroom by day by crawling into his window, and there
he finds a series of dark tunnels descending to an enclosed graveyard
where lie some old coffins. In one of these great boxes he finds the
Count with eyes open and stony, full of hatred but without the glas-
siness of death. Frantic, Harker flees, returning to his room to try
to think, knowing he must return to this hideous graveyard once
more to see if he can find the castle keys on the Count's body. When
he goes back again, he sees an even more gruesome scene. This time
Dracula is lying in the coffin looking younger, with a bloated,
bloodstained face, his body gorged with blood like a filthy leech
exhausted from lustful satiation. The thought that Harker was actually helping this monster arrange to go to London to victimize
millions for centuries to come drives him half mad, and he tries to
kill Dracula, but his horror paralyzes him, and when he hears voices

in the distance he flees and tries to escape by scaling the castle wall. Death by falling from the steep precipice is preferable to being victimized by these vampires.

Back in England Harker's fiancée, Mina, wonders why she has not heard from him. She worries about him and also about her best friend, Lucy, who has been besieged with bouts of sleepwalking, an old childhood malady. One night during sleep, Lucy wanders outside her house at Whitby by the sea. Mina, who has been visiting her, searches for her, and in the light of the full moon sees her silhouette in the churchyard of an old abbey, a place where they are fond of visiting. Rushing toward this spot, she sees the white-clad reclining figure of Lucy and a long black figure with a white face and red gleaming eyes bending over her. By the time Mina arrives the black figure is gone, but she finds Lucy gasping for breath and moaning, her hand touching her throat, which Mina later sees has been pierced, showing two tiny red points like pinpricks. On later nights Mina awakens to find Lucy at the window and a great black bat outside, coming and going in whirling circles.

Lucy's midnight sleepwalking takes its toll on her health, and she becomes so ill that an old friend, Dr. Seward, is called. Lucy's symptoms are strange: inexplicably, she seems to be suffering from a loss of blood. Seward calls in his old professor from Amsterdam, Van Helsing, a philosopher and metaphysician who is one of the most advanced scientists of the healing crafts. When Van Helsing arrives, he immediately notes the two punctures on Lucy's throat, asks Seward to watch her through the night, and returned to Amsterdam to do some research on this unusual disease.

The outer events at Whitby have also been bizarre. On a stormy night a derelict schooner arrives, its crew dead, the captain strapped to the helm with a crucifix tied in his hands. The only cargo aboard is a number of great wooden boxes filled with mold, and the only living thing a fierce brute of a dog, which runs away when it reaches land. The log of this Russian ship, the *Demeter,* links the murders to the specter of a tall, thin man whom the captain tries to kill but who disappears like a ghost. In the log the captain writes that he will fight with a crucifix, his only weapon against this fiend.

At Dr. Seward's hospital, a lunatic asylum, there is also a strange phenomenon—a madman who eats flies and spiders, who licks up blood, and whose mania is to believe he is under the power of "the Master," and who says, "The blood is the life."

Lucy's condition worsens the nights she is left alone, and several times the only way to save her is to give her blood transfusions from four strong men—her fiancé, Arthur, Quincy Morris, Dr. Seward, and the old professor. After his research, the professor brings an unusual cure—a necklace of white garlic flowers, which he places around her neck and warns her never to take off at night. On the nights she remembers to wear the garlic she sleeps, but when she forgets she is drained of blood again, and despite all the efforts of Dr. Seward and the Professor, Lucy dies after one terribly haunting night when she is found with the garlic torn from her throat. Her journal recounts night visions of a large black bat and the howling head of a great, gaunt gray wolf crashing through her bedroom windowpane. Strangely, in her funeral coffin Lucy looks younger and, her red lips glowing, more beautiful than ever. Meanwhile, the outer events in England continue. The newspapers report that a series of small children have been lured away from their homes at night. When found, they are injured with tiny throat wounds. Though too young to speak well, they all talk of "the bloofer lady." (In Cockney, "bloofer" means "beautiful.")

By this time Professor Van Helsing has done enough research to determine for himself the cause of Lucy's death. But to be sure, he collects all her letters and diaries and asks to see her friend, Mina, who he learns had been present on a night of Lucy's sleepwalking. Mina is now Mrs. Jonathan Harker. Harker had finally been traced to a hospital suffering from brain fever. On his recovery he and Mina married, and he gave her the shorthand journal he had kept, not sure whether it was a recording of dream or reality and too traumatized himself to talk of the events. By the time the Professor calls on her, Mina has read her husband's journal of his experience in Transylvania and, still concerned about her husband's health, hopes the Professor can help. The description of Harker's experience combined with the description of Lucy's unusual death leaves little doubt in both their minds that Count Dracula exists and is one of the Nosferatu, the Undead—vampires who live forever off the blood of others—and that Lucy's death is a result of Dracula's arrival in England. When Harker hears what the Professor has learned about Dracula he is relieved, for his brain fever was due to his doubt about the reality of what he experienced in Transylvania. Not knowing whether his experience was real or not, he felt impotent, in the dark, distrustful. The knowledge relieves him of his fear of the Count and frees him to act. Both he and Mina join the Professor in an effort to stop the evil blood lust of Dracula.

The Professor now tries to show his former student, Dr. Seward, as well as Lucy's fiancé, Arthur, and his friend (the three other men who once gave their blood to restore Lucy), that Lucy has been a victim of Count Dracula and thus has become a living vampire herself. But the Professor knows that before they can believe what he has to tell them they must first experience this themselves. As he says to the rational Seward:

> You are a clever man, friend John; you reason well, and your wit is bold; but you are too prejudiced. You do not let your eyes see nor your ears hear, and that which is outside your daily life is not of account to you. Do you not think that there are things which you cannot understand, and yet which are; that some people see things that others cannot? . . . Ah, it is the fault of our science that it wants to explain all; and if it explain not, then it says there is nothing to explain. . . . Let me tell you, my friend, that there are things done today in electrical science which would have been deemed unholy by the very men who discovered electricity—who would themselves not so long before have been burned as wizards. There are always mysteries in life.[3]

The Professor takes Seward and the others to the churchyard where Lucy lies in her coffin. There they find the coffin empty. On a series of successive nights they find Lucy returned to the coffin, then gone again, and nearby a missing child with throat wounds. As the evidence mounts up, the men have to accept that Lucy has been responsible for this and that she is a vampire. And indeed her appearance has changed, the former sweetness to cruelty and the purity to voluptuous wantonness, her lips now crimson red and dripping with blood, her eyes full of hellfire. Lucy is now only a nightmare of her former self, and the only way to free her soul is to kill her, Van

Helsing says, for as one of the Undead she is cursed to an eternal life of creating new vampires and multiplying the evils of the world. Arthur drives the necessary stake through her heart, the evil influence disappears, and a holy calm returns to Lucy's face.

By now the task has become clear to all—to find the author of this horror and to stamp him out. The vampire is strong and cunning and becomes only stronger as he sucks the blood of others. His cunning is more than mortal, for it has the growth of ages, and the aids of necromancy to command his dead victims. His heart is of the devil and he can within limitations appear at will in various forms, direct the elements, command the meaner animals, and at times vanish and become unknown. But to fail in this fight is not merely to lose a struggle of life or death; it is to become as him, "without heart or conscience, preying on the bodies and souls of those we love best."[4] As Van Helsing points out, there are clues to follow, but the task is long and difficult and filled with danger and pain. But there are strengths as well—the power of combination which the vampire does not have, sources of science, the freedom to act and think, the use of the hours of day and night equally—and above all, self-devotion in a cause, and an unselfish end to achieve.

The limitations of the vampire must be known and used. While he can fatten on the blood of the living, he cannot flourish without it. And while he throws no shadow, no reflection in the mirror, and while he can come in mist and on moonlight rays, while he can become so small as to come out from anything and into anything, and while he can even see in the dark, he is not utterly free and must obey some of nature's laws. He cannot enter anywhere at first unless someone bids him enter, and his power ceases at the coming of the day. He can change only at certain times, at noon or exact sunset and sunrise. And certain things render him powerless, such as garlic, the crucifix, and the branch of wild rose, which can confine him to his coffin. Thus, when his habitation is found, he can be confined and destroyed. Since he can do as he will in his coffin home, each of the boxes he has brought with him must be traced and found, his home earth sterilized so that he can no more seek safety in it, so that finally he can be found in the form of man between the hours of noon and sunset, when he is the weakest. The clues of his whereabouts are in the journals and diaries and letters kept by Mina and Jonathan Harker, by Lucy and by Dr. Seward. The details therein must be put in chronological order for comparison.

Mina offers to type up all the records, and with this information the men proceed to trace all the great boxes that Dracula brought with him on the derelict schooner. In order to protect Mina at this point, the Professor says she must be shielded from the dangerous knowledge henceforth. And although Mina feels this is a mistake, she accepts this decision. It is really Mina with her foresight, intelligence, and energy who has put the story together so that every detail shows the whole picture. But now, feeling her job is done, the men with their strength under the guidance of the Professor put all their energies toward tracking down Dracula. In so doing, they leave Mina unprotected and alone at night, when she begins to be assailed by dreadful dreams. In one she sees two red eyes staring at her in a pillar of smoky mist, just like the ones Lucy had described. Mina struggles against the force of these dreams, and finally takes a sleeping potion to get some sleep. But each morning she wakes up more weak and spiritless. Mina has been staying in Dr. Seward's quarters above the lunatic asylum, and finally one night Dracula uses the crazy Renfield to gain access to her. For Renfield, dependent on Dracula's power for his supply of living things to eat, can give Dracula the invitation to enter that Dracula needs. Renfield, who through all his craziness sees Mina's purity and respects her, tries to protect her from Dracula, but he is too weak and is found by Dr. Seward lying in a pool of blood, almost mangled to death. When Van Helsing sees him and hears his nightmarish story, he realizes Mina is under attack by Dracula, and he and Seward rush to her room. There they find Harker in a stupor on the bed beside Mina. By her side is a tall, thin man clad in black with a scar on his forehead—none other than Dracula himself—forcing Mina's lips to drink the blood from a wound above his heart. Startled, Dracula, his red eyes flaming with devilish passion, wrenches Mina away and springs to attack the Professor and Seward, but Van Helsing holds up the crucifix and the sacred host wafer, and Dracula is stopped and cowers back, finally disappearing into a mist. After Mina recovers, she tells how she had taken the sleeping draught but was assailed by horrible fantasies of blood and death and vampires, how the tall, thin man in black had entered in a mist and threatened the life of her husband if she screamed, how he bared her throat and drank the blood from her veins, and how "strangely enough, I did not want to hinder him. I suppose it is a part of the horrible curse that such is, when his touch is on his victim."[5] With the horrible realization that she is now "unclean," on call to do Dracula's bidding, she thinks to kill herself so she cannot do harm to others. But the Professor warns her that as long as Dracula is alive, now that she is contaminated by him she would only become one of the Undead and continue in the great chain of vampires, sucking upon the blood of humanity. The Professor exclaims:

> No, you must live! You must struggle and strive to live, though death would seem a boon unspeakable. You must fight Death himself, though he come to you in pain or in joy; by the day, or the night; in safety or in peril! On your living soul I charge you that you do not die—nay, nor think of death—till this great evil be past.[6]

Upon hearing the Professor's adamant words, Mina promises to continue to put her trust in God and strive to live until this nightmare has passed.

With Dracula's horror so fully revealed, all rejoin forces to track him down. Using Dracula's own access to Mina's psyche, the Professor hypnotizes her to see if she has unconscious awareness of Dracula's whereabouts. Under hypnosis Mina describes darkness, the lapping of water, the sounds of a ship, the feeling of death. From these unconscious sense perceptions and from his knowledge of Dracula's habits, the Professor deduces that Dracula is in the lost undiscovered great box he had brought with him and full enough of Mina's blood to survive for centuries, and that he is trying to return by ship to his castle in Transylvania, where he may lie undisturbed for centuries, only to return again. And since Mina is but a mortal woman, Dracula must be killed before her death if she is to be saved from the realm of the Undead. As Van Helsing exclaims, to kill Dracula in time is essential.

With great effort the men trace Dracula's whereabouts to a particular ship bound for Varna, the place from which the derelict schooner *Demeter* had embarked. Mina, with her detailed record keeping, her facility for reading maps and train schedules, and her ability to think and order facts, surmises the route back to the castle which Dracula is planning. And the new hypnotic power of intuition which she has gained by virtue of Dracula's terrible baptism by blood enables her and the Professor to find the dark, unknown way themselves so the place can be sanctified before Dracula gets there. Once this is done, Dracula will be prevented from entering his own castle, and if they can find him between the hours of noon and sunset, they have a chance to destroy him.

Once in Transylvania, Mina and the Professor head for Dracula's castle by land via the Borgo Pass, the route which Mina has so arduously traced out by map, while the others proceed by boat along a river to which they have traced the boat that carries Dracula in his great box. When Mina and the Professor spot Dracula's castle high up on the precipice, they stop for the night. Even the normally fearless Professor is afraid and draws a ring around Mina with the sacred wafer to protect her. For by now, this close to Dracula's castle, vampire traits have begun to show in her: she does not eat, her teeth have become sharper, a red scar appears on her forehead, and her laugh becomes low and unnatural. In the mist which begins to surround them appear three wanton women like the ones described in Jonathan Harker's journal. They try to lure Mina to them, but the holy circle keeps them from approaching her. All through the night this terror continues to the wailing of wolves. Come sunrise the Professor leaves Mina within the holy circle and proceeds to Dracula's castle. Once inside, he finds the graves where the three women lie in their vampire sleep and one empty grave that is Dracula's. As strong and purposeful as the Professor is, even he is paralyzed with fascination for these creatures. But hearing Mina's soul-wail in the distance, he wrenches his will away from the voluptuous beauty before him and performs the wild work of cutting off the head and driving a stake through the heart of each vampire woman. This done, the bodies crumble away into their native dust, and a calm seems to follow. After the sacred wafers are planted in Dracula's tomb so he can never again enter, the Professor rejoins Mina. From their perch atop the rock where they had camped, they see a gypsy cart with a great square chest headed for Dracula's castle. Behind, in pursuit of the cart, are four men soon recognized in the distance as Harker, Arthur, Seward, and Quincy Morris. Overpowering the gypsies with singleness of purpose, Harker jumps on the cart and opens the chest with all his force, flinging it to the ground, while Morris forces his way past the gypsies, who wounded him. The sun is about to set, but with a flash Jonathan cuts off Dracula's head while Morris plunges his knife into his heart. Before their eyes, Dracula's entire body crumbles into dust and passes away from sight with a final look of peace upon his face. The gypsies turn away without a word, and Mina, now freed from Dracula's power, leaves the protection of the holy circle and rushes to the four men. Morris is dying from his wound but in gratitude thanks God that he had a part in removing the curse of Dracula.

Seven years later the remaining members of the party are reunited. Mina has given birth to a boy, who was born on the day of Quincy Morris's death and was christened with Morris's name in his honor. The only traces left of that terrible time were masses of typewritten material, most of which had been burned by Dracula the night he entered the Harker's room. These could hardly serve as proofs of so wild a story. But as the Professor sums it up, with the Harkers' little boy on his knees: "We want no proofs; we ask none to believe us! This boy will some day know what a brave and gallant woman his mother is. Already he knows her sweetness and loving care; later on he will understand how some men so loved her, that they did dare much for her sake."[7]

The story of Dracula tells a mythic truth. Its characters are symbols of human experience; its actions are our actions. We have within ourselves all these figures, struggling with the forces of good and evil, the ultimate conflict of opposites at war in human existence. As such, Dracula, the Demon Lover in the psyche, is the epitome of the ultimate obstacle on the way to the wedding.

The tall, thin man in black allures with his penetrating, hypnotic eyes. He offsets us with his angularity—the elongated face, the aquiline nose, the pointed nails, the long, sharp teeth. His life in the shadows of the night, his ability to appear and disappear in the mist, tricks us and wears us down if we have not braved the unknown forces of the unconscious. In control, fearless except before the crucifix, demonically possessed (in lore he is said to be the son of the devil), with no remorse or guilt, with penetrating powers of the age-old knowledge of the supernatural combined with demonic fury, Dracula represents our own will to power—though to gain his power we must give up our will to his. Thus ultimately those who become his victims do not resist him. But then he comes from behind in the night when we are asleep, unconscious and off guard. Perhaps his greatest power is, as the professor says, that we don't believe vampires exist, that our rationality discards Dracula as mere superstition. Nevertheless, he continues to fascinate us. Since Bram Stoker wrote his novel in 1897, it has sold millions of copies, been continuously in print, and been the theme of numerous dramatizations. As described by Richard Geer, director of the stage version by Richard Sharp: "Dracula is the essence of evil's awesome attraction. He invites us to unimaginable pleasures, he offers us sensual immortality. We admire him and are horrified by our admiration of this elegant symbol of temptation."[8]

If we look at the other main characters in this story, we can see how the inner drama unfolds. There is Lucy, the victim—sweet and innocent, seduced by Dracula as she unconsciously wanders in her sleep at night. But this victim is dangerous, for her seduction by Dracula leads to her own replication of him, to her vampirism, which feeds off the blood of others as he fed off of hers. Lucy is a symbol of our own sweet innocence, the naive, unguarded side that wanders off unconsciously, thus giving itself over as a willing victim, which in turn victimizes others.

Then there is Renfield, the lunatic who lives numerically and quantitatively, eats living things, who want more and more, bigger and bigger living things, whose addiction provides Dracula with access to what he desires. Renfield symbolizes that side of ourselves assailed by our craving, be it for money, property, sex, alcohol, drugs, power, or victory—whatever addiction we have that invites the demon in to possess the soul.

The four strong men (Harker, Dr. Seward, Arthur, and Morris) are men of action who, with the Professor's guidance, physically put an end to Dracula's power, who with their combined forces drive the stake in the vampire's heart. Harker first makes the journey to Transylvania. He ventures forth into the unknown and unwittingly first experiences Dracula. He comes from the practical business world, from the ordinary, everyday realm of affairs. But when he encounters Dracula and is assailed by anxiety before this uncanny existence, he is conscious enough to write down his experience. Unlike the mass of humanity, he does not at first evade the strangeness of what he experiences, but alone he cannot bear up under the unexplainable, and in his confusion and doubt as to the reality of what he is experiencing he suffers temporarily from a nervous breakdown and falls into impotence and dark distrust. Once he accepts the reality of the Count and of his experience at the castle in Transylvania, he is able to act again. Harker symbolizes our potentiality to venture forth from our everyday world, to encounter the unknown, to face and keep a record of the unexplainable, no matter how horrible, and finally with understanding and courage to act.

Of the men who love Lucy and have given of their blood to save her, Dr. Seward is a former student of Professor Van Helsing's and a young scientist, representative of the rational spirit of his age. It is he who directs the lunatic asylum and who is trying to understand the cause of Renfield's mental disorder. But because he seeks rational explanation for all that he encounters, he is unable to save Lucy, and for a time even doubts the Professor. To him the Professor's ideas about vampirism are outrages against common sense. Seward represents the tendency of science to dismiss as nonsense what it cannot explain, the skeptical, matter-of-fact nineteenth-century scientific attitude that rejects mystery. This makes him unaware of the danger, and so it is through Dr. Seward's institution via Renfield that Dracula gains access to Mina. But Dr. Seward is also a caring doctor and a courageous man of integrity who can open his mind to new truths. He is the Professor's most conscientious and valuable assistant. In the battle against Dracula, Seward symbolizes our courage to be open and change our minds when faced with new phenomena and the persistence to transcribe and study for the sake of new consciousness.

Arthur (Lord Godalming), Lucy's fiancé, is a man of honor, rank, and money. It is through his efforts by way of his connections with the collective that much of the information on the whereabouts of Dracula in London is obtained. As Mina reflects, Arthur's efforts show the wonderful power of money when properly applied. For without Arthur's ability to get things done at the collective level and his generosity to use his money for a good end, the expedition to find Dracula could not take place. Arthur represents that force in the psyche that knows how, when, and where to use energy to achieve results in the world.

Quincy Morris, the American friend from Texas, is young and fresh, good-humored, a brave adventurer, a faithful friend. It is Morris who sacrifices his life in the final battle to kill Dracula. Morris is that brave, adventurous pioneer spirit that we need throughout life's quest.

Professor Van Helsing is the key facilitator in this inner drama. He is the hero, a mortal man of faith and wisdom, with open mind, kind and true heart, iron nerve, self-command, indomitable resolution, toleration, singleness of purpose. To these are added his knowledge of philosophy, metaphysics, medical science, mythology, ancient lore, and literature. He is a man of letters and one of the most advanced scientists of his day. The Professor believes in the mysteries of existence and knows that the greatest strength of the vampire is that people will not believe in him, that "in this enlightened age, when men believe not even what they see, the doubting of wise men would be his greatest strength. It would be at once his sheath and his armour, and his weapons to destroy us. . . ."[9] Van Helsing is a professor of the healing craft with an ability to be sympathetic, yet objective, that enables him to discriminate between the healthy and diseased parts of the soul. It is he who can distinguish between the person of Lucy and the evil force which has possessed her. Thus free of the bondage of pity, he can fight the state of possession, the evil force. The Professor symbolizes the force of consciousness which knows and uses the power of symbols such as the cruficix and the holy host, before which Dracula loses his power. Our inner healer, the Professor is a man of hope and courage who faces all he fears, with purpose, faith, and the wisdom of the ages, with reverence for the mystery of the divine, uniting all the available forces within the self in this battle with evil.

Perhaps the central character is Mina—intelligent, loving, loyal, an industrious and efficient worker, a person of integrity. It is Mina's love for Lucy and Harker, her diligently kept journal, her openness and trust in the Professor's wisdom, her admiration and respect for the bravery of the men, and her ability to make sense of the whole story through the morass of details and confusing events that make it possible to track down Dracula. It is also Mina whom Dracula desires most, whom he wants as his companion and helper, his queen of the night, whom he wants as "flesh of my flesh; blood of my blood; kin of my kin; my bountiful winepress." Mina is the "beloved," admired by all the men for that wonderful unity of heart, intelligence, and will forged by her own conscious work and integrity. What she says of women is true of herself: "We women have something of the mother in us that makes us rise above smaller matters when the mother-spirit is invoked." [10]

Mina is the one in us who gives birth through the difficult work of love, who symbolizes the human potential for creativity, the one who must say no to Dracula whenever he tries to possess us. The following dream of a woman whose husband had been dependent, taking her life's blood, provides an image of the Dracula drain upon the life force and creative birth and the adamant refusal one must make.

> I was giving birth, but my husband was sucking the birth fluid. When the baby was born he demanded I give it to him. I refused! I was not willing to give up my baby or let him suck away the lifeblood of my baby or myself any longer.

How is the way to the wedding blocked by the Demon Lover? What are some of the ways in which Dracula hypnotizes us? It is as if, after we have followed the arduous, unknown path through the woods, there behind the last tall tree looms the shadow of the tall, thin man. Is he the bridegroom or the Prince of Darkness? To know, we must recognize some of the forms his possession can take. Here are only four stories, four of a multitude of variations, but I hope they will provide insight into the ways of the last figure at the edge of the woods.

Dracula as Demon Lover is an archetypal symbol of addiction. For an addiction is a powerful demonic force which is master of the addict yet possesses an incredible fascination, a fascination whose pull addicts cannot break on their own once they are "bitten" by the substance to which they have given their will. And once they are in the power of this vampire who sucks the lifeblood from them, their only recourse is to admit their powerlessness over the addicting substance and ask for the help of a Higher Power. This is why Alcoholics Anonymous and Narcotics Anonymous are so effective in combating addiction, for like the Professor, who uses all the help he can summon—the various attributes of the strong young men, the detailed record keeping of Mina, and the faith in the spiritual power of the crucifix to fight Dracula—these groups summon up the combined power of millions of addicts who are recovering, who are fighting with the power of the spiritual sword and the cross against their dragons, and who, by virtue of their own spiritual progress and the love and communal compassion they extend to all addicts still bitten, provide an example of hope for recovery.

If you go to one of the numerous treatment centers for addicts, there you will find men and women of all ages trembling in fear about the power of the "love bite" to which they have succumbed. These men and women come from all strata of society: they range from physical laborers to professionals such as psychiatrists, university professors, and lawyers. Some have been in jail because of their addictions, some have lost arms and legs in automobile accidents, and some are just beginning to see where their path can lead them. Their love relationships have been jeopardized if not totally destroyed by their Demon Lover. Even the strongest-looking men and the wisest women quake before the grip of the Demon Lover on their life as they see their lifeblood draining away daily.

The dreams of one young man show this clearly. He was just twenty-two, had been taken by alcohol and various drugs since thirteen, and had entered a detoxification center and halfway house hoping he could recover. From a middle-class family in the Midwest, he hated his angry, alcoholic father and was trying to free himself from his possessive mother. He said his role in the family was scapegoat and rebel—a typical family constellation. He was longing for a love relationship, but so far his addictions had prevented his being open to love. Shortly after his detoxification he had the following nightmare, which woke him up and left him sweating and shaking in terror. One dream followed upon another within a week.

> I found myself inside a huge wine bottle. I was at the bottom, and there was a flood of its fluid around me. I saw the opening of the bottle above me, and I struggled desperately upward to reach this opening so that I could get out. But every time I started upward, the fluid forced me to the bottom again. I was trapped at the bottom of this wine bottle. I woke up in terror, afraid I would never get out.

This young man was terrified that he would be trapped in his addiction. In order to earn his way in the halfway house, he had gotten a job as a waiter in a nearby restaurant. Every day he was confronted with the torture of seeing wine bottles before him, and he feared he might one day reach for a glass of wine left unfinished by one of the customers. This daily torture is common to many alcoholics trying to recover from their addiction, for alcohol is everywhere. But as the AA literature says, one must learn to live one day at a time to deal with this. The next dream he had provides an image of the way such a person is cut off from love relationships.

> I was in the center of a ring. Around me on every side were bottles of liquor and drugs of every kind—all the drugs I had been using and more. There was so much alcohol and so many drugs I could not get out of the center of this ring. Encircling this ring was another, larger ring, and at its edge were many of my AA friends and sponsors and other friends and my family. They were all trying to get in to reach me, but they were so far unable to get through the circle of drugs and alcohol. I was desperate that all the drugs and alcohol would prevent them from reaching me and that I would not be able to get out to them.

The desperation of knowing that love surrounds one and not being able to reach out to it or let it reach in is a consequence of the way the Demon Lover operates. He erects so many walls and obstacles that the openings to love are shut off. This is an image of the Demon Lover's "ring of power."

The Demon Lover possesses in many ways other than through addiction. Jealousy is one of his chief tools. In love relationships this may be one of his most frequent manifestations. Consider the following dream.

> I am in a bare hallway and see a tall, thin, dark, cruel-looking man. I know there is a couple in love nearby and that the woman is pregnant, but I do not see them. I take an immediate dislike to the man and distrust him. Suddenly, when I look again, I see a prison cell. In it is the sadistic man sitting coldly behind a bare desk. With shock I see behind him the loving couple. They have hanged themselves in a suicide pact because they could not stand being trapped in this cold, cruel prison. Their bodies are yellow, and a note hangs from the foot of each saying that they had asked for help from a loving person but no one had responded. The dark, sadistic man looks ahead coldly and indifferently. In horror I wake up, anxious about my relationship with the woman I love.

The dreamer was a man who was very much in love. He had previously been in two committed relationships in which the women had betrayed him, while in his first marriage he had left his wife, betraying her. He also had had an intense relationship with his mother, who on the one hand had loved him too much, leaving him to contend with his jealous father, and on the other hand had abandoned him through depressions and through intense and time-consuming relationships with her friends, leaving him to look on in jealous longing to be part of her interesting life. The dreamer's fiancée was very much like his mother, having an active, interesting life. In addition, she was a recovering alcoholic. She herself had had a recurring childhood dream in which a tall, thin man dressed in black was chasing her, and she had spontaneously written a story about addiction in which the tall, thin man in black had seduced her father through giving him drink and her mother by giving her chocolate, leaving the little girl alone to face the man in black. The man felt his dream was a warning about a danger to the relationship coming from this demonic figure that seemed to be inside of them both. In the relationship the dreamer would become intensely jealous, fearing an eventual betrayal and again abandonment. His anxiety would be expressed as anger, and he would berate his lover. She would respond like his mother by withdrawing her feeling, repressing her anger, and suddenly becoming consumed by a terrible craving to drink, which represented her unconscious hostility toward her partner. It was as though there were a time bomb in the relationship which threatened to explode unexpectedly at any moment. The dream showed what would happen if it did—the loving couple dead in a prison cell, even killing the child of their relationship. But they had made a cry for help from a loving person in their notes. What stood in the way was the dark, sadistic man. This figure was strikingly like Dracula, closing off the channels of love—their own love and the love for and from others. What they needed to do was confront this Demon Lover who was sucking their love away and drive the stake through the cold heart of his vampirism. They sought to do this together through writing and painting about their common Demon Lover.

Still another way the Demon Lover can bite his victim is through a negative self-image and morbid self-doubt, which result in the refusal of love. One woman who was possessed by this sort of inner Dracula had a long relationship in which she and her lover played Dracula and his vampire victim to each other. She had had a father with a "mysterious, dark, enchanting mustache." He had left the family in Mexico to search for gold in Peru when she was three, and she remembered being happy until then. After that the family moved about in gypsy fashion, and her father would occasionally appear and then disappear. When he was present he would be judgmental and critical toward all his children, and connected with this behavior was an underlying alcoholic aggression. His negativity and criticism dominated her life, but underneath lay the early memory of the romantic dark mustache. This combination culminated in an erotic fascination with a dark, sadistic man within her.

The way this inner Dracula figure functioned was to tell her she was always wrong, that what she felt was a lie, that in essence she was no good, perhaps even "evil." This meant that she was incapable of love and that any love she received was an illusion. How, then, could she be capable of a genuine loving relationship? And how could she be good for anything at all in this world if she had within her the "demon seed"? As if to prove this to herself, she got into a habit of compulsive stealing, then hated herself for it. Although she was extremely imaginative and highly intelligent, she practically made a profession of underachievement. And she continually chose men who were inappropriate—the first a man limited by the Prince Charming identification, the second a sensitive man who lived in a world of shimmering fantasy cobwebs and saw her as a beautiful spider caught in the center. Behind these early choices lay the following image of herself, expressed by a poem from Peter Beagle's *The Last Unicorn,* which she adapted to be sung by a woman. She put this poem in the front of a journal she started writing in her early twenties.

When I was a young man, and very well thought of,
I couldn't ask aught that the ladies denied.
I nibbled their hearts like a handful of raisins,
And I never spoke love but I knew that I lied.

But I said to myself, "Ah, they none of them know
The secret I shelter and savor and save.
I wait for the one who will see through my seeming,
and I'll know when I love by the way I behave."

The years drifted over like clouds in the heavens;
The ladies went by me like snow in the wind.
I charmed and I cheated, deceived and dissembled,
And I sinned, and I sinned, and I sinned, and I sinned.

But I said to myself, "Ah, they none of them see
There's part of me pure as the whisk of a wave.
My lady is late, but she'll find I've been faithful,
And I'll know when I love by the way I behave."

At last came a lady both knowing and tender,
Saying, "You're not at all what they take you to be."
I betrayed her before she had quite finished speaking,
And she swallowed cold poison and jumped into the sea.

And I say to myself, when there's time for a word,
As I gracefully grow more debauched and depraved,
"Ah, love may be strong, but a habit is stronger,
And I knew when I loved by the way I behaved."[11]

Her dreams seemed to confirm this fate she imagined for herself. There was a dream of a deep, dark hole in the earth, and at its bottom was a dreadful black creature called the Skink, a creature so black and formless it could hardly be talked about. This dream brought a shiver up both our spines, but we did not retreat from this monster. We persisted and tried to define him, just as Dracula had to be identified with every means and limit possible in order to be confined so he could be destroyed. Many creatures in the psyche can be loved and transformed, but Dracula in his essence is one that must be destroyed so the good forces can come forth. One of the problems this woman had is that she *identified* with Dracula, and this is what kept her his prisoner. And so in therapy we had to work on dislodging this identification with the demon so she could gain a better image of herself, love herself, and give and receive love from others.

In her third relationship she came to know herself better. The relationship was with a perceptive man who was wounded himself. This man's heart had been wounded by his mother, who herself was Dracula-possessed but in the form of a fundamentalist Christian religion through which she projected that her son would be the coming Christ. This man had formerly been my client's therapist but had stopped working with her because he had fallen in love with her. And because he had become seduced by this beautiful woman, he couldn't be a Professor Van Helsing for her, thus enabling her to find her own Professor Van Helsing within. He was a very ethical man, and he told her the situation, so they stopped seeing each other for over a year. But one day they met, and with passion they decided to live together. Here were two intelligent, creative, well-meaning people, but the relationship as it was could not work out because for her he was still the therapist, though now he did not want to be. So when they lived together she took all his judgments and criticisms to heart, and her negative image of herself continued. And now he felt she was sucking his blood, as his mother had sucked his blood as a child, because she was still acting like his patient. There is a scene in *Dracula* in which, with his long, pointed fingernail, he cuts the vein above his heart and forces the victim to suck the blood from his central artery. This binds her to him and gives him access to her mind and will. Reflecting upon this relationship afterward, my client said that the Dracula in their relationship had done this, binding them together in vampire-to-vampire fashion for several years. Finally, with the help of a counselor, they realized they had to separate for a while in order to break this destructive pattern.

After the separation was effected, my client had a powerful image that came to her like a vision: "There was an ugly, deformed, and perverted old man sitting on my heart and eating it away." With a start she awoke from this vision and remembered a poem by Stephen Crane, "The Heart," which had always fascinated her.

In the desert
I saw a creature, naked, bestial,
Who, squatting upon the ground,
Held his heart in his hands,
and ate of it.

I said, "Is it good, friend?"
"It is bitter—bitter," he answered,
"But I like it.
Because it is bitter
and because it is my heart." [12]

Now everything began to come together in her understanding. Her bleeding heart, the inner image of the perverted old man sitting on it, her outer father, by now externally visible as a man degenerating from alcohol addiction, the magical mustache harder to see, and behind all this the archetype of Dracula, the Demon Lover, orchestrating the inner and outer drama of her life. She realized that while her heart was being eaten she could not give it to anyone. That was why she had become a vampire seductress, that was why she had identified with the Peter Beagle poem some sixteen years earlier, that was why now at forty she still had not actualized her potential for creativity in a meaningful profession or in a relationship.

Soon after she had made the intuitive connection between her outer father, the inner perverted old man, the archetypal Demon Lover, Dracula, and her own victim-vampire identity, she had a shocking experience. She went back home to attend her grandmother's funeral and had the following encounter with her father.

I stayed at my father's house last night. This morning he told me he had to tell me the dream he had had all night long. He may have said that he hoped it wouldn't shock me—or that I might think it was "silly." I said "I doubt it."

He said, "I dreamed I was kissing your pussy all night long. You kept saying, 'Don't stop! don't stop!'"

Then he told me that he would wake up and try to shake off the dream. "Did you ever have a dream that you couldn't seem to get rid of? I woke up this morning with a stomach ache. You kept saying, 'I'm coming, I'm coming.' You could, but I couldn't."

He said, "I have kissed [your pussy] at least a hundred times when you were a baby. You know, after your bath when you were all [clean] and powdered."

I responded rationally and with attempts at humor, and acted as if it weren't such a strange thing to be telling me. Now I feel like crying. My body could fly apart. I could go crazy. He will have to pay for my keep in an insane asylum. I may "go to pieces." I may be killed on this airplane flight.

We talked about sexual things the whole time I was there this morning. I told him about the miscarriage and three abortions. he said I was probably better off.

I keep feeling "Oh, my God!" but some part of me feels relieved to know that my problem with what has been termed "psychological incest" has a *real* basis. Should I wonder if he ever did more than kiss my tiny pussy when I was an infant? That's probably enough! Isn't it? Why did he tell me this?

This shocking discovery brought to mind a dream she had had years earlier, a dream which gave both an image of the actual incestuous violation by her father and the resulting image of herself which became internalized in her psyche. When she had the dream she had entitled it "Powder Baby."

A young, round, ripe little girl of about six or seven is standing beside me looking into a mirror. Her arms, legs, and belly are all full and firm and smooth. She literally leers into her image and while rubbing herself says, "I just *love* to put powder all over myself." She repeats this over and over with rolling eyes and a lascivious grin. Her one sadness is that it disappears too fast from her skin.

I am slightly surprised that so young a child is so voluptuous in appearance and so sensual in her tastes as well as being more than a little grotesque in her mannerisms. She, however, seems at ease with herself in my presence.

Up to now our therapy work had been in large part supportive while chipping slowly away at her terrible negative self-image. Suddenly, with the synchronous discovery of outer event and inner realization, the nature of our work together changed. She assumed her own positive identity, and now we could work together as sisters on the same path, an image which she had actually painted several years previous. She had always been fascinated with Dracula, and in the process of writing this book he had suddenly appeared to me independently several months before as a powerful archetypal image of destruction for human life and relationship. Avidly we reread the story together, each researching as much as we could about this Demon Lover. It was clear that she was a Mina, for she was very industrious and organized and had arduously been working to record her dreams for years. She needed only now to find those four strong men and professor Van Helsing within herself to drive the stake into Dracula's heart. For she knew now that although Dracula was a figure inside her, as he is in all human beings, he was *not* her.

In her Mina fashion she found the poems which to her expressed three levels of love. These stages of love emerged for her through the poems, as well as a fourth. The first stage was ecstatic love, the second was the shadow of this ecstasy, the third she called "back alone working on essentials of the heart," the fourth she called reunion. In this last relationship she had intensely experienced ecstatic love, followed shortly by its opposite, the crazy-making self-destruction in the relationship. At the time she found these poems she was in the third stage, back alone and working hard on the essentials of her heart. The fourth was still to come. Here are the three poems that touched her so deeply that she was able to see these patterns so clearly.

## ECSTATIC LOVE

Breathless, we flung us on the windy hill,
Laughed in the sun, and kissed the lovely grass.
You said, "Through glory and ecstasy we pass;
Wind, sun, and earth remain, the birds sing still,
When we are old, are old . . ." "And when we die
All's over that is ours; and life burns on
Through other lovers, other lips." said I,
"Heart of my heart, our heaven is now, is won!"
"We are Earth's best, that learnt her lesson here.
Life is our cry. We have kept the faith!" We said,
"We shall go down with unreluctant tread
Rose-crowned into the darkness! . . ." Proud we were,
And laughed, that had such brave true things to say.
And then you suddenly cried, and turned away.[13]

RUPERT BROOKE
"The Hill"

## LOVE'S SHADOW

The pain of loving you
Is almost more than I can bear.

I walk in fear of you.
The darkness starts up where
You stand, and the night comes through
Your eyes when you look at me.

Ah, never before did I see
The shadows that live in the sun!

Now every tall glad tree
Turns round its back to the sun
And looks down on the ground, to see
The shadow it used to shun.

At the foot of each growing thing
A night lies looking up.

Oh, and I want to sing
And dance, but I can't lift up

My eyes from the shadows: dark
They lie spilt round the cup.

What is it?—Hark
The faint fine seethe in the air!

Like the seething sound in a shell!
It is death still seething where
The wildflower shapes its bell
And the skylark twinkles blue—

The pain of loving you
Is almost more than I can bear.[14]

D. H. LAWRENCE
"A Young Wife"


ALONE WORKING WITH THE HEART

Now that we've done our best and worst, and parted,
I would fill my mind with thoughts that will not rend.
(Oh, heart, I do not dare go empty-hearted)
I'll think of Love in books, Love without end;
Women with child, content; and old men sleeping;
And wet strong plowlands, scarred for certain grain;
And babes that weep, and so forget their weeping;
And the young heavens, forgetful after rain;
And evening hush, broken by homing wings;
And Song's nobility, and Wisdom holy;
That live, we dead. I would think of a thousand things,
Lovely and durable, and taste them slowly,
One after one, like tasting a sweet food.
I have need to busy my heart with quietude.[15]

RUPERT BROOKE
"The Busy Heart"


Professor Van Helsing and his helpers can appear in many forms, and in this case the poem was one of those forms. The healing forces can also happen through a person, through nature, through almost any experience which opens the heart. The power of Dracula is to close the heart, to suck the blood away so it cannot function. Bu his power is not irreversible, as exemplified by this courageous and diligent woman. As I write now she is blossoming forth in her life, as a rosebud slowly opens to the light.

Inner creativity, the wedding within, is still another realm in which the Demon Lover can take his bite. Another of my clients came into analysis essentially with this issue. She was a very talented poet whose creative work was blocked. She had no problem with writing the poems: when she gave herself the time, vivid images poured forth in a torrent. But she rarely allowed herself creative time because of a guilt which was deep-rooted in childhood. Nor did she have problems forming the images which poured forth, but she had a fear of putting her poems into the world. When she came into analysis she was already aware of Dracula. She had been fascinated with this story as a child and was already aware how Dracula had played a part in her relationships.

When she was little she had had a very loving relationship with her father. He was a poet in exile from an eastern European country. But when she was five he died, and she felt guilty for his death as children often do. Her mother, who had been happy to stay at home and paint and be pampered by her father, now had to go out and work. Angry at this intrusion upon her pampered life, the mother made her daughters suffer for it. She criticized them if they day-dreamed or fantasied. She inculcated in them the necessity of work. Rita was so upset that she threw all her favorite dolls against the wall, breaking them to bits. One of her recent dreams shows a picture of the childhood influences operating upon her.

> My mother was kneeling over me while I slept, sucking blood from my neck like a vampire. I awoke and saw her move from me to my father's dead gray body lying beside me on a gray slab. After my mother finished sucking blood from me, she went over to my dead father and sucked blood from his neck, too.

In reality the mother had been sucking from the dead father, living off his death as a martyred victim and sucking the lifeblood of her three daughters. With this dream Rita realized that she had felt both abandoned by and guilty over her father's death. For that left her with no protection from the masculine. For this she had both hated God and ceased to believe in His existence. And the guilt about her father's death and her loneliness enabled her mother and later others to suck off her energy while she worked to support them. The first of these was her first husband, an artist and an eternal boy who let her support him. Later it was a woman friend to whom she gave continual mothering support. Both had in common that they had beautiful faces. What was it about the beautiful face that had so much power over her? In her second marriage she had not made the same mistake. Rather than marry a man with a beautiful face, she married a man of substance with a beautiful spirit. But when she found out she could not have a child, she asked the girlfriend with the beautiful face to mother a baby with her husband, for she wanted to have a beautiful child. The girlfriend moved into the home and became emotionally and financially dependent on Rita, until at last Rita and her husband felt that the lifeblood of their relationship was being sucked away. Finally the situation became so draining that the arrangement to have her friend mother her child had to be abandoned. About this time, Rita had the following dream:

> I was lying in bed about to give birth. When I looked up I saw three men with beautiful faces standing above me. They had cufflinks on their sleeves with my father's initials on them. The beautiful faces seemed evil, and suddenly the men rammed a rod up my vagina and killed the baby. I survived, but was horrified.

The three men, she was certain, were her mother's cruel, sadistic side, the part of her mother that did not want the daughter to have the creative life she could not have. And her father's initials signified his abandonment by death, resulting in the lack of protection coming from the masculine. In the story of Dracula, she reminded me, the Count only attacked the women when they were left unguarded by men. And the first victim, Lucy, had had her protective garlic removed by her sick mother. As a child and young woman, Rita had been like Lucy—naive, sweet, pure, and too giving, thus making herself vulnerable to being used. But now she was more like Mina, who, though a victim of Dracula, with consciousness tracks him down. She realized that she herself had tried to suck life from the friend whom she had wanted to give her the beautiful baby that she could not have herself. This recognition was important in tracking down the Dracula within.

Rita did a drawing of Dracula to see if that could reveal more. She drew a beautiful outer face and an inner face that was ugly. In the Richard Geer stage production of *Dracula,* such a change is shown dramatically. Dracula is an old, ugly man in his castle at Transylvania, but as soon as he sucks blood from his first victim he becomes younger and more handsome in appearance, until finally, when he arrives in England and approaches Mina, he is so appealing and erotic he is irresistible. Rita wrote this about the drawing:

> Looks beautiful but "feels" off or weird—something not right—this intuitive warning to stay distant is often ignored. Devouring, insatiable, seductive, evil, manipulative, beautiful, furious and jealous punisher. Comes as a lover, then turns to anger and destruction to be obeyed. Present when feelings of self-worth are absent.

When Rita courageously continued her work by having a dialogue with Dracula in active imagnation (a conscious confrontation with an inner figure), even more emerged. She had been intrigued with a certain combination that often makes for romantic illusion—the beautiful face which shows its lonely pain. So she asked him how he came into her life, and in her dialogue Dracula replied:

> I have come out of your mother's closet, up out of the deep bottom of loneliness, despair and guilt. She has been in the bottom of this despair without protection for years and so have you. You don't recognize me. You do not see my weakness or my evil side. You think of me as needy, as sad, as desperate, and that is true, but my need is to have you take on my burdens and such you try. You also cannot see how I want to imprison your talents, how I want you to serve me only. How envious and jealous I am of your talents. My need is to devour you. You can only be like a living dead with me—devoured and devoted. Never living your own life at all.

Dracula also told her she allowed herself to be a victim because she believed she was evil and that she should be punished, a belief which came from her childhood fear of having killed her father and overburdened her mother. From this dialogue with Dracula it emerged that her guilt extended to guilt for being alive, beautiful, and talented. She projected these qualities onto others and served them like a slave, keeping her own creativity in the realm of the "Undead."

The imprisonment of her creativity was revealed in another active imagination in which she had a beautiful baby and a boyfriend, and they all lived in a room with two doors. Her boyfriend could go in and out as he pleased, but she was afraid to go out with her baby, afraid they would shrivel and die. But she gathered up courage and did go out, and met a shrunken, dwarflike man whose eyes belied his appearance, showing kindness and wisdom. This was the one who had to be taken out that door and nurtured, not Dracula. Her creativity needed only to be taken out that door and nurtured and a fine contribution to the world of inspiration would be achieved. But to do that she had to recognize her state of possession from the Dracula influence. And although mourning and grief were healing, pity was not. Here entered the inner figure of Professor Van Helsing, a new protective father. He could discriminate the person from the state of possession (the mode of the Undead); he could distinguish between the person and the evil force. To make up for the dead father, she needed to develop an inner father with the objectivity, spirit, and compassion of Professor Van Helsing, who was humble enough to call upon the Higher Powers for help against the forces of evil.

We all have this battle with the Demon Lover to fight—be it in the form of addiction, or jealousy, guilt, doubt, or self-pity, or any of the other multitude states of possession which imprison us. And only if we are willing to consciously fight this battle, not just once but daily, will we be able to pass that final figure in the forest and reach out into the clearing so the wedding can take place.

*Where love reigns, there is no will to power; and where the will to power is paramount, love is lacking. The one is but the shadow of the other.*

C. G. JUNG

# 6

# *The Ring of Power*

The conflict between love and power is one of the mesmerizing "death dances" into which lovers most often fall on the way to the wedding. Power and possessiveness, the desire for control, are the fundamental obstacle on the way to the wedding—the temptation which we all have to confront. The desire for power prevents the openness to receive what is present, to receive the gifts of love that life offers us. The following dream of a woman who was planning to get married illustrates how ingrained the drive for power is.

> I was a queen on my way to the church to get married. Along the way spectators were cheering and I thought they were cheering for me—the first to get there. My consort would be there later. But when I arrived the groom was already there and he was a great king. I was disappointed and shocked with the feeling that I was not first, not the central figure in this wedding.

The dreamer told me she had wanted to get married but had unconsciously expected everything to stay the same. As the dream showed, she had wanted to keep the power, to be the queen, to be the ruler in control. Before she could exchange the ring of love with her betrothed, she had to give up the ring of power. This is the fundamental human struggle we have in relationship and in life. We want things our own way, trying to hold on to what we know so that we are in control. But most often we are held in the ring of power, which we try to control—a ring held tight by the tyrannical figures in our psyche.

Power is the temptation inherent in all of the archetypal obstacles we have encountered on the way to the wedding—the Ghostly Lover, Prince Charming and the Special Princess, the Bewitchment, and the Demon Lover. The Ghostly Lover holds us in its power grip of fantasy and fascination, and in trying to make a love object out of this transformative archetypal energy through which the soul can touch divine creativity and spirituality, we act as though we could possess the archetypal power, failing to acknowledge this as a blessing given to us. Only in letting go of the divine love as an object to be possessed, only in giving thanks for our opportunity to be here to participate in the mystery that is life and love, only in returning the gift of Being through our own praising in actual acts of love, creativity, and heroism can we transform the power of the Ghostly Lover into love.

The power of Prince Charming and the Special Princess is the power that collective images have upon us as well as the power of a secure and comfortable life in which everything is provided for us by others and through outer events and circumstances. This is the power of the practical world of materialism which sells the soul of love for comfort and security. Only by realizing that easy recipes for success and beauty will never give us the depth of love that comes from receiving the mystery of life, can we be free from "plastic" power and be open to nature's gift of love.

Through bewitchment the witch holds power by devouring us— our beauty, strength, and love. Hungry to possess, keeping her victims infantile, weak, and dependent, she casts a spell upon our creative powers, paralyzing our initiative. The witch holds us in her power through our fear of her, through her unpredictability and her power to cast spells which can hold us in a frozen state of indecision and keeps us from actualizing our potentialities, from living life. The only way to relate to the witch in her evil form is to act, to commit oneself to life and fight her spell.

The Demon Lover's power is seduction. He tempts us to give up our will to him even to the point of self-destruction. He possesses us by titilating, exciting us with the promise of a supernatural high; but once we have accepted his temptations, we belong to him and he drains and lives off our energy. Through the poison of his "love bite" we become addicted to his promises of false ecstasy, turn into vampires ourselves, and succumb to the will to power that destroys love. As with the witch, the only way to deal with the Demon Lover is to say no to his temptation of the will to power.

In my psyche the bewitchment of my energies for commitment seemed allied with the Demon Lover, the Dracula vampire who drained my life's blood away. It was as though I were entrapped in a tight ring of power, encircled in a spell of bewitchment. The two most powerful figures for me were the Ghostly Lover, who fascinated me through the power of romantic idealism, and the Demon Lover, who promised to give me control of that false state of ecstasy. I was held in a closed ring of power tightening around my heart, and so I could not receive the deep and open wedding ring of the holy grail or the alchemical vessel, or the ring of the world. This tight, controlling ring in which I was entrapped needed to be opened. For me the way went from the vampire, who negates the life forces, to the angel of Rilke's vision, who affirms all of existence. To break out of the tight ring that was strangling me, I needed to find an affirming image of feminine spirit.

I found this image in Brünnhilde, the heroine of Wagner's tetralogy of music drama, *Der Ring des Nibelungen*. Brünnhilde is a feminine spirit who broke the spell of the ring of power through her acknowledgment of the Higher Power of nature, thus opening up the heart for compassion, the ring of love. She embodies heart, courage, and wisdom—the warrior courage coming from her stepfather, the god Wotan; the instinctive, intuitive earth wisdom coming from her mother, the earth goddess, Erda; and her own heart, which was open to love. Shortly before I started writing the last chapter of this book, I had the following image of Brünnhilde during a vision quest.

I was in a raft which landed at the shore of a mountainous island. There, my lover met me. He was bare-chested, wearing only a loin cloth and a long bearskin cape around his shoulders. His eyes drew me inward, pulling me into the depths of his ancient wisdom, and I realized he was a priest who would initiate me into the ancient mysteries. He led me up a mountain, where we stopped halfway at the entrance of a cave. There he beckoned me toward him, put his bearskin cape around my shoulders, crowned my head with a silver-winged Valkyrie helmet, and presented me with a spear—the garments of Brünnhilde. Then he pointed the direction I was to go and bade me farewell. I went into a dark witch's forest. The tree branches were low and covered with cobwebs, and I had to bend down to pass through. As I came into a clearing I saw another cave, and at the entrance was "Dracula's Daughter," a witchlike vampire figure that had been harassing me for several years. As Dracula's Daughter taunted me, moving to the side of the cave, I took my spear and pierced it through her body, impaling her to a tree.

After this vision I was no longer afraid of this figure born of the combined dark energies of the Witch and Dracula, a figure which had held me in its tight ring of power.

The struggle between love and power is expressed at a deep archetypal level in *Der Ring des Nibelungen.* This work, which took Wagner over twenty years to complete, is a tale of the conflict of love and power, a conflict so overwhelming that it eventually leads to the fall of the gods and the destruction of the universe. But with this destruction comes the hope of understanding what went wrong so that there can be redemption and a rebuilding of the human world with a vision of love as compassion. Although the world of the gods crumbles because of its misuse of power, the last bars of the music suggest a promise of hope, inviting us, the spectators of this vast drama, not to forget what we have witnessed. *The Ring* shows us the figures in ourselves who opt for power and offers us a vision of the possibility of giving up the ring of power for the ring of love.

In the depths of the Rhine swim three mermaids who guard the precious gold of this great primeval river. A dwarf, Alberich, a creature from the caves far below the earth, sees the Rhine maidens in their play and, entranced by their beauty, tries to catch and possess them. The Rhine maidens elude his grasp and mock him, but when a sunbeam illumines the Rhinegold they rashly reveal that the gold, when forged into a ring, will bring its wearer power over the entire universe. But the price to be paid for this ring of power is the renunciation of love. Frustrated in his attempts to win the love of the Rhine maidens, Alberich curses love, seizes the gold, and disappears.

Meanwhile, in the heavens far above, dwell the gods. Wotan, ruler and father of gods and men, is entranced by the sight of Valhalla, a great palace for the gods which Wotan has ordered the earth-dwelling giants to build for him. The price he has paid for this enormous labor is to promise to give Freia, the goddess of love, youth, and beauty, to the giants. Although the contract with the giants is engraved irrevocably in sacred runes on Wotan's spear, Wotan thinks he can keep both Freia and Valhalla by tricking the giants. But the only way seems to be to rob the dwarf, Alberich, of his all-powerful gold and offer the gold to the giants in exchange for Freia. The giants agree to accept the gold in exchange for Freia and take her off as hostage. With the departure of Freia, the gods begin to age, and, fearing their death, Wotan descends into the earth to wrest the gold from Alberich.

In his underground cavern, Alberich has forged the ring from the Rhinegold as well as a magic helmet which can make its wearer invisible and able to transform into any shape. Through trickery, Alberich is persuaded to prove the power of the helmet by turning himself first into a huge dragon and then into its opposite, the smallest of toads. As a toad, Alberich is captured by Wotan and is forced to give all his gold, including the helmet and the ring, to Wotan as the price for his freedom. Enraged, Alberich puts a curse on the ring and all who shall possess it, and disappears. Wotan gives the giants all the gold except for the ring, which he wants to keep for his own power. But the giants demand the ring, too, and when Wotan refuses, the earth goddess, Erda, warns Wotan that the gods will be doomed if they keep the ring. So Wotan reluctantly adds the ring to the giants' hoard and Freia is returned to the rejuvenated gods. As the giants gather up their treasure, the effect of the curse of the ring begins its fatal course. The giants quarrel, and one is killed while the other hurries off with his hoard. Wotan, musing in horror at the curse of the Ring, nevertheless hails the sight of the glorious palace Valhalla and goes toward it, trying to drown out the voices of the Rhine maidens, who call out for the return of the Rhinegold to the depths of its natural home in the river. So ends *Das Rheingold*, the prologue to *The Ring*, setting the cosmic cause for the spell of the ring.

In *Die Walküre*, the second opera in the *Ring* cycle, the conflict of love and power comes to its height of expression. In the hopes of recovering the ring from the giants, Wotan has wandered on the earth disguised as a human and has fathered twin children, Sieg-mund and Sieglinde, by a mortal woman. Wotan, hoping to make Siegmund strong enough to retrieve the ring from the giants, has separated the twins in infancy and has put Siegmund through trial after trial of suffering, leaving him ignorant of his parentage and his destiny. Sieglinde he has simply abandoned, leaving her to enter a loveless marriage with Hunding, who is from another race. As the first act of *Die Walküre* opens, Siegmund, exhausted from his trials, seeks shelter from a raging storm in a house built around a great ash tree, stumbles in, and collapses on the floor. The woman of the house, who is Sieglinde, restores the wounded man by giving him water, and tells him she is the wife of Hunding, owner of the house. Inexplicably the two are overwhelmed by a mysterious attraction for each other. Siegmund is about to go, fearing he will bring misery to her, but Sieglinde asks him to stay. Just then Hunding enters and, after hearing Siegmund's story and seeing the amazing resemblance between him and Sieglinde, especially in their eyes, Hunding be-comes suspicious and realizes Siegmund is the enemy who has killed his brothers, who were forcing their sister into a detested marriage. As Siegmund tells his story he relates how he lost his sword while trying to protect this woman. Angrily, Hunding says that the laws of hospitality demand he offer a stranger shelter for one night, but in the morning they will fight. Hunding goes off to sleep, drugged by a sleeping draught Sieglinde has given him. Sieglinde returns to Siegmund, telling him of a one-eyed stranger who appeared at their marriage feast and drove a sword deep into the ash tree, saying that only a great hero would retrieve it. Siegmund now remembers his father had promised him he would find a sword in his hour of great-est need. Suddenly the door of the house opens after the storm, spring moonlight floods the hut, and, still unaware that they are sister and brother, the two embrace ecstatically in love. Recognizing her own face and voice in her lover and hearing her father's name when he calls out his father's name, Sieglinde understands that this is her long-lost twin brother and calls him by his true name, Siegmund. Drawing the sword from the great ash tree and calling it "Nothung" (the Needed One), Siegmund presents it to his sister as a bridal gift. Now they are united, both in blood and in love, brother and sister, lovers to be wed.

High on a wild rocky mountaintop, Wotan orders his favorite warrior daughter, the Valkyrie Brünnhilde (born of his union with Erda), to protect his mortal son, Siegmund, in the upcoming battle with Hunding. Wotan's hopes to regain the ring still rest in Siegmund. But Fricka, Wotan's wife, angrily berates him for condoning incest between the brother and sister, the breach of Sieglinde's marriage, and his own lawlessness in their marriage, and demands that he withdraw his aid from Siegmund. Although Wotan defends the love of Siegmund and Sieglinde in contrast to a marriage vow that binds those who lack love, and adds that Siegmund, free from godly protection and laws, is the hero who can retrieve the ring, Fricka wins the argument by pointing out that he has given Siegmund access to the magic sword. Withdraw the sword, Fricka says, and let him fight on his own. And, she adds, instruct Brünnhilde not to help him. Utterly dejected and inwardly in a rage, Wotan has to concede that Fricka is right. When Brünnhilde returns, he reveals to her the whole story of the ring and its curse. He tells her how, after the delights of young love had vanished for him, his spirit aspired to power and he sought to win for himself the world; how her mother, Erda, had warned him of the ring's curse and of the doom that was coming; how she bore for him Brünnhilde and her eight sisters, the Valkyries, the feminine spirits whose destiny was to care for slain heroes who would protect Valhalla, and with whom he hoped to break the fate of the gods' ignominious downfall. But now, he, Wotan, has been caught in his trickery by Fricka, and he must yield to her demands. And so he orders Brünnhilde to withdraw her support from Siegmund and allow Hunding to slay him. When Brünnhilde protests, Wotan warns her not to disobey his orders, or even she will suffer the horror of his wrath. Shocked and deeply troubled, she sets off in fear of her task.

In the gorge below she sees the lovers flee into a clearing in the forest. Frightened, guilt-ridden, and exhausted, Sieglinde falls senseless into Siegmund's arms. As he tenderly bends over her,

Brünnhilde approaches him, telling him he must die but that she will take his soul to Valhalla to join the other heroes. When he learns that Sieglinde cannot join him there, Siegmund refuses to be parted from her and angrily reproaches Brünnhilde for the coldness and hardness of her heart beneath her young and fair exterior. Brünnhilde is shaken by his reproach and stirred by the courageous devotion of his love. Experiencing the sacredness of love for the first time, she pledges to protect Siegmund and his love even though it means disobeying her father. But when the battle begins, Wotan appears suddenly and, furious at Brünnhilde's disobedience, shatters Siegmund's sword with his spear. Without weapon, Siegmund is killed in battle, and Brünnhilde hastens to save Sieglinde, fleeing with her to the Valkyries' rock.

When Brünnhilde reaches the Valkyries' rock, she begs her warrior sisters to save Sieglinde, but they refuse. Brünnhilde reveals that Sieglinde will give birth to Siegmund's child, who is destined to become the world's greatest hero, Siegfried. Handing the broken pieces of Siegmund's sword to Sieglinde, she sends her to seek a forest refuge to give birth to the new hero in the woods where the ring is guarded by the giant, knowing that Wotan's wrath cannot follow her there. Wotan is heard approaching with all the force of his wrath. The Valkyries at first try to hide Brünnhilde from their furious father, but when Wotan threatens them with the punishment he has decreed for Brünnhilde, they flee. She will lose her rights as a demigod and will be cast into a deep sleep on Valkyrie Rock, a helpless mortal, prey to any man who finds her. Brünnhilde pleads with him—she had only followed Wotan's heart in protecting Siegmund. If she is to be doomed to this fate, she begs her father to protect her with a ring of fire so that only the most fearless of heroes will dare to approach her. Relenting, Wotan agrees and, taking his beloved daughter in his arms, bids her farewell:

Now must I lose you,
you, whom I love so!
O radiant light in my darkness,
so blazing a fire
shall show your bridal
as never has burned for a bride.

Flickering flames
shall girdle the rock;
The terrible fire
will frighten the cowards.
The weak will flee
from Brünnhilde's rock—
yet one alone masters the bride,
one freer than I, the god![1]

With a final farewell, kissing her eyes, Wotan removes her divine attributes and commands Loge, the spirit of fire, to surround his beloved sleeping daughter with a circle of fire.

While Brünnhilde sleeps in mythic time on Valkyrie Rock, the new hero, son of Siegmund and Sieglinde, emerges in *The Ring's* third opera, *Siegfried*. Siegfried, whose mother died in childbirth, has grown up in a cave under the tutelage of the Nibelung dwarf, Mime, Alberich's brother. Mime has raised Siegfried to slay the dragon who now guards the ring in a cave nearby, planning then to kill Siegfried with a poisonous potion so he, Mime, with the power of the ring can be master of the world. Mime has taught Siegfried to forge swords, his own craft. He himself has tried in vain to weld together the pieces of Nothung, Siegmund's sword. When Mime gives the ignorant Siegfried the pieces of Nothung, Siegfried files them down and melts them, making a newly forged sword.

With Nothung newly forged, Mime takes Siegfried to the dragon's cave and goads him to kill the dragon. Alberich is hiding out nearby, hoping to regain the ring, and offers to protect the dragon if he'll give him the ring, but the dragon refuses. Meanwhile Siegfried's thoughts turn longingly to his mother, whom he never knew. But when the dragon awakens, the two struggle, and Siegfried slays the dragon, piercing his heart with the sword. In admiration for Siegfried's heroism, the dying dragon warns him that Mime is planning his death. A drop of the dragon's blood falls onto Siegfried's hand, and when he licks it, he suddenly understands the meaning of the forest bird's song that he had heard while musing about his mother. The bird tells him to take the ring and the helmet and that he now has the ability to read people's thoughts. When Siegfried hears the approaching Mime wish for his death, he kills him. Alberich, who had been arguing with Mime about who would eventually get the ring, laughs from afar. Meanwhile the forest bird tells Siegfried (who asks if it can find him a comrade) about Brünnhilde, the most beautiful of women, who lies sleeping on a rock surrounded by fire, awaiting the hero who has not learned to fear. Siegfried, who has never seen a woman, follows the bird toward Brünnhilde's rock.

At the foot of the Valkyries' rock, during a violent thunderstorm, Wotan summons Erda and asks her how to stop the terrible downfall of the gods. When Erda tells him to ask their wise daughter, Brünnhilde, Wotan tells her of the punishment and realizes Erda cannot help him to forestall the inevitable. Siegfried arrives, and Wotan angrily bars his way with his spear, but Siegfried breaks the spear with his sword, Nothung. He is the hero who does not fear! Wotan departs, and Siegfried moves through the flames to the rock where Brünnhilde sleeps. When he removes her armor, he draws back in astonishment. Now he learns fear with his first sight of a woman. But he kisses her and she awakens, asking who is this hero. It is Siegfried, he says, and joyously she revels in her love for him. Though she begs him to leave her untouched as the goddess she once was, human passion overtakes them, and the two embrace, hailing the ecstasy of their life and death together: "Love that enlightens! Death that is joy!," they sing.[2]

The drama of love and power comes to its completion in the *Ring* cycle's last opera, *"Götterdämmerung (Twilight of the Gods)*. The imminent fall of Valhalla is predicted by the three Norns as they spin the rope of fate. When the rope breaks they realize their power of prophecy is at an end and they return to their mother, Erda. It is dawn, and Brünnhilde and Siegfried awaken after their bridal night. Brünnhilde, knowing that Siegfried must pursue his heroic destiny, encourages him to go forth in the world to perform deeds of valor. Siegfried pledges his love to her by giving her the ring, and she gives him her horse, Grane.

During his adventures Siegfried approaches the castle of Gunther, king of the Gibichungs. There, Hagen, half brother of Gunther and son of the dwarf Alberich, is plotting to get the ring. Hagen's plot is that Gunther should marry Brünnhilde to consolidate his power. If

Siegfried is given a magic potion that makes him forget his love for Brünnhilde and fall in love with Gunther's sister, Gutrune, then he might be persuaded to win Brünnhilde for Gunther in order to wed Gutrune. When the unsuspecting hero takes the potion which Gutrune offers him, he immediately forgets Brünnhilde. Taking a pledge of blood brotherhood with Gunther, Siegfried agrees to the plan. Wearing his magic helmet, he will appear disguised in the form of Gunther and claim her as Gunther's bride.

Meanwhile, on Valkyrie Rock, Brünnhilde receives a visit from her sister Waltraute. In terror, Waltraute begs Brünnhilde to return the ring to the Rhine maidens. Wotan has warned that unless the ring is returned, the doom of the gods is sealed. But Brünnhilde, who has been banished from the gods by her father and is now under the full spell of human love, looks down at the ring on her wedding finger—it is the ring that Siegfried gave her, a ring symbolic of the rapture of their love. "Rather let Valhalla crash to earth," she says. "I'll not abandon the ring!"[3] In despair Waltraute leaves. Dusk falls and a stranger steps through the flames as Brünnhilde recoils in horror. It is Siegfried, disguised as Gunther, by means of the magic helmet. When she fends him off holding up the ring, he grabs it from her finger and claims her as Gunther's bride.

Back at the Gibichung castle, Alberich has forced his sleeping son, Hagen, to swear he will get the ring. This requires the destruction of Siegfried. Alberich recounts:

I—and you:
we're heirs of the world,
if I can count upon your faith,
sharing both my woe and wrath.
Wotan's spear
was split by the Volsung.
And through his great might
the dragon was slain.
He playfully picked up the ring.
Now he is lord of every power.
Valhall and Nibelhome
bow to his might.
Since this hero is fearless

my curses are lame.
He knows not how the ring is used,
he knows not its murderous might.
Laughter and love fill his heart:
joy in living is his.
Now we must plot
just how to destroy him.
The golden ring—
the ring—*that* we must capture.
A cunning, wise woman
lives for his love:
if she advise
that he return it
to the waters where
the Rhine-maidens live—
those girls who made me a fool—
the circlet then will be lost;
and no art will win it again.
Therefore delay not,
aim for the ring.[4]

When Brünnhilde is brought to the Gibichung castle to be
Gunther's bride, she sees Siegfried (now in his true form) wearing
her ring on his finger. Realizing she has been tricked, she claims
Siegfried is her true husband. But Siegfried, still influenced by the
magic potion, denies he has wronged her. Enraged, Brünnhilde accuses him of lying. But Siegfried dismisses her and leaves with Gutrune to prepare for the wedding. Confused, shamed, and furious,
Brünnhilde laments over the loss of her godly wisdom and her bondage to this man who has betrayed her. Determined to gain revenge,
she reveals to Hagen that Siegfried has one vulnerable spot: a spear
in his back will kill him.

While Hagen is planning to kill Siegfried during a hunting party,
Siegfried wanders off by the Rhine and encounters the Rhine maidens. They beg him for the ring, warning him of Alberich's curse—
that each of the ring's wearers will die. If he returns the ring, they
will hide it in the depths of the Rhine. "Only the waves cancel the
curse!" they sing.[5] But Siegfried dismisses their warnings as "woman's wiles," and the Rhine maidens, calling him a numbskull, swim

away, knowing that Brünnhilde, who will inherit the ring, will be wiser. Siegfried rejoins the hunting party and at Hagen's urging recounts his boyhood with Mime, his slaying of the dragon, and, after Hagen gives him another potion to restore his memory, his wooing of Brünnhilde. With the excuse of vengeance for the supposed betrayal of Gutrune, Hagen thrusts his spear in Siegfried's back. In his dying moment, his memory now restored, Siegfried hails Brünnhilde and their love.

When Siegfried's body is brought back to Gibichung hall, Gutrune accuses her brother, Gunther, of the murder. Gunther accuses Hagen, and the two men fight over the ring; Hagen kills Gunther and tries to get the ring from Siegfried's hand when Brünnhilde enters. Realizing now that Siegfried has been tricked and is indeed a true hero, she orders a funeral pyre for him, a holy flame that she will share. Musing on the curse of the ring and Wotan's responsibility for his death, she takes the ring and promises it to the Rhine maidens, to preserve it in its original home. Brünnhilde reflects:

He—purest
of heroes—betrayed me,
that thus a wife must be wise![6]

In the fire of sacrifice the ring will be purified and returned to its original source. Brünnhilde puts the ring on her finger and with her horse leaps into the fire, hailing Siegfried and their love with joy. As the flames blaze high, the river Rhine floods over, pouring its waters over the pyre. Hagen, still in pursuit of the ring, madly plunges into the flood while the Rhine maidens circle and play with the ring on the now-calm water. And, from the ruins of the fallen hall, the remaining men and women watch as the firelight in the heavens grows and the flames seize Valhalla, the palace of the gods.

Although the spell of power has finally consumed the gods, a cosmic enlightened wisdom is now possible. This is the wisdom of love that is compassion, a wisdom that is gained through Brünnhilde's original openness to the love of Siegmund and Sieglinde. And it is a wisdom in love that she has to learn through her own human experience of vulnerability and suffering. In the following lines, which were written by Wagner for Brünhilde to sing at the end but which were not included "because their meaning was already conveyed with the greatest clarity by the musical effects of the drama," as Wagner writes, Brünnhilde sings out her message to humankind.

You, flourishing life's
remaining race,
listen now to what I
have to tell you:
You'll see by the kindling fire
Siegfried and Brünnhilde consumed;
you'll see the Rhinemaidens
returning the ring to the deep;
to the North there
look through the night.
There, shining in the sky,
glows a sacred fire;
so understand
that you're watching Valhalla's end.
Vanished like air
is the race of gods;
without rulership
I leave the world behind;
my wisdom's holiest hoard
I assign to the world.
Not goods nor gold
nor godly state;
not house nor hearth
for lordly pomp;
not empty treaties'
treacherous bonds
for false tradition's
pitiless law:
blessed in joy and sorrow,
only love I bequeath![7]

The entire drama of *The Ring* shows the price of the course of power that we humans often pursue when we mistake power for love. The characters who gain possession of the ring show us those figures in ourselves who lose love for power. Alberich wants to possess the Rhine maidens for their beauty. Unable to accept that their beauty belongs to nature, to the Rhine, which symbolizes the flowing source of life and creativity, and is beauty that cannot be possessed by humans but only loved in awe, he becomes cynical and hateful when the Rhine maidens make a fool of him. So he renounces love for power, for control and mastery of the universe. As a dwarf, a cave dweller under earth, Alberich symbolizes that figure in us who wants to grab at love and beauty as a possession. And he is like the "perverted old man," that inner figure who becomes cynical when he cannot have what he wants and curses love. Although he has the knowledge and the craft to forge the gold into the magic ring and helmet, he loses them when he is tricked into showing off his power. In a man, in a woman, in a relationship, he is that one who does not honor the greater mystery of nature in humility but who wants to master it through his cunning, craftiness, and technique. He is the grabbing one, the underground manipulator who cynically curses love and opts for the play of power instead.

Wotan, the father and the ruler of the gods, is the wrathful one who overtly displays his power, who thinks that power is his natural right. His *notion* of love is narrowed to the delights of sexual pleasure; although he is a ruler of the heavens, he has not seen the power of spiritual love. When the delights of young love dwindle, he sees nothing higher than power over the world. Although he wants the pure love of Siegmund and Sieglinde to be possible, they are still only a means to his own selfish ends—to regain the ring. He does not really honor the integrity of anyone—he tries to trick the giants; he betrays his wife, Fricka, and he uses his daughters, the Valkyries, for his own power ends. Even Brünnhilde, the one whom he loves most purely, he sacrifices when she disobeys his orders, though she is following what she intuits to be his heart's love for Siegmund. Wotan is the one in us who betrays the heart, whose wrathful revenge destroys what he loves most. He is capable of tenderness: he is able to see the purity of heart in the love of Siegmund and Sieglinde and in the courageous act of Brünnhilde who has experienced and hopes to protect and preserve the sacredness of that love. But he cannot admit he is wrong! He remains self-justified to the end, even in the full knowledge that he has chosen a course of action that can only end in doom and destruction. He must have glory—the visible glory of the power of Valhalla before his eyes—no matter what the cost. Wotan is the one in us who destroys the love relationship because he does not want to give up his own power aims; the one who refuses humility; the one who will not acknowledge his guilt, that he has been wrong, or chosen poorly. He symbolizes the grandiose power drive which refuses to bow in humility before the Other and before the greater cosmic forces of nature.

The giants, who next gain possession of the ring, symbolize brute strength. They are stupid and do not know the value of the gold or how the ring may be used. They are interested only in sheer quantity. Amassing gold is their only aim, and once they have the ring they go to sleep. They do not even know the difference between the ring and the rest of the gold quantity. In us they are the stupid, sleeping ones who are unconscious of value, who sleep on gold we do not even try to transform. This is like sleeping on the gold of a love relationship, not seeing its value, and rather living unconsciously in the mass mentality of a quantitative existence. The giants are the inertial forces in ourselves whose quantitative material existence, whose sheer weight, oppresses us and pulls us back from the consciousness and growth of love.

Siegfried, the new hero, the hope of the future, is the one who wrests the ring away from the giant sleeping in the form of a dragon. In him, it seems, is our possibility; he is an innocent, unacquainted with the manipulative aims of power, with trickery. Reared without parents, he is an orphan and perhaps symbolic of the divine child within us. He is playful and has a natural relation to the singing birds of the forest. He has a natural courage and intelligence, has been taught the craft and discipline of forging, and is able through his strength, intelligence, and the diligence of his work to forge the new sword, Nothung. He is without fear, and even the dragon that he slays admires his courage. He symbolizes the intuitive ability to hear nature's songs and wisdom, and he has gained access to this hearing by being brave enough to slay the dragon and taste the dragon's blood. But Siegfried has never known woman; his mother died in childbirth, and Brünnhilde is the first woman he has ever seen. (At first he even mistakes her for his mother.) It is through his meeting with Brünnhilde that Siegfried first experiences emotional fear (the fear of the divinity of woman), and his overcoming of this fear initiates him into the realm of human love.

Siegfried is the heroic, fearless, primal masculine energy in us who is ready and able to bravely fight any dragon that *threatens* love. But he has not yet learned the wisdom of the feminine, so he does not fully understand what love is; nor does he understand the dangers of love. Thus he is easily tricked by the dark force of Hagan and takes the magic potion without a thought. His relation to love is still primitive: he is overwhelmed by Brünnhilde's wondrous beauty, then overwhelmed with Gutrune when he takes the magic potion. And, finally, when he encounters the Rhine maidens, he does not recognize their words to him as nature's feminine wisdom, but sees them merely as "pretty maids" who threaten a man if he does not succumb to their smiles and who would sting a man with scolding words. Siegfried is the hero in us who takes us beyond fear. But he is also the one who has not yet learned to discriminate within the feminine realm. He cannot discriminate between the physical feminine, which is seductive and therefore threatening, and the pure feminine receptivity of nature, which knows that nature's gold must be returned to its source and not kept for power. And so Siegfried is the unwed hero who must die because he has not yet learned nature's feminine wisdom. Siegfried takes us beyond fear but not beyond desire. He has not yet learned to listen to the feminine, the wisdom of creative fidelity to love.

Brünnhilde is the last one to have possession of the ring. She has had it twice—first when Siegfried gave it to her and then again when she inherited it after his death. It is through Brünnhilde that the lessons of love are learned—first in the love she has for her father, then in the sacred love she sees in the wedding of Siegmund and Sieglinde, next in her opening to human love in her own wedding with Siegfried and the dark passions that go with that love, and finally in the spiritual love of compassion, when she transcends human love and experiences a love that opens to the whole cosmos as she returns the ring to its natural source, the Rhine.

The daughter of Erda, the earth mother, and of Wotan, father of the heavenly gods, Brünnhilde is the child of the union of heaven and earth. In us she symbolizes the feminine spirit, uniting in herself the qualities of wisdom, courage, and heart. Initially she is a warrior maiden, a father's daughter who knows the wishes of his heart. But when she encounters the sacred love of Siegmund and Sieglinde, she grows beyond even this love to a selfless love that dares to disobey the power of his will. Although she accepts the punishment for her act of disobedience (the loss of her godhead), she courageously stands up to him for the integrity of her deed and appeals to his fatherly love to modify her punishment, so that if she is to wed it will be only to a fearless hero.

In her wedding embrace with Siegfried, the hero who fearlessly breaks through the ring of fire, Brünnhilde first experiences the passions of human love. It is in this ecstatic experience of being "in love" that she tries to possess the ring. For the ring is the symbol of Siegfried's love, a passionate love which has her under its spell. But as with all finite love, Brünnhilde experiences its end when Siegfried betrays her. She, too, falls under the spell of power—the power of revenge upon the man who has betrayed her. And it is through her wrathful revenge (not unlike her father's) that the new hero, Siegfried, is killed. In experiencing all the human passions, from ardor to revenge, Brünnhilde symbolizes our human destiny in love. But she also transcends this finite aspect of love as possession when she understands how Siegfried came to betray her and how in this grief she has grown wise. And in this understanding of our human suffering she attains an enlightened vision of love as compassion, which goes beyond possession and returns to nature what belongs to nature alone. Brünnhilde is that divine feminine spirit of love in us which understands human suffering and its healing wisdom through experience. Accepting the higher order of the cosmos, this spirit redeems love through restoring the ring to nature and celebrating the harmony of man and woman as, in a final act of self-sacrifice, Brünnhilde joins Siegfried in the redemptive fire of the wedding of their souls. She is that wondrous, wise woman in us who, born of earth and heaven, freely surrenders finite worldly power for the higher power of spiritual love.

The Ring is symbolic of the whole circle of nature, of the cycle of the seasons and of time, of the flow of the Tao, of the eternal return of all things to their origin. This circle of nature is cared for by the feminine nature spirits, the Rhine maidens, whose relation to the ring is joyfully playful, not possessive and controlling. It is when the masculine forces steal the ring for power purposes, because the love they want fails them and cannot be possessed, that the ring becomes a curse upon humans and the gods. As in the course of consciousness, there is a growth and transformation, a learning, in this process. The pure gold is formed and shaped into the circlet of the ring. A new masculine hero (Siegfried) emerges who can forge the sword of courageous consciousness. And the transformation of the feminine sky spirit (Brünnhilde) from father's daughter and warrior maid into a wise, wondrous woman of courageous open heart is achieved. So, too, is the growth of love from the possessiveness of selfish desire into that grand healing, redemptive love of compassion, the opening of the heart. And so when the ring is returned to nature, by the feminine spirit of earth and sky, Brünnhilde, the learning of love is there present for us, a vision of love for the way to the wedding of human and divine.

# PART TWO

# The Loving

The woman who is separated from her lover
Spins at the spinning wheel.

The Bagdad of the body rises with its towers and gates.
Inside it the palace of intelligence has been built.

The wheel of ecstatic love turns around in the sky,
and the spinning seat is made of the sapphires of
work and study.

This woman weaves threads that are subtle,
and the intensity of her praise makes them fine!

Kabir says: I am that woman.
I am weaving the linen of night and day.

When my Lover comes and I feel his feet,
the gift I will have for him is tears.

KABIR

*Love does not consist in gazing at each other, but in looking*
*outward in the same direction.*

ANTOINE DE SAINT-EXUPÉRY

# 7

# *Into the Clearing*

The journey through the woods on the way to the wedding winds around many obstacles and through varied terrains. The journey is unique for each person, but all who have started on their way share the excitement and ecstasy of a vision, the fear and trembling before the awesome mystery of love, and the agony of the struggle to find the way.

The obstacles we encounter on the way to the wedding are like rocks that, in changing the course of a rushing river, lead us into new ways of our being and love. Through encountering the obstacles, we grow and change into the adventure that our life and love are. Wendell Berry, in writing about the creative fidelity to the form in poetry and marriage, expresses it this way:

> . . . form serves us best when it works as an obstruction to baffle us and deflect our intended course. It may be that when we no longer know what to do we have come to our real work and that when we no longer know which way to go we have begun our real journey. The mind that is not baffled is not employed. The impeded stream is the one that sings.[1]

The obstacles and the suffering that goes with them are actually stepping stones on the way; they are an essential part of the way and form the very course of our journey.

A phase of the journey for my fiancé and myself, and what was required of each of us, was experienced on a mountain trek in Africa. Early in our relationship we decided to climb Mount Kilimanjaro.

The call of Africa, land where the Beast still roams, must have sounded deep in our psyches. This climb was the first vow we took together, and for each of us it required a different relation to existence, a way complementary to our usual modes. The climb was nontechnical but arduous and took about a week for the back route we had chosen. We started in the jungle, struggling up through mud and over tangled tree roots, through a veil of heavy mist, hearing the cries of animals around us. We climbed for five days, up from the jungle, through moorland, over a vertical wall of rock, finally through the clouds to our last base camp before the final ascent to over 18,000 feet. The last day's ascent was to begin at one o'clock in the morning. It would take many hours of climbing in the dark with flashlights, two steps up, then sliding one step back in the loose gravel rock to reach the top of this mysterious mountain. My chances of making it seemed slim. Compared with the rest of the group, athletes who had made climbs over 14,000 feet before, I was a mere beginner and had not trained properly. I had barely made it to the top of Mount Kenya (16,500 feet), the trial climb for this one. My lover teased me, saying I would never make it to the top of Kilimanjaro. As the trip physician, he had been asked to push people as quickly as possible to the top, and on the preceding days of the climb he ran up this mountain, attacking it like a beast, happy when he was the first to reach the base camp. I was usually the last to get there, panting breathlessly all the way. The trek leader looked at me doubtfully on the last night as he explained the dangers we would face. There was a guide prepared to take those of us who could not make it to the top along another route around the mountain to the camp where we would stay after the climb. At one A.M. we arose and for eight hours struggled up the mountain, slipping and sliding. In the dark we formed into different groups, proceeding at different paces. Angry at my lover for suggesting that I would not make it to the top, I determined not to give up on this challenge. I also knew in my heart that there was a muse on this mountain for me to meet; I knew that this climb was a symbolic testing ground for my commitment to myself and to the struggle of a relationship that had as many difficult and dangerous spots as this mountain. And so, step by step, breath by breath, I struggled slowly to the goal. Although I never knew if I would make it, the hardest part of the climb was about 17,000 feet when my lover called out of the dark down the mountainside behind me. *He* could not make it! An unexpected attack of severe altitude sickness had beset him. Later he told me his balance started to fail; his thought processes began to fade. Because he was a doctor he recognized the symptoms. The trek leader also agreed he must go back—he and an African guide would go with him. I despaired over what to do. Should I turn back and join him, or should I try to go on and reach the top alone? I knew that while he might want me to join him at this moment for comfort, later he would lose respect for me if I had not tried to reach the top. I also knew I had to try to climb this mountain for myself. I turned to the trek leader for advice. "Go on," he said, "there is nothing you can do now for your friend, and he will be safe with us." For me this was by far the most difficult moment of the trip. Was this love, to go on alone? Was it a part of the commitment or was it an "ego trip" to try to make it? Up to that point it had seemed clear: the task was to climb the mountain. I was confused. My heart sank. My will quavered. To go back would be easy. It was the loyal, loving, womanly thing to do. Or was it? Every step was harder to take; every breath shorter. But suddenly from somewhere deep within me the decision was made: Go on. Try to reach the goal. This was part of the wedding! So on I went in the agony of the struggle, and with the fear and trembling before the challenge of the mountain and the challenge of our soul relationship.

Finally I did make the ascent on Kilimanjaro, the mountain where the gods are said to dwell. And when I finally returned that last day to the base camp, my lover was there. But he was very depressed and angry with me. He was the only one on the trek who had not made it to the top. He accused me of being selfish for going on without him. I felt terrible, but inside I felt proud that I had met the challenge of Kilimanjaro. I felt empowered, as though a new life would begin for me. We spent an angry, silent night together, and the next day, still not speaking to each other, we continued down the mountain toward the jungle from which we had started, in unshed tears. Once in the jungle, my lover spoke to me again. He told me of a dream he'd had just before the trek.

I saw a high, spiritual mountain. Circling around the mountain from right to left at the cloud level was a pathway of heavy stones, each with a different archetypal symbol carved on the stone—one with a sun, one with a snake, and others with cryptic codes. Walking on the stone pathway slowly and silently were ancient spiritual people in flowing robes, circumambulating this holy mountain.

As my lover came down Kilimanjaro, descending through the veil of clouds and into the circular green area of the jungle, he remembered the dream, and its meaning suddenly became clear. Had he approached the mountain with serenity and spirituality symbolized by the ancient holy ones circling the mountain on the archetypal stone path, he would have been able to reach the top. He realized that his unrelated approach to the mountain had been his defeat. His rage turned to tears in silent acknowledgment of the meaning of this climb on Kilimanjaro for him. It was nothing less than the gentling of his warrior spirit, the gentling of the Beast; the acceptance of the patient, circling way rather than the hard, straight, direct line of attack; the recognition of vulnerability and a new, receptive relation to the feminine. I, too, had had a dream the night after I climbed to the top of Kilimanjaro. In the dream, a poet who had inspired me spoke, congratulating me on the climb. I knew this dream symbolized the meeting with the masculine muse on the mountain.

After our climb on Kilimanjaro our relationship changed. It now had a depth and a commitment that each of us was able to bring to the other and to the challenge of a soul relationship. We had faced death in the physical dangers of the climb—the unknown weather changes, the high altitude, the difficult terrain. And he had faced death very closely when altitude sickness struck and he could not go on, while I had feared his death in that agonizing moment. It was as though our individual and different journeys on this holy mountain existentially symbolized our soul journey with each other.

The experience of Kilimanjaro brought to mind *The Snows of Kilimanjaro* by Hemingway, a story of a marriage and of a life that was not a journey to the wedding until the end. The protagonist, Harry, is close to death in a camp on the plains below Kilimanjaro and is reflecting on his life and loves. He is tired, bitter, and angry about a life that has been wasted and is ending in bickering with his wife, a woman whom he is unable to love. His predicament has come about through a careless accident: he had scratched his leg on a thorny bush and neglected to attend to it, and gangrene had resulted. It symbolizes the way he has led his life—neglecting his talent to write and succumbing to the habit of not writing and working daily; marrying for comfort and security instead of love; letting the fat grow on his soul. As he lies dying, bickering with his wife, who refuses to acknowledge the truth of his approaching death, and blaming her for his wasted life, he reflects:

> She shot very well this good, this rich bitch, this kindly caretaker and destroyer of his talent. Nonsense. He had destroyed his talent himself. Why should he blame this woman because she kept him well? He had destroyed his talent by not using it, by betrayal of himself and what he believed in, by drinking so much that he blunted the edge of his perceptions, by laziness, by sloth, and by snobbery, by pride and by prejudice, by hook and by crook. What was this? A catalogue of old books? What was his talent anyway? It was a talent all right, but instead of using it, he had traded on it. It was never what he had done, but always what he could do.[2]

He had always quarreled with the women he loved, loving them too much, demanding too much, until the corrosion of continual quarreling wore the love out. And now his life was a lie; he was too tired to love, thinking nothing could hurt him if he did not care. Now he would not even care for death, he thought. As he says to his wife about love, "Love is a dunghill. And I'm the cock that gets on it to crow."[3]

With these bitter reflections, remembering all the stories he had not written, all the loves he had not loved, he felt death come close to him, first in a rush, then moving more slowly upon him, occupying the space around him; moving so its weight was upon his chest and he could not move or speak. His wife, thinking he slept, had the servants carry his cot into the tent. In the end—was it in dream or reality or still another realm?—he was in a plane flying through a storm when suddenly

all he could see, as wide as all the world, great, high, and unbelieve-
ably white in the sun, was the square top of Kilimanjaro. And then
he knew that was where he was going.[4]

. . .

Kilimanjaro is a snow-covered mountain in Africa. Its western summit
is called the Masai "Ngaje Ngai," the House of God. Close to the
western summit there is the dried and frozen carcass of a leopard.
No one has explained what a leopard was seeking at that altitude.[5]

In the end, facing death, despite his cynical life, Harry was that
leopard seeking a wedding with the divine in that high white open
dwelling of the gods. And his wife, awakened by a cry of the Beast
in the night, found Harry dead. She was left in fear and trembling
with the beating of her heart.

Neither Harry's life nor his marriage had the authenticity of a
"wedding," for he had never really looked within and faced the challenge of the mystery of his being. Nor had he and his wife looked
together at the mystery of their relationship. Instead, through a series of distractions made possible by money and security, they had
continually looked outside, until he had become cynical and she had
become desperate to please him. Facing death is the ultimate challenge of being human, for as Heidegger says, we are on our way to
death as soon as we begin to be. Death is at the heart of our being,
silently calling for our transformation. In the confrontation with
death, everything else is set in perspective. In the encounter with
death our soul meets divinity and has the possibility of vowing to
affirm life. This is the condition of every authentic wedding,
whether it is the wedding within oneself or the outer wedding with
the lover. In the inner wedding we face the deaths that come in the
joining of opposite energies that require the death of the old, static
identities for the new Being to emerge. In the outer wedding, when
our eyes meet and acknowledge the joining of two souls on a common path, the death of the I–It relation is accepted for the life of the
I–Thou love. Both Harry and his wife had avoided this confrontation until the end. They did not consider going on this soul journey
until the actual force of Death appeared to Harry at the end. Only
then did Harry know he, too, like the mystical leopard, was going
on the climb to Kilimanjaro, the House of God. And only then was

his wife awakened from her sleeping existence by the cry of the wild.

The dreams of one woman occurring over the long course of her analysis continually emphasized the importance of her own unique journey on the way to the wedding. When she began analysis with me she had already had several years of therapy and was living with a man whom she hoped eventually to wed. Over and over again in her dreams she would start on a journey with her boyfriend. But inevitably they would become separated and she would have to journey alone, often through frightening places with terrifying figures. After dealing with these situations on her own, usually she would reunite with her lover at the end of the dream. On her dream journeys, like Psyche, she would pass through many dangerous terrains—through underground tunnels, darkened corridors, and war-torn territory; through the woods along a creek filled with large, revolting black water snakes, into a no-man's-land of battling renegades, past savage cossacks and the "KGB," who wanted to destroy her relationship. And many times in her dreams she had to face death. She confronted many figures from the past—her dead aunt and uncle, who had raised her to be a "good girl"; girlfriends from her school days whose "armored amazon" approach to life had negated her own, more feeling puella sensitivity; and old boyfriends between whom she felt torn, some representing the cultural, intellectual side of herself and others the warm, familial, emotional side. All were figures whom she now felt were inner parts of herself to be conversed with and integrated. In many of the dreams she had to fight for herself against the threatening figures. In one dream she had to use an armed revolver and "bodily weaponry." Her dreams continually emphasized that she needed to do things herself, pick the design of her life herself, and choose her own path. One of her dreams imaged it this way:

A. and I are together heading toward a place where I have business to do. I feel caught in anxiety because it is something I really need to do on my own, and yet I'm afraid to tell him this for fear he won't understand. But I do tell him when he raises the question. He doesn't feel he belongs on this mission with me. He does understand, and I feel relieved and free.

Growing up with her aunt and uncle because her father had died unexpectedly early in her childhood and her mother had been institutionalized before that, this woman was brought up to be a good, dutiful daughter. Her aunt and uncle were kind, but she was taught not to express her feelings of anger and aggression, not to assert herself. By nature she was very sweet and feminine with a high degree of aesthetic sensitivity. She was interested in the history of the arts and culture and wanted to live the life of a homemaker and hostess. She had a natural way of pleasing people, was very charming and attractive, and lived much of her life in the "darling doll" role. While this was in large part natural to her personality, she had been taught not to fight, and it was exactly the role of "warrior queen" that was emphasized in her dreams. Her life demanded this of her as well. She never chose men of wealth and so, after losing a small inheritance, she was forced to earn her own living. Like many women nowadays, who after years of marriage are confronted with divorce and must learn to forge their own way in the world, this woman was confronted with this task earlier, before she had married. Because one side of her secretly wished to be taken care of, to marry a man who would support her, some of the figures she had to confront on her journey reflected these dangers—the dullness of the "Miss America type," the nonsense of the "educational race course," the superficiality of the "middle-class hippies," the banality of the "beautiful people." In one dream she was working her way down through a path inside a rocky mountain to a foreign land, a rocky desert notorious for its dangerous, savage inhabitants. She was with her boyfriend, and both had to be alert for two dangerous groups— some Arabian-like savages and some "beautiful people" from the international jet set, all decked out in gold chains and safari hats, dangerous because they were so detached from earth. In this dream her boyfriend, whom she was afraid the beautiful people would scorn, was left in the shadows and she had to learn from them how to get along in the world. But ultimately she hoped to reunite with her beloved. In another dream she was left in a barren desert to confront an exquisitely dressed aristocratic actor, to whom she was initially attracted but who she later learned was the murderer of countless young girls whom he first had seduced.

The contrast between the beautiful people and the beastly savages was a theme in many of her dreams and reflected a split in her family heritage—one side stemming from an aristocratic, sophisticated city line, the other from cruder country folk. Much of her individuation work was to integrate these two sides. Because she herself was beautiful, the danger from that side was the greater for her, and she had to learn to value her own beastly side. One of her dreams gave her a striking image for this.

> I am with my boyfriend at an outdoor café that is well integrated with Nature. A. leaves to do something and I talk with a young woman who, it seems, was my first Jungian analyst. She is single but very much wants to be in a relationship with a man. But she feels so unattractive, although it is hard to understand this because she is a lovely person. Only when I take a more distanced look at her do I see her difficulty. On each side of her nose on her human face is a circle-shaped boar's tusk. It would, I realize, take a remarkable man, a man of real depth, to see her beauty beyond the appearance of these boar tusks. Somehow I feel she is part of me. I spot a man who was my former therapist and invite him over to chat. I like him but feel reserved in his presence. Somehow I don't trust him to understand that part of me. I hear that he and his wife have divorced and that he is a single man. This upsets me, as I had expected that he would have been more of a man and able to make a lasting commitment. Then I find A. up the hill in what seems to be a school building. Bright green grass seems to be growing at the seams of the marble walls and floors. And it was only a few years ago, I muse, that this was a new and pristine building. I'm amazed that it has been allowed to go like this. It seems to be going back into Nature. I realize that this is the Jung Institute. A. and I are both amazed, although he seems to have some grasp of it that I do not. I like it that he feels a connection with this place—something which I had always felt he didn't have. His face wears a seriousness that comes of profound sincerity, of knowing about the depths of his life, which gives me hope and security.

This dream showed her that she had the power of the boar's tusks and that her inner lover (symbolized in the dream by her boyfriend) was a man of depth, appreciative of Jung, who had been a guide for her in her search for spirit, able to see beyond appearances, able to make a soul commitment to her, an inner bridegroom who would make the vow at the wedding within. This inner wedding, she realized, was a prerequisite for the worldly wedding with her lover. Her way to the wedding had to be slowly approached by the careful integration of all these sides of herself, culminating in valuing the beauty of the boar tusks, which symbolized the aggressive warrior-queen side of herself. Previously she had had a dream that her boyfriend wanted her to wear white pants at their wedding. In the dream she had been shocked and repelled, for she wanted to wear a dress expressing her femininity. But now wearing the white pants at the wedding had meaning, for they symbolized a newly integrated warrior side.

If the inner wedding is not reached before the outer wedding takes place or during the course of a marriage, the marriage frequently breaks up because it lacks the depth of a soul relationship. Many men and women in our time and culture are making their way to the wedding after the trials of divorce. Recently I gave a workshop in which most of the participants were women in their late forties. Many had lived through their marriages as "darling dolls," had realized the lack of depth in these relationships, and were now seeking the way to wed the inner muse of creativity. As one woman going through the breakup of a twenty-year marriage expressed it: "I am not looking for an outer relationship right now. I just went out on a date with a very nice man, but realized how ridiculous this was for me right now. I need time to be alone—time to discover who I am." This woman knew she needed to wear the bridal veil for a while so she could make a vow to herself, at her own holy wedding within. After years of a marriage that did not celebrate the divine mystery of two human beings joined in a vision quest together, she knew her own soul's journey toward the divine wedding within herself was a prerequisite for an authentic wedding with a soul partner in the outer world.

The mystery of the wedding is expressed by Denise Levertov in her poem "An Embroidery":

> Rose Red's hair is brown as fur
> and shines in firelight as she prepares

supper of honey and apples, curds and whey,
for the bear, and leaves it ready
on the hearth-stone.

Rose White's grey eyes
look into the dark forest.

Rose Red's cheeks are burning,
sign of her ardent, joyful
compassionate heart.
Rose White is pale,
turning away when she hears
the bear's paw on the latch.

When he enters, there is
frost on his fur,
he draws near to the fire
giving off sparks.

Rose White catches the scent of the forest,
of mushrooms, of rosin.[6]

Together Rose Red and Rose White
sing to the bear;
it is a cradle song, a loom song,
a song about marriage, about
a pilgrimage to the mountains
long ago.

Raised on an elbow,
the bear stretched on the hearth
nods and hums; soon he sighs
and puts down his head.

He sleeps; the Roses
bank the fire.
Sunk in the clouds of their feather bed
they prepare to dream.

Rose Red in a cave that smells of honey
dreams she is combing the fur of her cubs
with a golden comb.
Rose White is lying awake.

Rose White shall marry the bear's brother.
Shall he too
when the time is ripe,
step from the bear's hide?
Is that other, her bridegroom,
here in the room?

*Venus and the Mother Goddess merge in a wild raging wind
and scour the deep canyon walls for the betrayer. When they
emerge into civilization they find the object of their feminine
wrath.*

*He is wealthy. He is ill. He is sleeping on the couch in a
fabulously elegant room. He is blonde, shrunken, possibly
mad. He is dying.*

*His face—bland and babyish—begins to kaleidoscope
when faced with the presence of the goddesses. In moments he
has become ten thousand men—my fathers, my sons, my
lovers.*

"Venus and the Mother Goddess,"
Dream of a Woman

# 8

# *The Missing Bridegroom and the Woman in Black*

Where is the bridegroom? Who is the new bride? These are questions I continually hear from my clients and friends, questions I ask myself. Recently I gave several workshops on the wedding theme to various groups across the country. When I asked if anyone had had wedding dreams, the response was overwhelming. But what was most striking was the continuity of themes—the "Missing Bridegroom" and the "Woman in Black." A number of people had dreams in which the bridegroom did not show up and the dreamer realized it was not time for the wedding. In other dreams a substitute bridegroom appeared, but the dreamer knew it was not the right person. And sometimes the dreamer had no idea who the bridegroom was. In two of these dreams a phenomenal happening occurred. When the dreamer, in each case a woman, went to the ceremony to be married, she found the one she was to marry was herself. In another dream a woman was preparing for her wedding and was all dressed in white. But suddenly she realized the wedding was really to be her death, and she was then dressed in black. Another woman dreamed her fiancé was getting married but the bride was not herself—it was a strange, dark, and powerful woman.

As we talked more, the Woman in Black emerged as a key figure at the wedding. One woman had the following dream.

I am at the wedding of a friend, a blond woman. The ceremony was about to take place when all eyes turned to a magnificent Grecian-like staircase. An elegant woman dressed in black and blue descended slowly. Her dress shimmered and she wore a black heart at

149

her hip. This dark woman with the black heart at her hip demanded our attention.

Who was the lady in black? Why was the bridegroom missing? We didn't know, but the mysterious feeling of these dreams suggested a significance that was more than individual, a meaning that went beyond the individual dreamer's life and was showing us a picture on the universal human level.

Before the wedding could occur it seemed as though the mysterious Woman in Black had a message to be heard by all. The ancient Sumerian myth of Inanna, Queen of Heaven (Ishtar), the goddess who descends to the underworld where she meets humiliation, suffering, and death by facing Ereshkigal, Queen of the Netherworld, was recalled by many women in the seminar.[1] These women felt that a dark, powerful side of the feminine, the "dark goddess" side, had been split off and rejected by the patriarchy and consequently had become a frightening force in the unconscious. Mythologically this dark goddess figure has always appeared in many cultures; as Kali, Hindu goddess of destruction and creation: as Persephone, Greek goddess of the underworld; as Lillith in the Bible; as Babayaga, the witch of Russian fairy tales; and Ereshkigal, Sumerian Queen of the Netherworld. But in the lives of women and men this fearsome feminine figure has often been left to dwell in the darkness of the night world. The myth of Inanna's descent to meet the dark goddess—her initiation there and reemergence from the underworld after Ereshkigal's suffering is acknowledged and her power recognized—is an archetypal expression of a journey that must be made before the wedding. This is why the woman in black and blue with the black heart at her hip is the center of attention in this wedding dream. The power of the dark feminine, that which enables a woman to say no and assert her needs for development—not out of the armored control of righteous self-justification but out of the soul's dark descent to face death—must be present for a relationship to have depth and ground. And it must be present in both the man and the woman. In the myth a substitute is required to meet Ereshkigal in the underworld if Inanna is to return to the upper world. Inanna chooses Dumuzi (Tammuz), her primary consort. But Dumuzi, who prides himself in the pleasures of his high place, tries to flee. Relentlessly pursued by the demons, in one version of the story Dumuzi turns to his sister for help and she offers to go in his place. At last Inanna allows the two to share the time in the underworld.

The man, too, must descend and meet the dark goddess, just as the virginal Persephone must wed Pluto, Lord of the Underworld. He must bear the rage and the tears of his own "depth-dark sobbing," as Rilke expresses it, to be truly present at the wedding. Perhaps this is why the bridegroom was missing in so many of the dreams—he must first meet the dark woman in himself before he can wed.

The 1984 film *Paris, Texas* expresses a man's descent into darkness, a descent which finally brings him before his own powerlessness and mortality and which finally enables him to speak with honesty, openness, and humility to his ex-wife, to make amends for the way he has treated her, and to open up the possibility for a soul relationship. As the film begins, the protagonist, Travis, is wandering lost and near death in the desert. He stumbles into a lonely gas station on a remote road in the lunarlike landscape, passes out in exhaustion, and is taken to a country clinic. Travis is mute, but the doctor finally traces his brother, Walt, in Los Angeles. Travis has been missing for four years, and the brother and his wife have cared for his son, whom he abandoned when he mysteriously disappeared. By the time Walt reaches the clinic in southern Texas, Travis has disappeared again. Walt finally finds him walking cross-country in a dazed condition, unable to speak. He asks Travis why he disappeared so mysteriously, but Travis looks blank and does not respond. During the long drive back through the desert to Los Angeles, Travis wanders off once again, as though trying to flee back into the barren solitude from which he has come. But Walt finds him and asks Travis if he remembers his little son, Hunter. Travis opens up to his caring, nonjudgmental brother with silent tears when his son is mentioned, but is still unable to tell his story.

Once in Los Angeles, Travis and his son, now seven, meet. Their encounter is difficult at first—confusing and upsetting for the shy and distrustful son, despairing and painful for the father, who slowly begins to remember what happened in the dark preceding years. Their silent reconciliation occurs when Walt shows some home mov-

ies. As a scene of Travis, three-year-old Hunter, and Jane, Travis's
ex-wife, appears on the screen, Travis's sunken memories reemerge
and he looks upset and dazed as from a dream. Seeing his father's
startled reactions, Hunter understands and calls Travis "Dad." After
this Travis recognizes he is "looking for *the* father"—for his own
internal father and how to be a father, and he becomes more confident in his approach to his son. Walt's wife, Anne, tells Travis that
Jane had asked Anne to care for Hunter and has been wiring money
from a bank in Houston for the boy's future. Remembering his former rage at Jane as well as his love, Travis decides to try to find her
so that she and Hunter can be reunited. Taking Hunter with him,
he sets off for Texas, where he traces her to a place in Houston where
she works—a peep-show club where lonely men go to look at
women through one-way windows and try to live out their fantasies.
The men cannot touch the women and the women cannot see the
men. Travis enters one of the booths and keeps asking for different
women until Jane finally appears through the one-way window. She
is surprised that this man does not want her to undress, but she
listens and tries to draw him out. Travis leaves wordlessly in rage
and tears while Jane continues to talk, not realizing he is gone. He
goes to a bar to get drunk, to flee the humiliating memories of their
relationship, of his own mad jealousy and possessiveness, of his fears
of betrayal. Drunk, he tells Hunter about his parents and his own
origins in "Paris, Texas," where his father and mother first made
love, where he was conceived, and where he himself went four years
ago to buy a vacant lot, hoping to rebuild a house of love based on
his fantasies. He tells Hunter about his simple mother and his father's projections on her, a story which he himself partially reenacted
with Jane.

> Oh, God. My mother, not *YOUR* mother, but *MY* mother, was
> *NOT* a fancy woman. She was . . . she never wanted to be a fancy
> woman, she never pretended to be a fancy woman . . . she was just
> . . . plain. Just plain, and good. But my Daddy, see, my Daddy, he
> had this idea, he had this idea in his head that was kind of a sickness
> . . . He had this idea about her and . . . he looked at her, but . . .
> he didn't see her. He saw this idea. And he told people she was from
> Paris. It was a big joke. But he started telling everybody all the time

and, finally, it wasn't a joke anymore. He actually believed it. And, one day, he actually did believe it. And my mother . . . oh, God, she would get so embarrassed. She was . . . she was so shy.[2]

When Travis recovers from his drunken relapse, he tapes a message to his son, thanking the boy for showing him how to be a father. But he also tells his son that he belongs with his mother, that it was Travis who tore them apart, and that he would try to bring them back together, that he was afraid of walking away, but even more afraid of not facing his fear. "I love you, Hunter," he says. "I love you more than my life."[3]

Once again Travis goes back to the club and enters a peep-show booth to talk to Jane. He tells her his story: He was wildly in love with a young, very beautiful girl of seventeen who loved him, too. They were always together and turned everything into an adventure. He loved her more than anything and couldn't stand being away from her. So he quit work to be with her, but the money ran out and then she started to worry. He became torn inside and started drinking. He knew he had to work, but he couldn't stand being away from her; when he was, he started to get crazy, to imagine that she was seeing men on the sly. Finally, he started accusing her, yelling at her, smashing things in their trailer. Then to test her he started staying out late to see if she'd get jealous. She was worried about him, but she didn't get jealous, and that made him even madder, because if she wasn't jealous it meant to him that she didn't love him. When she became pregnant, he believed again that she loved him because she was carrying his child. He stopped drinking and got a job, hoping to make a home for her. But after she had the baby she started to get mad and irritated. And no matter what he did, he felt he couldn't make her happy. For two years he tried to make things like they were when they first met. But finally he gave up and hit the bottle again. He was drunk and mean, and she was enraged. She felt trapped and told him he wanted to keep her a prisoner by making her have a baby. She wanted to escape—in her dreams she would try to run away from him and he would always stop her. When he heard this, he knew he had to stop her before she left him forever. So he tied a cow bell to her ankle so he could hear her at all times, thus tying her down even more. But she learned to muffle the sound and sought even more desperately to escape. One night he heard her, caught her, tied her to the stove, and listened to her scream, and to her son scream, too. But by now he couldn't feel anymore; he only wanted to sleep. He was lost in a deep, dark dream, and when he awoke he was on fire. His bed was burning and his wife and son were gone. Not once looking back at his burning home, he ran into the desert until there were no signs of people anymore, into the dark desert wasteland.

Though she cannot see the stranger who is telling his story, Jane knows who he is, for it is her story, too. In tears she cries out his name and presses her face to the glass. He turns so they are face to face and sees his features reflected in hers. He tells her to turn off the light in her room to see if she can see him. It works—the mirror reverses; now she can see him but he cannot see her. She tells him her simple story—that she didn't have what her son needed, that she didn't want to use Hunter to fill up her loneliness, and so she left him in the care of Walt and Anne. And finally she couldn't stand the pain of seeing her son grow up and missing him, so she asked Anne to stop sending pictures of him. She used to talk to Travis even though he wasn't there, imagined them talking together, talked to him in vivid dreams. "I hear your voice all the time. Every man has your voice."[4] And then finally everything faded—his voice, his image—and she gave up and started working at the club.

After she finishes her story, Travis tells her where Hunter is, that her son needs her now, and then he leaves. Jane sits in silence for a while, then goes to the hotel room where Hunter is. When he first sees his mother, he is stunned, but then he runs to her and hugs her in joy and they tenderly embrace and together "turn and turn in joyous circles."[5] From the car-park roof Travis looks on at a distance, gets into his car, finally smiles, and drives away.

*Paris, Texas* is the story of a man's descent into the darkness of his own jealousy and rage, of his inhuman attempt to possess his wife, of his fantasy image of her, which never allows him to see who she really is or recognize her needs for independence, but which instead tags her like a cow, a piece of property, until she is so enraged and desperate she has to run away, leaving a house on fire behind her. In the mirror of his wife's desperation, rage, and abandonment he encounters these dark faces of the feminine within himself. His agony is so excruciating that he loses everything, even his memory. He drowns in his drunkenness, burns in the fire of his jealous rage, and dries out in the desert of his alienation. His is a long "night sea journey," four years of alchemical dissolving, burning, drying out, and re-forming into a new being. The healing comes through the masculine, and not through "confrontation" but through love. The love of his brother and of his son helps him to find "the father," to transform the wound inherited from his own father, who tried to find his identity through a projection on his own wife, the projection of "Paris," city of beautiful women and glittering sophistication, and perhaps of Paris, the Trojan man who stole Helen, symbol of beauty and power, from the Greeks, thus instigating the Trojan War. Commenting on the film, Wim Wenders says that one of its subtexts is "man insisting on a certain image of a woman . . . that's how the peepshow came up: Travis is sitting in front of a screen, and she's on the screen, or behind it, and is really the object of his imagination."[6] The transformation that Travis undergoes requires him to recognize that he has been relating to his wife as an object and that his desire to possess her has been a domination through violence, that he's reached his bottom and has to face humiliation. Travis's desperation forces him to be honest. He faces his emotions, his loves and his longing, his vulnerability and his violence, and through the depth of his deflation he is finally able to love—to make amends to Jane and to freely give her their son. When I first saw this film I found myself shedding tears of pain for this helpless, humiliated man, who reminded me of my wounded father and the ways in which I was like him, and tears of gratitude for his redemption—for the man with heart who Travis courageously chooses to be as a result of this dark descent. Here was a man, I felt, finally ready to be a bridegroom at the sacred wedding for now he had consciously met the woman in black within.

The Woman in Black is often angry and in mourning because she has been neglected. Often men are afraid to meet this dark woman because they're afraid they'll lose their soul to her. So they connect their soul with the Special Princess, a lighter image of woman they know and can control, a collective image. One man I worked with told me the following story of his encounter with the dark woman. He was in love with a woman who needed to be free to explore her own life. His feelings of insecurity arose, and all his old teenage jealousies flooded him. He had worked in analysis for some time and thought he was through with these feelings, but here they were back to plague him. As he told me his history with women, several things emerged. He had always been attracted to glamorous, sexual women, the Hollywood-image type. He had no trouble meeting such women, but now, in his thirties, he had had only three intimate relationships with women. The first was as a teenager, and it ended when his girlfriend joined a religious movement that disallowed their marriage. The second relationship led to marriage, but with it came his growing lack of interest in intimacy with his partner. This was a pattern he was noticing in himself—before he had "won" the woman, he was all afire with interest. Once she was "his," he began to lose interest. He and his wife divorced but parted friends. The third relationship was the present one, and he wanted to work on these issues. In this relationship he had experienced both poles— the sense of detachment when the relationship turned toward com- mitment, and the overwhelming feelings of jealousy when he felt his lover going toward her own independent life.

For some time the images of the feminine had been changing in his dreams—from sexual seductress to a more ordinary woman who, however, had a sense of soul. But around the time of his jealousy he had several dreams of women betraying him. I wondered if these might not represent his inner woman, who led him on and then turned fickle, for in his creativity he could not commit to one proj- ect. Enormously intelligent and talented, he wanted to compose music and write books, and had already begun to do so. But he couldn't stay with a project long enough to complete it and get it out into the world. He was not quite able to commit to the wedding on either the inner or outer level. Nor did his family dynamics seem to clarify this dilemma. But he had the following dream of a "dark woman" who seemed to have a message for him.

I was standing behind a glass wall partition watching cars go by. There was a traffic jam, but in the car directly in front of where I was standing was a black woman. She looked somewhat androgynous, for she had masculine hair growing out of the side of her face, like a day-old beard. Ordinarily this would have bothered me, but to my surprise I felt a deep soul connection with her, like a deep love for a friend. The traffic wasn't moving, so she reached through an opening in the glass wall and handed me a note. She thanked me for helping her, but said she had to go. Then the car behind her broke down and the traffic was stopped for a while. Just then the glass wall opened, so she drove through what was now a larger opening in the glass. Her car was full of older women who seemed to be in their sixties, women both black and white. I came over to the car and met these women, shook their hands, and felt the enormous energy of their human caring.

The dreamer associated the black woman with a deep instinctual level of his soul. Although she did not look like the woman of his "dreams," it was she with whom he felt the soul connection, she who was able to reach out to him through the glass wall, symbolic of the distance he had felt toward women, the barrier that kept him from commitment to the outer woman and to his own inner feminine inspiration. The car that broke down from behind he associated with obstructions from his own past, the jealousy, envy, insecurity that blocked his way in relationship. His current experience of returning to these feelings brought all this up for him, but it also brought him into relationship with the black woman and the compassionate older women in her car. He was in love now, in love with the mystery in his soul. Perhaps with the relation to the dark woman he would no longer be caught between dreams and reality but rather be free for a committed relationship to both.

After he had this dream, he realized that his childhood was not so uncomplicated as he had thought. His mother had always offered him unconditional love, which did not require him to give anything in return. He had always gotten all the attention he wanted from her. It struck him that in his marriage he had been expecting the same attention and unconditional love and that he had given only when he wanted to do so. And recently, when he wasn't getting the attention he wanted from his lover because she needed to attend to her own needs, powerful feelings of jealousy and infantile possessiveness arose. He paid attention to this new revelation from his psyche. When he went back to visit his lover the next time, he had insight enough to work with his jealousy and was able to accept that she needed to pay attention to herself—her occasional inattentiveness to him didn't mean that she didn't love him. It was as though his encounter with the dark woman in his dream was a corrective to the too positive, too all-giving mother. The dark woman introduced him to the feminine and to women as individual human beings with their own personal needs for freedom and development. In loving the dark woman, he could now truly love women in their individuality and he could love the creative muse in himself.

A woman who made the descent to meet the dark woman in herself told me the following story of the crumbling of her first marriage—a union of Prince Charming and the Special Princess—and the divine wedding she had after her descent. She and her husband had been very much in love during the first four years of their marriage. He was the Prince Charming she had always wanted, a "golden boy" who had been both a football player and ballet dancer in college; he was bright, cheerful, and healthy. The first day she saw him she thought, "There's my husband." Together they lived out their golden dream of marriage—to live off the land and have a happy family. They became the managers of a farm in the Midwest but found that living their shining dream brought them darkness. Disasters hit, one after the other. The first year the wheat crops burned up; the next year they were frozen by hail. The canteloupes got a strange fungus. And all their checks began to bounce. After two years of frustration they gave up the farm and went to a meditation retreat. There the fantasy of their marriage crumbled and each came face to face with himself or herself. The husband decided to devote himself completely to the meditative life. This threw the woman into her descent. She felt rejected: "It was worse than if he'd fallen in love with another woman." Her false, happy persona crumbled. "In my marriage I had been bright, sunny, tidy, a helpmate, always there and always good." When they finally acknowledged the marriage wasn't working, the dark side emerged. Although she had been in love, the sexual relationship had been disappointing to her, and the anger which she had been stifling came out. She began to drink heavily, and her wildness emerged at parties. She began to feel as though she were two persons: by day a precious princess, gentle and contained; by night a wild woman who was so angry she was beginning to destroy herself and everything around her. Her wild drinking resulted in a series of physical accidents. She hit her head three times and got concussions. The left side of her body became temporarily crippled. The pain was so excruciating she felt as though her soul were leaving her body. And the humiliation was overwhelming.

In desperation she tried traditional medical treatment, to no avail. Then she went to an acupuncturist who tried to balance the energy forces in both sides of her body. As the balancing of the dark and light forces occurred, she had a series of transformational dreams. In one she made love with a mysterious woman, for her a symbol of the divine feminine within herself. In another she confronted a dark, witchlike woman who, in the dream, was married to the man she loved, and she expressed her anger fully and effectively. Then she had a dream in which she gave birth to a baby girl who could walk and talk—a symbol of the feminine divine child.

Now she was beginning to feel the balance of dark and light forces within herself. She could express her anger, acknowledge her dark side, and accept the mystery of herself as a woman, as the fascinating new feminine being who was continually unfolding. She felt, in particular, the mystery of her womb—"the dark space that is quiet and still and can create for others."

She remarried, and this marriage was based not on fantasy of Prince Charming and the Special Princess, but on the spiritual transformation work the partners had done within themselves. Several months after the marriage she had a magical wedding dream which symbolized the divine wedding within.

> I am at a Chinese wedding. Someone said the wedding would be postponed until the special bread was ready. I was invited to the bakery where the wedding bread was being made, and noticed I was wearing a white dress. The bakery was magical inside, with red lacquerwork like the inside of a Chinese basket. We could hear the baking of the bread. A friend of mine, a wise old woman with a wonderful marriage, said the wedding stick her husband gave to her

was gold. Then a man approached and said, "The wedding stick is from the *Malleus Maleficorum* ["The Hammer of the Witches," a medieval witchcraft manual] and is the stick of alchemy."

The golden wedding stick symbolized for this woman the power of the creative phallus she now felt within herself. Through her descent into darkness and her encounter with the dark woman in herself (alluded to in the dream image of the witchcraft manual), she had, like the alchemists who wanted to transform base matter into gold, transformed the dark forces in herself into the creative phallus. Now the power of the inner bridegroom was present.

The image of the Missing Bridegroom, which has emerged in so many women's dreams, comes to mind again and again when women ask: "Where are the men who are developed and who understand women? Where is the man both sensitive and strong, the man who is not afraid of his suffering, who is not afraid of challenge, the man who seeks creativity and change, who seeks the developed woman?" Many women nowadays who have made the descent cry out this question with the rage of the Woman in Black. Yet, while the focus of their question is the outer man, most of these women are at bottom asking where is that man in themselves, where is the inner man of heart and courage, where is the deeply sensitive inner bridegroom? And men, I find, are seeking this kind of model for themselves, and also ask, "Where are the women with deepening strength, independence, and sensitivity?"

Rainer Maria Rilke made the descent the missing bridegroom must make. The poet devoted most of his life to understanding and expressing the soul's journey toward love and beauty, and he faced the ravages of his "depth-dark sobbing" and met the dark lady of lament. Then he could affirm life and see both love and death as essential to the creative process. He envisioned the relationship between men and women this way:

> . . . some day there will be girls and women whose name will no longer signify merely an opposite of the masculine, but something in itself, something that makes one think not of any complement and limit, but only of life and existence: the feminine human being. This advance will (at first much against the will of the outstripped

men) change the love-experience, which is now full of error, will alter it from the ground up, reshape it into a relation that is meant to be of one human being to another, no longer of man to woman. And this more human love (that will fulfill itself, infinitely considerate and gentle, and kind and clear in binding and releasing) will resemble that which we are preparing with struggle and toil, the love that consists in this, that two solitudes protect and border and salute each other.[7]

Rilke provides many men and women with hope and inspiration in their long and lonely journeys to find love—with others and in themselves. For Rilke understood through his own experience the descent into the depths of inner solitude that was necessary for a life of love and creativity. He was a man of heart, of courage and tremendous introspection and insight, born of his willingness to live and love the questions of existence. A man who understood women as well as men, he honored and was in awe of the mysterious difference between the sexes and the even greater mysterious divine unity in which they are wed and through which they create. And most of all he understood that the agonizing loneliness over which so many of us despair is really a learning experience, a secluded time of preparation for love. One woman who was in deep despair over the breakup of a love relationship, a breakup which reflected for her the failure of all her relationships and ultimately the failure of her own life, found solace in reading Rilke's *Letters to a Young Poet.* "Rilke's words comforted me in my suffering," she said; "they affirmed my being and helped me realize I was not at a dead end in my life, but that my very suffering was deepening my soul in its search for love." For all who are waiting for love to happen, expecting it to come miraculously from the outside, Rilke has this to say:

. . . the future enters into us in this way in order to transform itself in us long before it happens. And this is why it is so important to be lonely and attentive when one is sad: because the apparently uneventful and stark moment at which our future sets foot in us is so much closer to life than that other noisy and fortuitous point of time at which it happens to us as if from outside. The more still, more patient and more open we are when we are sad, so much the deeper and so much the more unswervingly does the new go into us, so much the better do we make it ours, so much the more will it be *our* destiny, and when on some later day it "happens" (that is, steps forth out of us to others), we shall feel in our inmost selves akin and near to it. And that is necessary. It is necessary—and toward this our development will move gradually—that nothing strange should befall us, but only that which has long belonged to us. We have already had to rethink so many of our concepts of motion, we will also gradually learn to realize that that which we call destiny goes forth from within people, not from without into them.[8]

Rilke's life-long journey into the depths where the soul learns the work of love shows a way to the divine wedding in which the Woman in Black and the Missing Bridegroom can be reunited. It illumines the way for all of us, whether that inner wedding leads to marriage or to a single life devoted to the outer expression of the holy longing.

*How should we be able to forget those ancient myths that are at the beginning of all peoples, the myths about dragons that at the last moment turn into princesses; perhaps all the dragons of our lives are princesses who are only waiting to see us once beautiful and brave. Perhaps everything terrible is in its deepest being something helpless that wants help from us.*

RAINER MARIA RILKE
*Letters to a Young Poet*

# 9

# *Beauty and the Beast*

"Beauty and the Beast" is the story of a couple's journey on the way to the wedding. It is a story which shows a fundamental obstacle to both the inner and the outer wedding, and the transformation of that obstacle into the existential vow of creative fidelity to the mystery of life and love. This tale of transformation rings true for many of us: for the man who needs to have faith and trust in his soul, that she will remain true to him; and for the woman who needs to learn not to be deceived by appearances, that the terror of being trapped by an ugly beast within may conceal the wealth of love that can transform them both.

Deep in the forest dwells a Beast so terrifying that many maidens fear to make the journey through the forest on the way to the wedding. And the Beast, who is longing for a bride of beauty to transform him, is himself afraid that no maiden will dare to brave him. For the Beast's voice is so gruff that it resounds "in a tone that might have struck terror into the boldest heart, though he did not seem to be angry."[1] The Beast wears a veil of ugliness and anger which conceals his inner beauty, and the maiden who will wed him must be able to see through that veil to the mystery of him, of herself, and of their relationship.

Beauty is the youngest daughter of a rich merchant who has given his six sons and six daughters everything they fancy. But suddenly this prosperous father is beset with misfortune. His house burns to the ground, and all his ships are lost at sea. From the greatest wealth, he falls into the most dire poverty. At first his children cannot adjust. They expect their friends will be sorry for them and help, but instead the friends blame this change of fortune on their extravagance.

The family must now live in a rough cottage deep in a dark forest, seemingly the most dismal place on earth. The children have to work, the sons in the fields and the daughters like peasants, and all wish only for their former wealth—all, that is, but the youngest daughter, who has the gift of bravery, cheerfulness, and gaiety, the gift of song and dance. When the father has news that one of his ships has come into port, all the children believe they will once again have wealth except Beauty. Each child asks for jewels and dresses, but Beauty, who only wants her father to be safe, asks for nothing. When her father insists that she choose something she wants, Beauty asks for a rose, her most beloved flower, which does not grow in the dismal forest where they live.

When the father reaches the port town, he finds that the ship's goods have been taken by former companions who believe him dead. On his terrible journey back, beset with storm and snow, he becomes lost in a deep forest. At night he follows a track which leads him to a palace immersed in deep silence and peace. Though everywhere else it is winter, here the sun shines, birds sing, flowers bloom, and the air is soft and sweet. In the palace a good dinner is served in luxurious surroundings, and in ecstasy the merchant thinks to himself, "All this must be meant for me!" When he sees a hedge of exquisite roses he remembers his promise to Beauty and selects one for her. Just then he hears a strange noise behind him and turns around to see the frightful, angry Beast, who berates him in a terrifying voice for insulting the kindness of his hospitality by stealing one of his flowers, and threatens to punish him with death. The merchant tries to pacify the Beast with excuses and flattery, but to no avail, and in despair he thinks that Beauty's simple request has cost him more than a king's ransom. He tells the Beast about his daughters' requests, and the Beast replies that he will allow the merchant to live if one of his daughters is courageous and loves him enough to save his life by coming willingly to live with the Beast in the palace. The Beast gives the merchant one month to keep his promise and reminds him that if one of his daughters does not come of her own choice, the merchant will lose his life and there is no escape. Dressed in a luxurious mantle and riding on a splendid horse, the merchant returns and, thinking sadly to himself how little Beauty knows the cost of her rose, tells his children about his misadventure. The daughters blame Beauty, and the sons say they will kill this terrible Beast. But Beauty, who is very distressed, offers to live with the Beast to save her father's life. At first everyone protests, but Beauty is firm, and at the month's end she mounts the horse, which seems to fly back to the Beast's castle. Although she is anxious, she cannot but admire the amazing and wonderful things she sees in the Beast's palace. Her father is with her, and when she hears the Beast approaching, she clings to him in terror. But she hides her fear when the Beast appears, and she talks to him sweetly. Although she is terrified by his voice, she says she has come willingly to stay with him. Pleased at her response, the Beast allows her father to go and to take with him all the riches he can carry. That night, after weeping herself to sleep, Beauty dreams that a handsome young prince comes to her, telling her that she will be rewarded for all she has suffered, but that she must not be deceived by appearances, and he hopes she will find him, no matter how he is disguised. "Be as true hearted as you are beautiful, and do not desert me from my cruel misery," he says.[2] Then a beautiful, stately lady appears in her dream and reminds her not to be deceived by appearances.

During her stay with the Beast, Beauty is treated kindly and royally. But she thinks her dream means that the horrible Beast is keeping the prince a prisoner. In the rooms of the palace Beauty finds amazing things. One room is filled with mirrors reflecting herself, there is a bracelet reflecting the prince of her dreams, then a gallery of pictures with a portrait of the prince, a room with musical instruments of all kinds, a library with a lifetime of books to read, and finally a room lit with ruby and diamond candlesticks in which a delicious supper is all laid out. After supper the Beast appears and asks her if she could be happy in this palace and whether she would marry him. Concealing her terror, Beauty replies that she could indeed be happy in this beautiful palace. Still, although she is afraid to anger the Beast, she refuses his proposal of marriage. That night, she dreams the prince asks her why she was so unkind to him.

The next day Beauty discovers new rooms—one of art materials of every sort, another of rare birds so tame they fly to her shoulder, still another room which provides every entertainment she might desire—pantomimes, dances, music—all so gay that she need never feel lonely. But even though the Beast appears kinder, she still has to say no to his offer of marriage. And every night her dreams of the prince continue, dreams in which he constantly tells her "to distrust appearances, to let her heart guide her. . . ."[3]

But soon Beauty longs for her father and her family. She knows that despite his ferocious looks and dreadful voice the Beast is really gentle, so she asks him to let her return home for two months and then she will return to him. The Beast agrees, but says he will die if she does not come back. When Beauty goes to sleep that night she has another dream of the prince, but this time he says to her sadly and wearily, "Are you not leaving me to my death, perhaps?"[4] Beauty assures the prince she will return to the Beast and even die to save him from pain, for he is kind even though he is ugly. Beauty wakes up the next morning in her father's house, and all are glad to see her. When Beauty asks her father what her dreams of the prince might mean, why the prince constantly asks her not to trust mere appearances, her father replies thoughtfully that the prince must mean that she should marry the Beast, for he is kind and gentle. Beauty thinks he may be right, but she still is in love with the handsome prince and not the ugly Beast.

In her two-month stay at home Beauty finds she is bored despite all the wealth her family now has once again. And not once does she dream of the prince. But she still delays her return to the Beast until one night she has a dismal dream that he is dying in a cave. So that night she turns the ring the Beast had given her and firmly says she wishes to return to the Beast's palace. When she awakens she is back again in the palace. She anxiously waits for the Beast to appear at supper as he always did before. When he does not, she is frantic and searches through the paths in the garden. Suddenly she comes upon the shady path she had seen in her dream. When she sees the cave of her dream, she rushes in and finds the Beast—asleep or dead, she does not know. In panic she bends over him, saying, "Oh, Beast, how you frightened me! I never knew how much I loved you until just now, when I feared I was too late to save your life." "Beauty," he says faintly, "can you really love such an ugly creature as I am? I was dying because I thought you had forgotten your promise."[5] But he reassures her and says he will join her after supper. Beauty, surprised that he wasn't angry with her, is reassured by his gentle voice and goes back to the palace.

That evening after supper the Beast joins Beauty and asks her about her trip. And when it is time for him to leave, again he asks her to marry him. This time Beauty says yes, and when she does there is a blaze of light and firecrackers and guns in salute. When she looks to ask the Beast what it means, there is no longer a Beast but her long-loved prince. Then up comes the stately lady of her dreams, who says to the prince's queen mother (who suddenly appears), "This is Beauty who has had the courage to rescue your son from the terrible enchantment."[6] The queen rejoices, thanking Beauty, and the next day the wedding is held in splendor.

"Beauty and the Beast" in some ways is a counterpart to the drama of Prince Charming and the Special Princess, but here the rescue comes from the feminine side. The story also shows a progression away from the collective—the rich father has lost his money and material goods, and the secret riches are found instead in the heart of the woods. It is because Beauty asks for a natural gift—a rose, a symbol of spiritual love—rather than something to be bought with money that the transformation unfolds the way it does. In this story the masculine principle, in the form of the Beast, is enchanted and must be transformed.

The Beast is ugly in appearance, and he can be angry, terrifying, revengeful (he threatens to punish the father by death), self-righteous (he accuses the father of insolence because he picked a rose and was ungrateful for his hospitality), unforgiving (unless he receives recompense, a daughter, for the rose), and fearful of abandonment (he is afraid to let Beauty leave). But underneath this exterior he is kind, gentle, and generous, as Beauty learns during her stay at the palace. And he is infinitely rich, with a magical palace of rooms containing intellectual, artistic, musical, and creative possibilities and which is surrounded by blossoming orange trees and flowers though it is winter everywhere else. The task of redemption for Beauty is twofold: she must overcome her fear and be courageous and, as she is told repeatedly in her dreams, she must not be deceived by appearances. Pure and innocent, she does not know the tremendous cost of the rose—she must learn to love the Beast. While this may seem difficult for Beauty, the Beast has his tremendous transformation challenge, too. Despite all his power, ultimately he must allow Beauty to leave and learn to trust that she will return. At first Beauty comes to the palace only because of his threat against her father's life. As long as he keeps Beauty there only by virtue of his power over her father, he will never know if she loves him or not, for he has not allowed her a free choice. His transformation requires that he let her go and also open himself up to vulnerability, the ultimate vulnerability of death.

The story of Beauty and the Beast makes a great deal of sense to me as a reflection of the tasks for men and women of our culture. Women have not been allowed to have their own "Beast" because men have been so entranced by the collective image of beauty. They want a woman who is young and pure so they can project the beauty of the soul onto her. This saves them from the labor of love that soul work requires. The woman who accepts this projection is also saved from facing her inner Beast, with its anger, possessiveness, and power. But at the same time she misses discovering the magical rooms in the Beast's palace, the rooms of creativity. The Beast is in part the primal masculine power and sexuality she has in herself. This can be very frightening because it embraces so much assertive energy. Many women who live through men allow the man to carry this creative power for them. Sometimes, by adapting like the "darling doll," they will stay with a Beast-like man out of fear, letting him dominate them. In the story, Beauty first has to get to the Beast's house, and that happens originally not of her own free choice but as a condition of saving her father. She has had a good father, but one who did not have the Beast developed in himself. So, not having learned about the Beast from her father, she has to go to the Beast herself. Many women who do not get into relationships or who "cannot find the right man" are in terror of being trapped by a man's power. Thus they unwittingly make themselves unavailable for relationship. I did this myself after my first marriage and managed to stay out of a committed relationship for fourteen years! In that fourteen years, though, I painfully discovered and excruciatingly experienced the Beast in myself.

Once Beauty gets to the Beast's house, she has the opportunity to see all the riches and creative possibilities he possesses, as well as his hidden kindness and gentleness. And her dreams tell her not to be deceived by appearances. Even so, she cannot accept that the Beast has the prince side of which she dreams. At first she separates the two, thinking that the Beast is keeping the prince a prisoner. She still longs to go back to the world of her father, despite all the wonderful things she has seen. Like many women who want the protection of the father or the patriarchy, Beauty is not yet ready to stand on her own. So she pleads with the Beast to let her go home, and sadly he agrees, though he says he will die if she does not return in two months. In order to gain her own power, Beauty has to come back to the Beast of her own free will. Love can transform the Beast, but it cannot be a love born of fear. When a woman stays in a relationship out of fear—be it fear for economic security, fear of being rejected, fear of being alone, fear that she does not have the inner strength to withstand life's demands, fear of standing up to her partner—she betrays herself and does not find the prince within. To transform the Beast she has to return to him of her own consciousness and will, with the power of her love. Beauty is able to overcome the dread of the Beast through her love, which recognizes the Beast's vulnerability. As in Beauty's case it often takes separation to be capable of courageous love and a genuine choice. In a mature relationship it is necessary to separate from the other internally, to act strongly from one's own center. This is often the hardest thing to do, for we want to merge together in an ecstatic "in love" state. Rilke expressed this necessity for separation beautifully in *Letters to a Young Poet*.

But learning-time is always a long, secluded time, and so loving, for a long while ahead and far on into life, is—solitude, intensified and deepened loneness for him who loves. Love is at first not anything that means merging, giving over, and uniting with another (for what would a union be of something unclarified and unfinished still subordinate?)—it is a high inducement to the individual to ripen, to become something in himself, to become world, to become world for himself for another's sake, it is a great exacting claim upon him, something that chooses him out and calls him to vast things.[7]

In the tale of Psyche and Amor such a separation is also necessary to build up strength. This story has a "Beauty and the Beast" theme within it. Psyche is taken by the wind while asleep to a palace where she falls in love with the mysterious owner. But she is not allowed to see him; she can only make love at night. Her sisters plant the seed of suspicion that he is a monster and urge her to light a lamp to see him so she can kill him. When she sees him by light she realizes he is the god Eros (Amor). But the price she must pay for her knowledge is separation, for the condition of their being together was that she not see him in the light. She then is given four tasks, and in each she is assailed by despair and enormous fear. The tasks involve sorting a heap of seeds that seems infinite (which represents the act of conscious differentiation); gathering fleece from raging rams that can be approached only at night (gaining strength via patience as opposed to direct confrontation); filling a crystal bowl with water from a river flowing between the upper world and the underworld (forming energy and containing it); and finally a descent into the underworld to gain the secret of beauty from the dark underworld goddess, Persephone. This last task requires that she save the cakes and coins she is given for this dangerous journey for herself. She must avoid giving them away so that she can later ascend with the secret of beauty from the underworld. In this story the tasks give Psyche the strength to be independent of others and the formation of her own identity, and they are necessary for her to unite with Eros.

Once separation is achieved, then it is possible to make a real choice. For Beauty this involves going back to the family house and finding that it isn't so interesting. It lacks the magical rooms of the Beast's palace, and at home she doesn't even dream of the prince. She also realizes that she genuinely cares for the Beast, despite his ugliness. Finally, she is able to distinguish between external appearance and inner beauty. Beauty herself has had external beauty, and without being able to make this distinction she would never be able to acknowledge her own inner beauty, the beauty of the feminine center. Many women suffer from feeling they are not beautiful compared with the collective image of beauty projected by men via the mass media. And, seduced by these plastic images, many women seek their prince in external appearance, too, forgetting the inner beauty of the Beast in the dark forest. What Beauty discovers, symbolic of the feminine spiritual center, is that her real beauty is her courageous vulnerability, her readiness to be open to the mystery of the unknown. It is this quality that finally saves the Beast when he is dying—that Beauty is willing to die to save his life. This is not love born of fear but love born of courage. Now she is not afraid to accept his marriage proposal. And when she does, her wedding with the prince can take place. It takes consciousness, choice, and transformation for a woman to relate to a man in his entirety and not just to the idealized fatherly side that the woman may want. Moreover, through Beauty's journey and meeting with the Beast, the father has developed in this story, too. At first a pleasing but naive man who valued material appearances and never encountered the Beast, he learns to see the value of the Beast, acknowledging this princely possibility within himself, and even blesses Beauty's wedding to the Beast.

Many men of this generation have turned from the "macho" image of manhood, as Robert Bly has pointed out, toward their softer "flower child" side, which women said they wanted. But then women became disappointed in men when that primal masculine power was missing. Bly says that integration for a man entails reconnecting with the "wildman"—that primitive energy lying deep within the instinctive masculine, a dark energy which at the same time shines through the hair as a spiritually radiant energy, dangerously creative.[8] The Beast-Prince with his magical rooms of creativity is an image of such energy. Only when Beauty can love the Beast, in herself and in the man of her choice, will the positive power of the "wildman" be accepted as an integral part of relationship.

Often men need to hear from a woman that their "Beast" is beautiful. But this requires that they also be open to hear it. A woman who was in the process of acknowledging and valuing her own beast-like side put it this way: "My boyfriend thinks he's a beast, often acts like one, and then feels guilty. If only he'd open up I could tell him how beautiful he really is."

Rilke felt the Beast had a natural relationship with divinity, a relationship to which we aspire but can never totally achieve because as humans we are creatures of "the between." Unlike animals, which look into eternity, we encircle the unbroken unity, looking backward, seeing before us the *no* inherent in our existence. As Rilke expresses it:

> With all its eyes the creature-world beholds
> the open. But our eyes, as though reversed,
> encircle it on every side, like traps
> set round its unobstructed path to freedom.
> What *is* outside, we know from the brute's face
> alone; for while a child's quite small we take it
> and turn it round and force it to look backwards
> at conformation, not that openness
> so deep within the brute's face. Free from death.
> We only see death; the free animal
> has its decease perpetually behind it
> and God in front, and when it moves, it moves
> into eternity, like running springs.[9]

For Rilke the animal's close, almost medial relation to nature, to the Whole from which it came, constitutes its superiority to humans. "Within the wakefully-warm beast there lies the weight and care of a great sadness,"[10] and that longing in animals links them to us in our vulnerability.

The Beast in its deepest being is that part of us which we fear, the horrific aspect of existence which threatens our ego control, that naive brute openness that weds us to the divine without suspicion, without control, without ego conditions and manipulations. When we fear the Beast, when we are afraid of the vitality of the life force which it presents to us, when we are afraid of that great unity of life and death which the Beast's being vibrates, we frequently try to put it behind bars, objectifying it to ward off its danger, protecting ourselves, yet all the while fascinated with it like spectators at the zoo.

In Rilke's poem "The Panther," the Beast is a caged one, its beauty imprisoned, its great life energy encased and numbed.

From seeing the bars, his seeing is so exhausted
that it no longer holds anything anymore.
To him the world is bars, a hundred thousand
bars, and behind the bars, nothing.

The lithe swinging of that rhythmical easy stride
which circles down to the tiniest hub
is like a dance of energy around a point
in which a great will stands stunned and numb.

Only at times the curtains of the pupil rise
without a sound . . . then a shape enters,
slips through the tightened silence of the shoulders,
reaches the heart, and dies.[11]

To free the panther's princely power we must, like Beauty, give up our fear, face our mortality, learn to be in "the open realm," and dance in the sacred space with the Beast. This dance with the Beast is essential to the creative wedding within and the wedding of the outer creative relationship.

One of my own waking dreams long ago led to dancing with a creature which I regarded as the most beastlike, horrific, and frightening of all—a cockroach. In the dream, like Psyche, I had gone in search of a soulmate and had climbed a tall tower to see where I was going. At the top I met a wise, stately, queenlike woman who led me to the edge and pointed out toward the ocean and then to the edge of the sea where there was a raft drawn by a giant swan. In search of the Eros I sought, she said, I was to take a sea journey on this raft. She took me back down the tower and over to the raft, which I boarded, whereupon the swan headed out toward the open sea. After quite some time the swan suddenly dived underwater, and under I went too, and finally we reached the entrance of an underwater cave. There a witch took me inside the cave. We went through a series of dark tunnels, and in one I saw a wild boar chained to the dark, dank wall, pawing the ground furiously. Then the witch led me into a circular room and there was a giant cockroach. I was frightened and repelled, but the witch pulled me toward the cockroach and, taking one of his hands, forced me to take the other, and started a round dance with the three of us. We danced around and around in the tiny round room, faster and faster, when suddenly the witch stepped aside, leaving me to dance alone with the cockroach. Hardly able to bear it, I closed my eyes, but when I opened them once more the shell of the cockroach cracked open and out stepped a handsome prince, with whom I danced in amazement.

For me the cockroach represented my father, for when he came home drunk in the middle of the night, beastlike and violent, the cockroaches would be running about. I had come to associate cockroaches with this beastly side of my father, and I hated and feared them more than any other living creature. In coming to terms with my father, I had to come to terms with this beastly side of myself. Dancing with the cockroach, an ancient creature that is an age-old survivor, led to the dance with the prince.

A dream in which she had to encounter the Beast occurred for one woman just when she had made the existential vow to her soul's creative process.

> I am on a boat. It's the end of a world war. We land at the inlet to an island, traveling inward into the island to find a place to start our new life. The terrain is canyonlands, something like the Grand Canyon. Off to the left I get a glimpse of a giant Beast, a Cyclops, who seems to be either following us or leading us. He's flirting with me, teasingly engaging me as we walk along. I'm afraid and cry out, "Why is this horrible Beast here? Will he hurt me? Will he kill me?" when a voice replies: "This is your spiritual Beast!"

This dream had meaning for her on both a personal and a universal level. She was a very brilliant and medial woman with the gift of dreams which frequently told the soul's story, as do the dreams of poets. Up to now in her personal life she had lived for others, sacrificing the expression of her own creative vision. But now, as she approached midlife, her psyche was demanding that she change her life. Her psyche demanded nothing less than an existential vow, a commitment to transformation. For her this involved accepting her medial powers and giving expression to them in the world. Her mother had had this gift of dreams and refused it, encaging her pantherlike power, which turned against her in a deadly, debilitating depression which she unconsciously communicated to her daughter; hence the daughter's sacrifice of her own creative vision and expression. She had even had a dream in which her mother announced to her brother and herself that she had a special power of knowing, something like ESP, that she was afraid of, considered horrible, and had spent her whole life trying to suppress, keeping it from the world. This was the reason, the mother told her children, that she had never developed herself. The dreamer said, to the amazement of her mother and her brother, "Don't you realize that this power can be used for the world's good and for transformation?" This was the existential vow that she had made at the time of the Beast dream—the commitment to make the journey inward, to face the death of her old self for the rebirth of her new being in the world. On the personal level, the end of a world war reflected the end of an old era in her life, the death of an old self at war with itself. The boat journey reflected the voyage into the unconscious and the responsible acceptance of the life she found there. Taking the path to the center of the island to begin a new life was the new path she had chosen, the path inward to the center of the self. And the giant Beast to her left, the Cyclops who was flirting with her, was the open-eyed Beast of spiritual vision, which was hers to wed. Though the journey might be frightening and awesome, she was now courageously committed to the challenge of creative fidelity to the mystery of life.

The vow to find her feminine spirit, entailing an intense struggle to relate to the Beast inside herself, was a central theme in the life and dreams of another of my clients. She was a naturally gentle and loving woman, but her powers were being drained by an inner Beast which was so frightening that she would go to any lengths to please people and avoid confronting her own anger. This pattern seemed to come from having an alcoholic father who went into unpredictable violent rages, and a sweet "Doris Day"-type mother, who tried to hide the chaos in her life from the outer world and who projected onto her sweet and gentle daughter a "golden girl" image, which corresponded to the daughter's blond, blue-eyed appearance and to her innate temperament. As a consequence, the daughter was cut off from her own rage. It only showed in the times she got drunk and in her choice of partners—women who were dark and angry. The access to her own dark powers of assertion was so closed off that she developed a phobia of speaking in public, so devastating that it barred her way in job interviews or any situation in which she needed to present herself. Her voice would fail her!

Shortly after she began analysis, she had a series of dreams of "meeting the Beast." She met wounded, bloody animals, then a man-eating shark that tried to kill her. But the following dream, which led her to confront the Beast in herself and in the collective judgments of society, brought out some central issues in her struggle to integrate the Beast.

> I am a visitor in a large mental institution. A nurse offers to take me on a tour of the locked ward in the back of the hospital. At the very back, imprisoned behind bars, a small gorilla leers mockingly at me. Suddenly the gorilla grows to the size of King Kong, breaks through the bars, grabs the nurse, and runs wildly through the hospital. Desperate to warn the hospital officials, I run into the first room I see. A group of male psychiatrists are discussing the case of "the lesbian" in pathological terms. A female mentor of mine is there and shakes her head in agreement. I feel betrayed, but still I try to get their attention to warn them about the wild, giant gorilla on the loose. But they do not see or hear me. I run on to get help when I realize the entire hospital is in danger. It is now a ship in deep waters, floating perilously, and I dive underwater to try to secure the anchor so the hospital will not submerge.

The dream imaged the enormity of the Beast she had to confront in the form of her own rage and the rage of many women at the collective patriarchy, which, like Beasts, judged her as pathological for being a lesbian instead of acknowledging the beauty of her feminine nature. It also had significance for her on the collective level, for it reflected the attitudes of the psychiatric patriarchy, unaware of the giant gorilla running loose in their institutional judgments, judgments which threatened the stability of the mental hospital system. The dreamer was herself a therapist who worked within this system and had felt insecure in her own authority, losing her voice before authoritative figures who spoke only from the masculine, whether they were men or women. She was also afraid of the negative judgment of women, symbolized by the female mentor in her dreams, and this came in part because her mother had never been able to accept her as lesbian. But ultimately the giant gorilla on the loose was her own inner Beast power.

To deal with this Beast she made a gorilla mask and danced out his rage, which was a rage at her father for having acted out the Beast in his drunken violence, a rage at her mother for having put up with this and for wanting her daughter to be a person she wasn't, a rage at her former lovers for having acted out their Beast, and finally a rage at the patriarchy symbolized by a figure named "Mr. Tyranny." Later, in another imaginative movement, she came closer to the Beast and felt its loneliness and sadness. She felt tenderness toward the Beast, moving both as the Beast and as herself, when finally, as she danced in the shadows reflecting from some bars on a window, her dancing shadow merged with the Beast's behind the bars.

Working with her inner Beast took years, but gradually she was able to separate from her dark, possessive lovers. This required a period in which she lived alone and acknowledged these dark forces in herself. It was as though she had gone to the Beast's palace when she lived with her early lovers, discovered there were riches there, but realized she had to leave to find herself. After a few years of separation and work on her inner gorilla, a change in her life took place. Suddenly she became more confident, fell in love with a person more suited to her, and became more assertive at work and in interpersonal relationships. Her dreams reflected this. In one dream she was walking along the ridge of a grassy green hill (one that she loved to walk along in waking life) when all of a sudden she took a tumble and rolled down to a level place in the middle. As she recovered from her fall she looked up to find a hairy, dwarflike man who looked at her knowingly. Perhaps this was a version of the "wildman"; in any case he seemed to be a miner with some ancient wisdom. After this she had a series of dreams about animals—rescuing them, being chased by them, confronting them. The most striking was about a ferocious wolf.

I was in a house when I heard a loud commotion. Outside was a herd of hoofed animals running aimlessly. I was afraid they'd crash into the house, so I started running away from them. I realized they were running blindly and in terror because a huge wolf was pursuing them. Then I realized the wolf had turned his attention to me and, terrified, I tried to outrace him. But soon we were neck and neck. Finally, as I was running, I looked over at the wolf and directly into his eyes. He gazed back and seemed to smile and, as my look mirrored his, I suddenly felt empowered by a wildness in myself. After this deep and soulful look passed between us, we ran on together.

This woman, who had run away from the Beast all her life, was now beginning to feel the power of the Beast and to love him. She was now ready for the inner wedding of Beauty and the Beast, for now she could love him within herself. This love was a soul love, a divine love, and brought to mind the beginning lines from Francis Thompson's poem "The Hound of Heaven."

> I fled Him, down the nights and down the days;
>   I fled Him, down the arches of the years;
> I fled Him, down the labyrinthine ways
>   Of my own mind; and in the midst of tears
> I hid from Him, and under running laughter.
>       Up vistaed hopes I sped;
>       And shot, precipitated,
>   Adown Titanic glooms of chasmed fears,
> From those strong Feet that followed, followed after.
>       But with unhurrying chase,
>       And unperturbed pace,
>   Deliberate speed, majestic instancy,
>       They beat—and a Voice beat
>       More instant than the Feet—
> "All things betray thee, who betrayest me." [12]

Pursued by the power of the divine wildness, no longer fleeing from it, now she felt this power within herself wed to her femininity.

Another woman, an artist who had a good marriage relationship, but who was struggling to stand by her creativity in the outer world, dreamed she made love with a beautiful white seal and the two swam together in the sea. The dreamer felt this white seal was like an animal goddess, a mystical muse whose graceful feminine instinctuality would guide and accompany her on her creative sea journeys. This woman had originally come into analysis to work on relationship problems in her first marriage. After this work was done she was able to separate from a marriage that had not been fulfilling on the instinctual level and eventually remarried a man who appreciated her both as creative and as a woman. Several years later she came back into analysis to work directly on her creativity. At this time she was painting urns, which she felt showed the receptive flow of the feminine. She also had the possibility to publish a novel which expressed the confusions of a woman who had grown up under the stern rule of a puritanical minister father. Although her creative work was flowing out freely from the feminine center, she was still afraid of the critical judgments of her father and the cultural collectivism that put down her feminine nature. This dream of making love with a sea creature, the graceful, mysterious white seal, symbolized her wedding with the divine feminine muse and affirmed her in her creativity.

For a man, the story of Beauty and the Beast may be even more illuminating. Men in our culture have been either labeled Beasts or emasculated (the Beast taken out of them). In this story the Beast is searching for his soul. He wants a woman who is brave enough to come of her own accord to his domain and who loves her father enough to make this choice willingly. But there is a condition in his desire, for he still retains the power in this relationship since it is he who has set the conditions. For many men, giving up control and possessiveness is the greatest challenge, as it was for Travis in *Paris, Texas*. Such a man wants the beauty of the soul, but thinks the way to find it is external, through marrying a beautiful young woman, whom he then tries to possess. Frequently the beautiful young woman he finds is insecure and looking for a father herself. So he tries to hold on to this woman through financial or emotional dominance, and is often in continual fear that she will leave him. More obviously, this pattern is seen in relationships between an older man and a younger woman, but it is often a part of relationships which do not necessarily look like this from the outside.

What is really at issue for the man is to relate to his own soul. As in the story, the Beast has to let Beauty leave to see if she will come back of her own free will. This means giving up his control, allowing his vulnerability to show, even risking death as the Beast does. It means assuming a receptive role, allowing the feminine in himself to be. Internally, Beauty as his soul symbolizes the nonpossessive. All she asks for is a rose, the symbol of spiritual love. For a man to find his inner rose means being more gentle to himself, letting go of the controlling demands he makes on himself, and accepting himself both as Beast and Prince. There is a paradox here for the man: he has to be able to let the soul go to have it come back to him. This may mean letting go of a soul-image projection on a woman and of his attempt to possess her.

One man dreamed he was at the top of an ancient castle tower. Under a great white silken veil in a round bed elevated on stone lay the body of a woman. He thought she was dead. In the tower a white bird was flying around. Then, a few nights later, he had the same dream, but this time he opened a window and let the white bird fly out. To his surprise in a while the white bird returned and flew back in. When the bird returned he knew the woman wasn't dead. Mysteriously the veil lifted, and there was the woman, alive. He associated the dead woman with the loss of his soul. His attempt to keep the white bird in the tower he felt was his attempt to possess his lover, to keep track of her all the time. He was jealous of all the friendships she had, and he traced this feeling to his childhood. His mother had had many friends, many of whom were very creative. When her attention turned away from him toward these friends, he felt abandoned and that he had lost his soul, his meaning in life. Although a man with great intelligence, an extraordinary fantasy life, and a great potential for creativity, he felt inferior. He was always afraid that some man with greater creativity would come along and take his mother–wife–lover–inner femininity away. So he tried to hold on to his lover by dominating her through anger if she spent time with someone else. He was like the Beast in this respect. Within his inner palace he had all the magical rooms of creativity, but he was projecting it onto his lover, who was an artist. At the time of the dream she was engrossed in sculpting for an exhibition and so her time and energy were directed away from him, even though she was not occupied with her friends. He was being confronted with her creative process and was caught in a conflict of opposites. He wanted her to create, but he also wanted her all to himself. In the course of analysis, and especially through this dream, he realized that to relate to her he had to let her be, and that this would also free his own access to actualizing the creative in himself. Just as the Beast had to let Beauty go to find out whether she really loved him, and in that process open up his vulnerability and even open himself to death, so this man had to look at the woman under the veil and at the possibility of death, and open the window of his tower of fantasy, allowing the bird to fly out. And with the window open, the bird was able to fly back in. It was as though he had to lose his soul to gain his soul. Once feeling his own creative soul, he did not have to fear losing his lover—either to her own creativity or to her friends.

When a man caught in possessiveness acknowledges the possibility that the woman may leave, he is acknowledging her freedom of choice as an individual. In the past the man has been used to choosing and making decisions. So he has to recognize that the woman can choose and to trust that she will choose him. Until he is able to let go, his possessive, controlling Beast side will not be transformed into the Prince. Letting go means he opens himself to being corrected; it means an acknowledgment that he is not always right. Ultimately, when the Beast lets Beauty go and return of her own free choice, he has opened himself up with humility before the mystery of life and love.

After telling the story of Beauty and the Beast, I have often been asked how we can distinguish the Beast from the Demon Lover. For the two may seem to be alike—and the Beast may offer creativity, but the Demon Lover will suck the creativity away and kill us. Here one feels the difference! Ultimately, the Beast is able to let the woman be free; he allows her to choose. He does not try to make her into his own image, as does Dracula, who turns his women into vampires like himself, feeds on their life energy, and makes them his slaves. In living with the Beast, love, generosity, creative vitality, and spiritual radiance are felt and shared. The Beast offers the elixir of life, while the Demon Lover feeds off one's energy and leaves one to the living death of the "Undead."

While I was writing about Beauty and the Beast I realized how much this was my own soul's wedding story, one path I had to follow on my way to the wedding. Writing the story brought me into the heart of the forest and deeply into the forest of my own heart. I had wanted a relationship desperately, but I never seemed to find the man with whom I could fall in love. A voice kept saying to me the same words of frustration I would hear from many of my woman friends and clients: "Men are undeveloped, not interested in individuation; all they want are mindless, beautiful young women they can dominate. Men are Beasts!" This voice was the voice of my mother, my grandmother, and the angry, suspicious, jealous sisters inside me, of the wounded woman who had suffered from abandonment by my father and from his own bewitched and encased Beast, never transformed into the princely power that was his potential. When I realized my father was wounded, that he needed to be redeemed in me, I took my first journey into the woods to the Beast's domain, and there I also encountered the Beast in myself. In the process of coming to terms with my father's Beast I had to experience and redeem my own, and this, surprisingly, brought me to the revisioning of my feminine spirit as well. It was as though the psyche had asked for the rose that the father found in the Beast's garden without my even realizing I had asked for this rose or what its cost might be.

Writing *The Wounded Woman* was my first journey to the Beast's domain. Like Beauty, I had to take the journey into the forest to the Beast's palace to redeem my inner father, whose beautiful Beast was bewitched, and to free the primal princely potency, to find the instinctual man of heart in myself. This journey was not only mine, I found, but a journey of the psyche for other women as well. After this difficult way I found a new center, a rose center, a bud that could open its petals and begin to receive the warmth of love. And so, miraculously, I was able to meet the man of heart who was now suddenly there and waiting to be wed. Here in this relationship was the deep potential for a true marriage of Beauty and the Beast. The man I met was a man of depth and creativity, of introversion and fantasy, a man who knew the soul of the Beast of the woods, who could growl and grumble as well as play the music of love. In our first year together we even lived in a rose-covered manor house, a magical place in the heart of the redwoods, a place with many rooms for fantasy and imagination. But I was often afraid of this dark, mysterious, many-roomed house deep in the woods. For I still had Beauty's fear of the Beast, fear of his rage and masculine primal power, fear that my freedom would be lost. In this relationship I now had to learn to consciously use the power of my inner Beast, the power of assertion that had previously been lost in both my father and myself. Both for the outer wedding of our potential marriage and the inner wedding with the divine, the Beast had to be faced, loved, and wed so the sacred union with the divine prince could occur. Using the power of my inner Beast meant learning to separate within the relationship, to maintain my own feminine center and freedom without fleeing, so that we could share our sacred space together. During this time I had a number of dreams in which mysterious women made love with me, dreams that symbolized for me the sacred wedding with my feminine soul. I also had a dream in which my father taught me how to conjugate the Latin word for love, *amare*. My beloved had his learning time in love, too—he had to learn to trust and allow his "Beauty" to be free, to learn that his soul cannot be controlled or possessed in a woman, but has its own life and time and movement, a life to which he had to be open and gentle so that he might receive it. During this time he dreamed about a large, beautiful circle divided into squares. But two squares were missing. The missing squares represented for him the parts of our relationship in which we were at war. In the dream he realized that instead of his fighting against me, we needed to fight together to make the circle of our love relationship whole.

Within us all, Beauty and the Beast must meet and have their sacred wedding. In the story this happens when Beauty and the Beast each face their own mortality: when the Beast is willing to be vulnerable and take the risk of death, when Beauty is willing to die to save his life. A wedding within brings us to the acceptance of mortality, an acceptance of the higher powers of life and death. A wedding in the world, if it goes beyond appearances, brings each partner before his or her own death, for it requires the giving up of ego needs and wishes for the higher powers of the soul relationship. Ultimately Beauty and the Beast is a wedding of human and animal, a wedding call (vocation) blessed by the divine mystery within us. The wedding joins the dark masculine soul of the Beast and the feminine spirit of Beauty. At this wedding these two dance with each other; they make a vow to each other, and that vow is a dance in the mysterious ring cycle of life and death and love.

# PART THREE

# *The Wondering*

A god can do it. But how, tell me, shall
a man follow him through the narrow lyre?
His mind is cleavage. At the crossing of two
heartways stands no temple for Apollo.

Song, as you teach it, is not desire,
not sung for something yet in the end attained;
song is existence. Easy for the god.
But when do we exist? And when does he

spend the earth and stars upon our being?
Youth, this is not it, your loving, even
if then your voice thrusts your mouth open,—learn

to forget your sudden song. That will run out.
Real singing is a different breath.
A breath for nothing. A wafting in the god. A wind.

RAINER MARIA RILKE
*Sonnets to Orpheus*

*Only one who has lifted the lyre
among shadows too,
may divining render
the infinite praise.*

*Only who with the dead has eaten
of the poppy that is theirs,
will never again lose
the most delicate tone.*

*Though the reflection in the pool
often swims before our eyes:
Know the image.*

*Only in the dual realm
do voices become
eternal and mild.*

RAINER MARIA RILKE
*Sonnets to Orpheus*

# 10

# *The Divine Wedding*

The man or woman searching for a soulmate is seeking the divine, and often looks for the divine in a concrete person who has divinity within. But the human loved one, like the lover, is also finite and lives in the ordinary realm, thus ultimately disappointing when compared with the vision of divine love. This is why, in German romanticism, romantic love has to end in the *Liebestod* (love in death) as in *Tristan and Isolde, The Flying Dutchman,* and *Swan Lake.* Only in the eternal realm apart from ordinary life can this pure romantic vision be reached. In the everyday world with a concrete person, such a pure love cannot last. Disillusion is inevitable.

But the pure-love vision of romanticism, though it is symbolic of a divine love that will accept death, when literalized, is based on a dualistic conception of life and love, as is its opposite—the "purely" practical attitude which abhors mystical longing and mystery because it cannot be mastered and obtained completely. This practical notion of love and life results in materialism, a banal, lifeless existence drained of the primitive vital life force. This dualism—the split between the finite and the infinite, the temporal and the eternal, the outer and the inner, matter and spirit—was challenged by the existential philosophers Nietzsche, Kierkegaard, and Heidegger.

In my own search for the soulmate I entered into the passionate longing of the German romantics. I also drank the "love potion" like Tristan and Isolde. I became enchanted by the spell of wine—a potion which first brought me the ecstatic longing for the winged love that soars eternally, the promise of total union—a potion which later became a poison for me and threatened death. On the physical level I suffered from the disease of alcoholism, a disease afflicting my father and my grandfathers. On the emotional level I suffered from a dualism that split life and love off from death, that always sought the eternal realm and avoided the ordinary. When the physical component of my disease threatened my life so intensely that I knew I would die if I did not give up the love potion of wine, by now my most powerful Ghostly Lover, I was forced to look at life and love and death again. While I never ceased to believe in a Higher Power, my longing for the god I could never reach turned to rage, a rage that now was directed by the Demon Lover. For the mystery of the Ghostly Lover had been consumed by the power of the Prince of Darkness. Until I lived through this rage long enough to recognize the demonic lover who, like Dracula, was draining me of my life's blood and love and was turning me into a vampire like himself, I fought life's mystery with my old controlling dualism, a dualism which objectified love and mystery by splitting it off from finitude and earth's exigencies. Even though philosophically I subscribed to a view which acknowledged living in the tension of the dual realms of human and divine, even though the words of Heidegger, Jung, and Rilke gave me insight and solace, my captured will and passions belonged to the demon of dualism.

Finally, I had to learn through my tortured years of longing that love could not be literalized; that love could not be found forever in the loved one as object. Love was not a possession I could own. There was, I learned, a dark death in the heart of love, a deep death through which I had to let myself descend before I could meet with love which was not power, before I could meet with love which was whole and holy. For me this meant surrendering my particular versions of love, my inner obstacles—the Ghostly Lover who, when literalized, led me not toward the soul but away to an unobtainable love, and the Demon Lover who had captured my soul and was draining my life's blood, keeping me away from both love and death in that inauthentic existence of the Undead. Despite all my knowledge as a philosopher and Jungian analyst, it took years for me to accept this existential truth in the blood of my being. And even now

I must relearn love daily; every day I must renew this vow to the truth of existence.

Those fourteen years of solitude, while I wore the veil of tears and journeyed down the deep descent into the dark, awesome caverns of my being, were the very years of learning love. Those difficult years allowed me to treasure love and to value the struggle it would cost me. I learned I had to fight for love, to be a warrior woman in the realm of love, and, like Brünnhilde, to return the ring of possessive power back to nature daily as a redemptive sacrifice for the love of compassion. This required a daily sacrifice of my ego power wishes to possess that pure love in the loved one; to accept the devastating battles with my lover as part of the whole of love. I had to learn to honor my longing for the divine love while giving up the ideal of total consummation in this one finite person whom I loved. Finally I came to realize I could not "get" love in the lover, but together we could find love *with* each other. Together, living in the mysteries, we could learn love. There are times of battle in this love, times of boredom, times of dark descent and wondrous, winged times of inspiration and ecstasy. Together, now, we travel with our holy longing, wandering with wondering, in a ring cycle that spirals ever downward and upward simultaneously, circling that still point at the center of our being.

This way of wondering, of living daily in the tension of the opposites, of living an authentic life that tries to honor with awe and loyalty the mystery in the whole of existence, is for each of us the way to the wedding. For ultimately, the wedding we have with each other is grounded in the wedding with the divine. We human lovers need to be grounded in the great transcendent love of compassion. To wed means to join, to unite two different beings in a sacred search for meaning in their lives. Every soul wedding brings us before Being, before the ground of the soul. It is this soul wedding, the inner wedding, the royal or divine marriage, which for Jung is a symbol of the culmination of the individuation process. It is a symbol of the supreme and ultimate union, a symbol in alchemy "which is supposed to bring the work to its final consummation and bind the opposites by love, for 'love is stronger than death.'"[1] Ultimately the divine wedding represents the union of opposites through love and is an archetype found in most cultures, religions, fairy tales, and mythologies as well as in dreams.

One man, in the beginning of his analysis, dreamed that he had been invited to the royal wedding of the king and queen. The royal couple was there and all the attendants were richly appointed. But when he looked down at his clothes he saw he was wearing old jeans and felt out of place. Upon awakening, he realized that he was not prepared for the divine wedding, and had a lot of work to do on himself before he could attend this sacred event. A woman had a dream that she was at the royal wedding, even helping the king and queen rehearse the ceremony, but realized her body was infested with worms. She was still in the process of suffering, in the dark *nigredo* of the alchemical process of transformation, wearing the veil in readiness for the vow of affirmation. She was still suffering but was now able to see the golden light of the royal wedding of opposites within herself.

The divine mating, the mystical marriage, is, according to Jung, an *a priori* image, an archetype at the very heart of our human existence. It is that vision which inspires the soul's sacred journey to the divine. And while we most often first project the divine wedding as a mystery to be found outside us, ultimately we come to find that the dance of the divine wedding is a wedding within.

The veil, the vow, and the ring are symbolic elements of the inner and outer wedding. In wedding ceremonies the veil is a traditional symbol. Originally the bride was veiled to protect her from evil forces so she would be pure for the consummation of the union. Eventually the veil became a symbol of constancy, a sign of consecration to the holy state of matrimony. Just as "taking the veil" was a sacramental symbol of dedication to the religious life for a nun, so in a wedding ceremony it symbolized the inviolable fidelity to the sacred marriage. In its association with the sacred, the veil separated the one to be wed from the outer, profane influences.[2] When one wears a veil, one's gaze is shielded from the distractions of the external, collective world and is turned within. The veil represents that time of inward dwelling, that part of the journey which is traveled alone, often in agony. And often the veil is a veil of tears. One woman, at the start of her journey to find herself, spontaneously had the image of wearing the veil like a Muslim woman. Now she saw some symbolic meaning in a custom which previously she had thought barbaric. She felt she needed the protection of the veil for the long and tender time which she was entering. The veil time is a time when one makes a vow to the Self, to the creative process of one's own unique life's journey on this earth. It is a time of deepening, of soul work, of energy turned inward.

This time of receptivity is reflected in the fairy tale of the Handless Maiden, whose veil of tears protected her from the devil, while she was waiting for the wedding.

In this tale both bride and groom take on the veil. The Handless Maiden, who has been sacrificed by her careless father to the devil, protects herself from the devil through her veil of tears. For the devil cannot possess the person who has purified herself with this holy water. But in trying to possess her, he has her hands cut off. When she leaves her father and wanders into the woods, handless, she is protected by the angels and fed until the king of the land discovers her, falls in love, and makes for her temporary hands of silver. The two are wed, but then war devastates the land and they are separated when the king must leave to fight. Again the devil interferes. Hating now this woman he could not possess, he gives the king false messages that say his wife has betrayed him and should be killed. When finally the king loses faith, he accedes to the devil's request and asks his mother to kill his wife, who he now believes has betrayed him. But the mother, who with her heart knows the purity of the Handless Maiden, protects her by sending her off into the forest to wait and give birth. The Handless Maiden waits in solitude, again with the veil of sorrow, and gives birth to a son named Schmerzenreich, ("one who is rich in sorrows"). When the war is over and the king returns home, he realizes he has been tricked by the devil, and he, too, wanders for seven years, wearing the veil. And when, one day, the two meet in a clearing in the wood, the wife, whose hands have grown back naturally during her time of waiting in the veil, sees that he, too, now knows the meaning of the veil and honors the mystery that is between them. When the king's veil is finally lifted and he recognizes the faithful, loyal love of his wife, and the child of their union, "Rich in Sorrows," the two are reunited and have a second wedding, a divine wedding to celebrate their love, loyalty, and faith.

As in this fairy tale, the veil protects us and gives us the sacred time to make the vow to loyal and lasting love. With the veil on, we gaze at the inner mystery and are ourselves veiled in mystery from the outer eyes of those who look at us, from the observer who would objectify our identity. And the groom, because he cannot see the bride's face, is also drawn to go inward to the mystery of his own soul. The veil expresses the mystery inherent in the wedding for both the bride and the groom. And as a symbol of the unknown, the veil emphasizes the mystery of the Other to whom one makes the vow.

In the outer wedding, the veil preserves the mystery of the bride for herself and for the groom. For the one wearing the veil it casts the gaze within, preserving a time for meditation. Wearing the veil before the outer wedding union is consecrated symbolizes that sacred time when we look within ourselves as we do the inner work of individuation, of uniting the opposites within us. This is the inner wedding that prepares us for the outer wedding with the soul's work in the world, be it in a marriage (the lovers), a single life dedicated to God (the saint), political action (the hero), or creative contribution to human culture (the scientist and the artist). The veil symbolizes the mystery of the wedding within, the time of venture into the inner mysteries of life and love and death. The veil is the time of preparation for the vow.

The vow is that part of the wedding which is an active affirmation of meaning which transcends the individual. The vow is a vow to the Other, be it God, a beloved, a child, or one's work in the world. The vow to the Other is a necessary part of individuation, essential for wholeness. Jung expresses the necessity of the vow this way:

> The unrelated human being lacks wholeness, for he can achieve wholeness only through the soul, and the soul cannot exist without its other side, which is always found in a "You." Wholeness is a combination of I and You, and these show themselves to be parts of a transcendent unity whose nature can only be grasped symbolically, as in the symbols of the *rotundum*, the rose, the wheel or the *conjunctio Solis et Lunae* (the mystic marriage of sun and moon).[3]

The vow is an affirmation of relationship and ultimately of the human longing for transcendent wholeness. The vow is often made in fear and trembling, for we do not know where the mysterious Other will lead us. That is why anxiety is invariably the mood before the wedding. One man told me the only time in his life he had ever had an anxiety attack occurred right before his wedding. Suddenly, without warning, he was engulfed in a nameless anxiety which left him trembling. A woman who was about to get married suddenly had dream after dream in which she had to flee pursuers who might trap her. The anxiety in the dreams corresponded to her anxiety in waking life—was she making the right choice? For me the time before the vow was a time of fear and trembling. I was afraid I would lose the freedom and independence for which I had struggled so desperately in my four decades. Anxiety before a soul wedding, be it inner or outer, is natural because it means the death of ego control, enabling one to make the vow to the greater mystery of love and of life.

Anxiety is the mood which breaks into our controlling egos, breaks open the rigid static ways we tend to waste our lives, according to Heidegger. Human beings, in his view, dwell in a dual realm. They are creatures of the practical world in which they must learn to control their environment and their lives in order to survive. Technology and much of progress are based on this aspect of existence. But humans also belong to a greater whole—the whole of Being, which transcends control and defies attempts at rational description. Although we encounter this greater mystery, especially in the experiences of love and of death, toward which we move as soon as we are born, most humans find it easier and safer to follow the path of control, which produces fast and immediate results and seems to offer security. This is why many of us opt for the practical marriage, warding off the divine lightning of the soul wedding. Anxiety is the mood through which the divine lightning of love strikes, opening our clutching and controlling hands so that they might receive the sublime but inexplicable revelations of the mystery of Being, and thus requiring an acceptance of death, a readiness to die to old ways and formulations, a readiness in love (as we saw in "Beauty and the Beast") to die for the Other. This is the source of the anxiety, the fear and trembling, we experience before the vow.

According to Heidegger, Rilke is a poet who has clearly realized that the destitution of our time comes from not accepting that death, pain, and love belong together. Speaking of Rilke's poetic expression of the mysteries of the veil and the vow in the *Duino Elegies* and the *Sonnets to Orpheus,* Heidegger says:

> Along the way Rilke comes to realize the destitution of the time more clearly. The time remains destitute not only because God is dead, but because mortals are hardly aware and capable even of their own mortality. Mortals have not yet come into ownership of their own nature. Death withdraws into the enigmatic. The mystery of pain remains veiled. Love has not been learned. The time is destitute because it lacks the unconcealedness of the nature of pain, death, and love. This destitution is itself destitute because that realm of being withdraws within which pain and death and love belong together.[4]

The dualism that was preventing me from making my vow to the divine wedding, from making my affirmation of life and love, was as Heidegger describes it. But I had not opted for the practical. In my pure, romantic vision, I had idealized love and death so much that I had absolutized them, thinking their unity was possible only in the eternal realm (as in the *Liebestod* of the Flying Dutchman and Tristan and Isolde). In seeking the romance of mystery, I had absolutized the mystery itself, thus losing mystery, losing the hard way of living in the tension of the dual realm. I had separated pain from love and death. My learning about love required me to live and endure in the struggle of the opposites. And then I came to see the dance of the two vows.

In a soul wedding there are two vows—the concrete vow to the Other and the existential vow to life. The two vows need to rest in each other, to dance in harmony. Without the existential vow to the mystery of life and love, the personal vow has no sacred space in which to rest and move. Without the personal, particular vow to the Other, the existential vow has no special ground or place to grow. It becomes vague and rootless, and seeking mystery, it often objectifies it, losing it instead. The concrete vow is the medium through which the existential vow is made. For some the medium is the relationship to another person; for others the concrete vow is primarily through the medium of their work in the world; for still others it may be through a spiritual community or through a spiritual practice of meditation. The Buddhist monk who sits reciting mantras, the couple who pledge their life and love to each other, the artist whose vow is continually expressed in a painting or a poem or a song, the person who contributes to social growth through the devotion of work and action—all in their unique way affirm the vow to existence.

Images of the existential vow in wedding dreams were shared in one workshop I gave recently. These dreams of the vow emphasized the importance of commitment to the soul's journey and the continuity of that commitment. One woman dreamed that when she arrived at her wedding, she realized the external wedding was not the important thing; rather, it was the commitment to her soul's journey that mattered. Another woman, who had just celebrated a wedding with her lesbian lover, had an ecstatic dream vision in which the sky was a profusion of brilliant, exuberant colors as in a painting by Chagall, and all was united in the image of a woven thread, symbolizing for her the existential continuity and unity of their divine love commitment.

In feudal times, a vow was made by the weaker person to the stronger in return for protection. This extended from serf to lord to king to God. The vow was an acknowledgment of powerlessness and of trust in the other to use his power wisely and honestly. In our time, though economic and societal circumstances differ, there is in the vow still an inherent acknowledgment of vulnerability and humility to the Higher Power of the mystery of the Other and the soul relationship. In a wedding each person is humbled before the mystery of the wedding, before the union of two unique beings. But through this humility, each shares in the mystery and becomes stronger. To vow does not mean to give up one's center. A vow, if it is genuine, can only be given out of one's center, and it strengthens, protects, and reinforces that center.

Sometimes we denigrate the vow because we focus upon more external aspects of the vow that are transitory. Some of the men in one workshop criticized vows based on changeable feelings or vows that were legalistic. For in such vows the heart of the mystery is lost; we are back in the practical, transitory realm alone. In response, another man pointed out the necessity of the inner vow to the soul, both for a meaningful individual life and for a community. As he said, without the vow we would have an uncommitted life and an uncommitted society ruled by the trickster. The surrender of transitory ego wishes is essential for the vow, and this requires an acknowledgment of who one is in the face of death. And thus we face the discipline of the vow.

The discipline of the vow entails a daily renewal in our human lives. A newly married couple told me that each of them, independent of the other, had recurring dreams with the same motif after their wedding. In these dreams they had to go through the wedding ceremony again, even though it was apparent that they were already married. Both partners felt that the dreams were reminding them of the necessity of the daily renewal of their wedding vow. Someone else told me he had to renew the vow to his wife daily. He did this by confronting his dark fantasies of anger, jealousy, and possessiveness, trying to transform them rather than be their slave. By this daily work on himself he was able to renew the depth of his commitment.

In Buddhist practice the vow is a way of heightening awareness. By taking the vow, one forms a vessel in which the energy of a relationship or a creative work is contained. When I made a vow to write this book, I set aside a daily time and space in which I sat with pencil and blank page. Because I kept to the discipline and structure of my vow, the words emerged, words which changed my life and brought me to a higher awareness. And, more important, the vow I made to the new soul relationship formed the vessel for a transforming love. Wendell Berry likens the vow in a marriage to the form in a poem. In each the vow forms an alchemical vessel for transforming energy. The discipline and structure and the daily renewal of the concrete vow in the practical world form the vessel for the existential vow to the flow of the mystery. As Berry expresses it:

> Properly used, a verse form, like a marriage, creates impasses, which
> the will and present understanding can solve only arbitrarily and

superficially. These halts and difficulties do not ask for immediate remedy; we fail them by making emergencies of them. They ask, rather, for patience, forbearance, inspiration—the gifts and graces of time, circumstance, and faith. They are, perhaps, the true occasions of the poem: occasions for surpassing what we know or have reason to expect. They are points of growth, like the axils of leaves.[5]

The vow to wholeness, to the whole of existence, is symbolized by the ring. As a circle, the ring gives us an image for the roundness of life, the circular cycle of the seasons, the fullness of the cycle of growth and transformation, of death and rebirth. It is an image for the cosmic marriage, the wedding of heaven and earth. The ring draws the eye to the center—the center of the Self and the center of the mystery of Being. With the exchange of rings in the wedding ceremony, the ecstasy of the union of two souls, the ecstasy of the I and the Thou, is enacted.

In the inner wedding, the ring is a symbol of union with the divine. Women's dreams frequently contain the motif of the ring in a wedding in which the woman is joined with her divine feminine self. The full cycle of healing and the wedding of the masculine and feminine within was shown in the image of a ring of blood in the following dream of a woman.

> I am in the forest, standing in silent awe before the fragile beauty of a gentle doe. Suddenly there is a shot; the doe falls wounded to the ground, and a hunter emerges through the brush. Angrily I berate this man for carelessly wounding this beautiful being of nature. The hunter is horrified at what he has done and hopes to heal the wounded doe. He tells me to fill a cup with the blood flowing from the wound and give it to the dying doe to drink. I am suspicious! This man has wounded the doe. Perhaps with these words he is trying to trick me into killing her. I hesitate when the doe speaks. She tells me that this ring of blood is nature's way of healing.

Like the doe, the dreamer in life had been wounded in her feminine instinct by her father, an alcoholic whose angry, violent, and unpredictable outbursts had so frightened her that she was unable to assert herself. And like the doe, she was gentle, receptive, and feminine by nature. Her erotic relations were with women, and the collective patriarchal judgment against lesbianism constituted another wound. When, in the dream, she shouted angrily at the hunter who shot the doe, she finally felt her power of assertion against the aggressive masculine. No longer was she afraid of his power. But she was afraid of his trickery. When the doe spoke and she allowed the hunter to help in the healing of the wound, she was able to forgive the masculine for wounding her feminine instinct and to realize that there was a cycle of healing and a source of life flowing from the wound itself. For her this dream provided an image for the wedding of the masculine and feminine within, and the doe's drinking of blood from its wound imaged a ring of healing, an ancient ritual of Christianity—the drinking of the blood of Christ as a holy sacrament.

*Did she not tell you when she charged you then—*
*the bridal bed that awaits for us within*
*is of the underworld? I have said farewell,*
*farewell upon farewell.*
*No dying soul could bid more pure farewells.*
*I wedded*
*that all that buried lies under my husband*
*should flow, distill, resolve. —*
*Lead me away, for I will die for him.*

RAINER MARIA RILKE
"Alcestis"

# 11

# *The Veil*

The wedding of Rainer Maria Rilke was a wedding within. Rilke's bride was his poetic imagination; his was a marriage to the muse. All his life Rilke struggled to find meaning in a world he found replete with war, disruption, and the torn existence of human finitude. For many years he wore the veil of tears.

When I first read Rilke in my early thirties, I was living in Zurich, not far from many of the places where he wrote. He influenced me so powerfully that he became my inner bridegroom, my inspiration, my masculine muse. Plunged deep into the unconscious, in despair I was searching for life's meaning, but without the resources to find my way out of the night sea into which I had fallen. Rilke's novel *The Notebooks of Malte Laurids Brigge* reflected what I felt at the time—the pain of the world, a sensitivity that sometimes could not endure the horrors of the streets, and a deep, hopeless suffering that was crying out for the existence of the divine to show itself. And yet there was the incredible beauty all around, too, so much that I was looking for a soulmate to share my search with me. But nowhere did I meet him. So Rilke, through his writing and the transcendent beauty of his poetic images, touched my soul and helped me to understand and endure this period. He became my inner soulmate.

As I experienced it, Rilke's life and work were devoted to the search for soul, and he went wherever that search took him. He was looking for the wedding between human and divine, and he actualized this wedding in himself through his struggle by writing to express this theme for others. And so his vow was to the word, the word that would give expression to the human search for meaning.

Rilke's search reflected for me the inner search that was happening in myself, and that was necessary to prepare me for the inner marriage to my creative muse, the man of heart, and the outer marriage to the man who would be my life's companion. This time of preparation was a solitary time, a time of looking inward, a time when I put on "the veil" and encountered life and love and death. It was a time of fear and trembling before the great mysteries.

The time of the veil for me was long, about fourteen years. The veil time differs for every person. For some it may be much shorter. For Rilke it lasted nearly a lifetime. In my practice I hear the sufferings of many men and women, how they long for a relationship, how alone they feel without one, and the torture of not knowing whether they will ever meet anyone they can love or who can love them. I, too, went through this torment, doubting whether love was possible, whether I was capable of loving anyone, whether I could even love myself. And under it all was the greatest doubt— was there, after all, meaning in our finite human existence? Was there a Higher Power, an eternal dimension to our lives? Was love possible? Or was there only death?

These were Rilke's life-long questions, too. And his struggle to find and affirm meaning in human existence and to transform fleeting energies into something eternal was the great challenge and significance of his life and work. The ground of Rilke's divine wedding was his acceptance of the ultimate unity of life, love, and death.

Rilke's final acceptance of this unity grew out of much personal suffering, which finally deepened to the point where it touched the mystery of human life. In this realm where the personal and universal meet, his affirmation emerged. Rilke's individual way to this region was through writing, particularly poetry, the expression of his life's quest as well as the guide. Like Orpheus, who descended into the underworld to bring his love, Eurydice, back to life, Rilke descended into the abyss and in accepting death reaffirmed his life. This is the descent made by Travis in *Paris, Texas*—the descent of the Missing Bridegroom—and that must be made by all of us on the way to the wedding.

Rilke's way to the wedding, to the marriage of human and divine, required of him an inner solitary journey. *The Notebooks of Malte Laurids Brigge* is the intense expression of this search to find life's meaning. This semiautobiographical novel reveals the thoughts and feelings of a sensitive young man, alone in Paris and struggling to maintain meaning amid the meaningless and horrifying suffering which he encounters every day. In the notebooks, one is immediately confronted with the fundamental issue of life and death, for dying is physically and spiritually everywhere in the streets. On the first day Malte sees a man swaying and sinking to the ground, dying as a crowd gathers in curiosity, a woman about to give birth in the squalid streets, and a sick, greenish-skinned baby. These everyday occurrences in this city of many hospitals seem to symbolize the condition of humankind. Malte is horrified and begins to change inwardly. He reflects: "I am learning to see. I don't know why it is, but everything penetrates more deeply into me and does not stop at the place where until now it always used to finish. I have an inner self of which I was ignorant."[1] Confronting the fear and horror and suffering of the city, Malte begins to confront himself as well, which brings him to confront the meaning of life and death. As he sees physical death and "living death" all around him, he begins to reflect on dying. The impersonal relationship to life that he observes everywhere seems to end in an equally impersonal death; the people who are dying never realize that their death is their own and something of dignity, "that one had one's death within one, as a fruit its kernel."[2]

Overwhelmed, Malte begins to realize that fear and suffering are the basis upon which he must grow, and that he must learn to write of it. Up to now, he realizes, he has expressed nothing of life. The verses he had written were merely the outcome of youthful feelings, not life experiences. So the lonely, fearful twenty-eight-year-old Malte, who is just "learning to see," begins to reflect upon the origin of poetry.

For verses are not, as people imagine, simply feelings (those one has early enough)—they are experiences. For the sake of a single verse, one must see many cities, men and things, one must know the animals, one must feel how the birds fly and know the gesture with which the little flowers open in the morning. One must be able to think back to roads in unknown regions, to unexpected meetings and to partings one had long seen coming; to days of childhood that are still unexplained, to parents whom one had to hurt when they brought one some joy and one did not grasp it (it was a joy for someone else); to childhood illnesses that so strangely begin with such a number of profound and grave transformations, to days in rooms withdrawn and quiet and to mornings by the sea, to the sea itself, to seas, to nights of travel that rushed along on high and flew with all the starts—and it is not yet enough if one may think of all this. One must have memories of many nights of love, none of which was like the others, of the screams of women in labor, and of light, white, sleeping women in childbed, closing again. But one must also have been beside the dying, must have sat beside the dead in the room with the open window and the fitful noises. And still it is not yet enough to have memories. One must be able to forget them when they are many and one must have the great patience to wait until they come again. For it is not yet the memories themselves. Not till they have turned to blood within us, to glance and gesture, nameless and no longer to be distinguished from ourselves—not till then can it happen that in a most rare hour the first word of a verse arises in their midst and goes forth from them.[3]

Malte Laurids Brigge begins to open himself to all of life, the horrifying and the lovely, the terrible and the tender, the dying and the living. In opening himself, the question is whether he can endure the tension of these opposites and ultimately give them some personal creative expression. For Malte, this expression is through writing; his task is to transform his experiences into something meaningful, to endure through the task of transformation.

Malte's journals reveal his enormous struggle to stay open to experience and to maintain his dignity. His memories go back to childhood, to the deaths he experienced in his family, and to his loves. As he grows inwardly, outwardly his health becomes poorer. His inner suffering increases. His encounter with death becomes so powerful that he begins to feel the difference between himself and the dying breaking down: when he sees a quiet man with a gray, strained face slumping at the next table, Malte feels this man withdraw into death and recognizes that the only difference left is that he still defends himself against death, while the other "defended himself no longer."[4]

Malte tries to save himself by writing. But he begins to feel that soon even the writing will disintegrate, that his hand will be unable to form the words, and that even the words themselves may crumble into meaninglessness. The danger of his task shines more vividly before him. One of his most vivid descriptions is that of the man with a tic; it shows the extent to which a human being with some abnormality cannot fit into the collective. The desperate attempt to adapt ends in humiliation as a crowd laughs mercilessly.[5]

By accident Malte is drawn to follow this man, who tries to cover up a strange hop by pretending to trip over something in the street and who almost succeeds by willpower in containing the jerking. Malte takes on his anxiety, identifies with him, and tries to help. But he is powerless. Finally the man can contain the jerking no longer, and as the wild movement breaks out all over his body while a crowd gathers to watch, Malte leaves, empty and broken. For this man's struggle to endure and fight against this powerful absurdity symbolizes Malte's struggle to contain and endure the almost inevitable victory of the terrible imperfection of human existence. On this springlike day Malte, having just overcome an illness, had ventured forth like a child, hoping to see children joyfully launching brightly colored sailboats on the lake. But instead he encountered the humiliation of the hopping man. Malte writes in his notebooks:

> I asked for my childhood and it has come back, and I feel that it is just as difficult as it was before, and that it has been useless to grow older. . . . Today I really did not expect it; I went out so bravely, as though that were the simplest and most natural thing in the world. And yet, again there was something which took me like paper, crumpled me up and threw me away, something unheard of.[6]

This experience corresponds to the hopelessness people often feel during the waiting time of the veil.

The tension between his childlike faith and openness to existence begins to break Malte's spirit. Vulnerable and dependent, he is not able to consciously stand through these experiences, from which most of mankind has fled. Rilke believed that this capacity to open to life and to endure is the destiny of all human beings and that the attempt to express and share it is the task of the artist. About the challenge of openness to life, Rilke wrote:

> The vision of the artist had to steel itself so far as to see in terrible and apparently only repulsive things the Existential, which, in common with all other beings, *has value*. As little as any selection is permissible to him, so little is it permitted to the creator to turn away from any form of existence whatever: a single rejection anywhere on his part forces him out of the state of grace, makes him wholly sinful. . . .
>
> Ah, we count the years and make occasional cuttings of them and stop and begin again and hesitate between both. But actually everything that befalls us is of one piece, in whose correlations one thing is kith and kin with another, fashions its own birth, grows and is educated to its own needs, and we have ultimately only *to be there,* simply, fervently, as the earth is there, in harmony with the seasons, dark and light and absolutely in space, not demanding to be cradled in anything but this web of influences and powers in which the very stars feel safeguarded.[7]

Malte's difficulty is not the human failure of being unable to release one's ego control of the world, for this more common failure avoids the confrontation with death and with the dark aspects of oneself and existence. Malte rather confronts the horror of existence, but in giving up his ego borders to be able to see, he is so overwhelmed by this dark and demonic side that he is unable to keep his identity and falls victim to the dark side of the whole. At this stage, Malte is in the depths of a great descent. An entry in his journal, appearing shortly after his encounter with the man with the tic, describes the experience.

> The existence of the horrible in every particle of air! You breathe it in with what is transparent; but inside you it precipitates, hardens, takes on pointed geometrical forms between your organs; for whatever of torment and horror has happened in places of execution, in torture-chambers, mad-houses, operating-theatres, under the vaults of bridges in late autumn: all this has a tough imperishability, all this subsists in its own right and, jealous of all that is, clings to its

own frightful reality. People would like to be allowed to forget much of this; sleep gently files over such grooves in their brains, but dreams drive sleep away and trace the designs again. And they wake up gasping and let the gleam of a candle melt into the darkness, and drink, like sugared water, the half-light solace. But, alas, on what a ledge this security rests! Only the slightest movement, and once again vision stands out beyond the known and friendly, and the contour but now so consoling grows clearer as an outline of terror.[8]

The struggle of the man with the tic is the struggle we all have—to maintain the center of our strength in the face of our wounds. Sometimes, like the man with the tic, we try to conceal these wounds and adapt to a collective image. But sooner or later we are discovered, and often humiliated. Accepting the wounds and learning to wrest our healing from them is the very ground upon which we must learn to win the soul. This is one of the greatest challenges in human relationship and loving. Rilke says it is Malte's very descent into the abyss of suffering and despair that could have made possible the highest ascent into bliss. This descent into the abyss is a necessary part of the inner wedding that enables men and women to endure the great tensions of a soul relationship.

But Malte is consumed by the struggle, as was the man with the tic, and at the end appeals to the mother to provide peace. In his return to that original openness and vulnerability, he loses himself in the longing for the primal protection and peace of the mother, instead of taking the fight upon himself. Just so in challenging human relationships, partners often lose heart. They long for unconditional parental love, the security of paradise. If they give in to this archetypal longing, the adult relationship is lost. Of course, in all our renewals, the continual return to our past, our source, is necessary. But the return that yields transformation must be conscious so that integration occurs. It is the conscious acceptance of life and death that opens the way for love.

The prominent theme at the end of the notebooks is that of love. The love of women, whose devotion is so great that they understand God as "a direction of love, not an object of love,"[9] emerges as a model for Malte. They have learned to let go, to give up the concrete loved one and open themselves to the eternal, so that a complete sacrifice, abandonment, and, finally, openness take place. For, as Malte defines it in this last entry, love is to learn to love, "to love is to endure."[10]

Rilke believed that love and the acceptance of death were very close, because both carry us into a conscious relationship with the whole of Being. If we try to possess the loved one, we lose love because we try to trap it in a finite cage. And the same with death: it is because we fail to see the unity of life and death, and make death an object to be feared, held off, and evaded, that we have lost our primordial relationship to the source of all that is. Rilke writes:

> . . . Nature, however, knew nothing of this banishment which we have somehow managed to accomplish—when a tree blossoms, death blooms in it as well as life; every field is full of Death, who reaps a rich harvest of expression from its prone countenance, and the animals pass patiently from one to the other; all round us Death is at home, he peers out at us from the cracks of things, and the rusty nail that sticks up out of a plank does nothing but rejoice over him day and night. And love too, which bedevils our arithmetic so as to introduce a game of Near and Far—in which we always show ourselves so far, indeed, from one another that it seems as if the universe were crowded and ourselves alone full of space—love too has no regard for our divisions but sweeps us, trembling as we are, into an infinite consciousness of the whole. Lovers do not live from any sundering of the Actual; as though a partition had never taken place they break into the boundless capital of their hearts; of them one can say that God is nourishing to them and that death does not harm them: *for they are full of death because they are full of life.*[11]

This task which stands before Malte is the immediate, primary, indeed the *only* task for humankind, according to Rilke. And it is this task which Malte, in his extreme consciousness of it, was perhaps not quite able to endure, although he achieved the vision of it from which most have fled. In the last entry of the notebooks he is still struggling, realizing that to be loved is to be consumed, and that the real challenge is to love, and endure, even through all despair. He begins the work of labor that love is and hopes to be able to love God.

He had found the philosopher's stone, and now he was being forced ceaselessly to transmute the swiftly made gold of his happiness into the lumpy lead of patience. He, who had adapted himself to space, like a worm traced crooked passages without outlet or direction. Now that with so much labor and sorrow he was learning to love, it was shown him how trivial and careless up to now all the love had been which he thought to have achieved.[12]

Though the book ends in the struggle with despair, Rilke himself was concerned that people understand Malte in an "ascending" sense and not fall into a despair like his. Speaking of the paradoxical nature of the notebooks, Rilke wrote:

> Once, years ago, I tried to tell someone whom this book had frightened how I myself sometimes regarded it as a negative, as an empty form, the hollows and depressions of which were pain, despair and saddest insight but whose cast, were it possible to produce one (like the positive figure obtained with bronzes), might perhaps be happiness, the most definite and certain serenity. Who knows, I ask myself, whether we do not always emerge as it were at the back of the gods, separated from the sublime radiance of their faces by nothing save their own selves, quite close to the expression for which we yearn but standing exactly behind it? Yet what else does this mean except that our face and the face of the gods look out in the same direction and are at one; how then should we approach the gods from the front?[13]

Rilke came to see Malte's despair as a "strange, darksome, ascent into a remote and deserted part of heaven."[14] He wrote this in December 1911 from the castle at Duino, a few months before the sudden inspiration with which he wrote the first verses of the *Duino Elegies.* Still in deep despair, having undergone two infertile years after finishing *Malte,* he even questioned the value of work. How could it be that after so much work, done in response to a profound inner call, he was still at the mercy of desires, feelings, and forces he could not comprehend? Like so many of us who search for years for meaningful relationship and work on our inner conflicts with the hope of finding it, he lost heart when the end did not seem to be in sight. (I had the same experience when, after writing *The Wounded Woman,* there was no immediate result. I had to learn to wait a little longer.)

Writing *Malte* had been an attempt to deal with his own despair. Rilke had to let Malte perish in order to save his soul, feeling the psychological necessity to sacrifice his inner compulsions and psychic dead-ends to let the new and redeemed possibility emerge. In *Symbols of Transformation* Jung points out that in the process of development, when one's ideal is about to change, the figure embodying the old ideal has to die, in a sense, and that this produces in the person presentiments of death.

Malte was for Rilke such a symbolic inner figure, an inner conversant whom he had to confront for many years and to whom he had to give form and shape. Rilke felt strongly that despair could be transformed by art and poetry and in this way be redeemed. He expressed this view in "Requiem," a poem written to and in memory of Wolf von Kalkreuth, a promising young poet who had committed suicide at the age of nineteen.

> O ancient curse of poets!
> Being sorry for themselves instead of saying,
> forever passing judgment on their feeling
> instead of shaping it; forever thinking
> that what is sad or joyful in themselves
> is what they know and what in poems may fitly
> be mourned or celebrated. Invalids,
> using a language full of woefulness
> to tell us where it hurts, instead of sternly
> transforming into words those selves of theirs,
> as imperturbable cathedral carvers
> transposed themselves into the constant stone.
> That would have been salvation. Had you once
> perceived how fate may pass into a verse
> and not come back, how, once in, it turns image,
> nothing but image, but an ancestor,
> who sometimes, when you watch him in his frame,
> seems to be like you and again not like you: —
> you would have persevered.[15]

As the poem ends, "Who talks of victory? To endure is all." [16] Had
Kalkreuth been able to endure his despair—to wear his veil—long
enough to transform it through his poetry, Rilke suggests that this
tragic, premature death might have been avoided. Shaping the figure of Malte was an attempt by Rilke to shape and transform his
own experience, to affirm life. He writes: "Poor Malte starts so deep
in misery and, in a strict sense, reaches to eternal bliss: he is a heart
that strikes a whole octave: after him all songs are possible." [17]

After he completed *Malte*, Rilke felt that a new period in his development had begun. He felt that the struggle with Malte together
with his work with form would provide a fruitful basis for further
poetic expression. But instead there followed the empty, infertile,
and uninspired two-year period which threw him further into despair. He traveled, but his heart was not really in the experience. He
longed, during this period, for human companionship, though at
the same time he felt that it would only disturb the possibility for
creativity. He especially longed for love which was capable of giving
but expected no return.

During this period Rilke's despair extended to the province of art
itself. As many men and women who feel marriage to be their life-
long vocation enter into despair and bitterness when that deep relationship seems to elude them, so it was for Rilke and his writing.
At one point he even exclaimed, "Art is superfluous, can art heal
wounds, can it take away the bitterness of death? It does not assuage
despair, it does not feed the hungry or clothe the shivering." [18] Just
as lovers have to let go of the loved one as an object they can control
and possess, just as the Beast had to let Beauty go, accepting separation, so Rilke had to let go of art itself and face the death that
could open up the new.

In this condition of extreme emptiness, Rilke went to a castle
high on the rocky cliffs above Duino on the Adriatic Sea. There he
had the solitude and seclusion he needed for creativity, but with it
came the danger of self-confrontation. Yet to face his own emptiness,
his longing for love, and his failure to create was all he had left.
Entering such a dark night of the soul, as Rilke voluntarily chose to
do for the sake of what he felt to be his life's task, is one of the most

essential tasks in the human journey. This dark night may be forced upon one—or perhaps, more rarely, it is freely chosen—but in any case it is the way of the transformation process. And, as the paradox of human nature would have it, the way down is at the same time the way up. Jung explains:

> Whenever some great work is to be accomplished, before which a man recoils, doubtful of his strength, his libido streams back to the fountainhead—and that is the dangerous moment when the issue hangs between annihilation and new life. For if the libido gets stuck in the wonderland of this inner world, then for the upper world man is nothing but a shadow, he is already moribund or at least seriously ill. But if the libido manages to tear itself loose and force its way up again, something like a miracle happens; the journey to the underworld was a plunge into the fountain of youth, and the libido, apparently dead, wakes to renewed fruitfulness. [19]

And so it was with Rilke. Suddenly one stormy day while he was walking along the windy bastions of the Duino castle, preoccupied with a letter he had to write concerning some practical matter, he heard a voice calling out to him in the storm. The words he heard became the first line of his profound poetic cycle, the *Duino Elegies:* "Who, if I cried, would hear me among the angelic orders?"

The tormenting question of Rilke's life, the tormenting question of Malte and indeed of all human beings struggling to make a commitment to life in this perishable and confusing existence, is: "How is it possible to live when the fundamentals of this our life are so completely incomprehensible? When we are always inadequate in love, wavering in our determination and impotent in the face of death, how is it possible to exist?" [20] This cry issues forth in its most powerful expression in the *Duino Elegies*.

When Rilke wrote the *Elegies,* the First World War was a reality. Now, seven decades later, humankind is faced with the possibility of nuclear holocaust, the destruction of the entire human race. We are always face to face with the imminent reality of death—in our lives, in our loves, in our human community. But often we evade it. Rilke's conscious descent to face this deep darkness in our existence reveals a firelit path of passion for life and love for those of us who choose to follow him.

In the *Elegies,* the cry is the veil that remains while the vow to the mystery of life and love and death is made. Without the veil the mystery is lost, and with it the possibility for the sacred marriage with the soulmate. For the soul is lost when mystery is taken away. The veil, in preserving the inner mysteries, allows the sacred time and space needed for the soul's wedding. For an artist like Rilke, the soul's wedding is with the divine muse, and the work of art is an affirmation of the union of heaven and earth, a vow to divine creativity. For Rilke, the ecstasy of the wedding came with inspiration, culminating in the *Duino Elegies* and the *Sonnets to Orpheus.* But Rilke wore the veil of darkness while he wrote *The Notebooks of Malte Laurids Brigge* and even after that for the ten years it took him to give birth to the *Elegies.* Just as the veil with its fear and trembling, its deep despair before the reality of death, was the prelude to the ecstasy of the vow for Rilke, so it is for lovers. Only if the veil is there can it be lifted. Only then can we experience the divine ecstasy described by the poet Rumi:

This is love: to fly toward a secret sky,
to cause a hundred veils to fall each moment.
First to let go of life.
Finally, to take a step without feet.[21]

*To praise is the whole thing! A man who can praise*
*comes toward us like ore out of the silences*
*of rock. His heart, that dies, presses out*
*for others a wine that is fresh forever.*

*When the god's energy takes hold of him,*
*his voice never collapses in the dust.*
*Everything turns to vineyards, everything turns to grapes,*
*made ready for harvest by his powerful south.*

*The mold in the catacomb of the king*
*does not suggest that his praising is lies, nor*
*the fact that the gods cast shadows.*

*He is one of the servants who does not go away,*
*who still holds through the doors*
*of the tomb trays of shining fruit.*

RAINER MARIA RILKE
*Sonnets to Orpheus*

# 12

# *The Vow*

One night while I was in my lonely room in Zurich, deep in the despair of the veil, the *Duino Elegies* saved my life. Night after night I had been ruminating upon my wounds, the terrible injustices of my childhood, and my seeming inability to accept life on its terms despite all the work I had done inwardly and outwardly to transform myself in readiness for the soul relationship that always seemed elusive. On this particular night I awoke from a troubled sleep at four A.M. and, almost as though someone had singled it out, my eyes fell upon a volume of the *Duino Elegies,* a book I had brought with me to Europe but so far had been unable to read. That night I read it from beginning to end and found hope in these poems, through which Rilke transformed his despair into affirmation, thus celebrating a vow praising the mysteries of the Higher Power. Rilke's vow was made with the full recognition and acceptance of the cycles of life and death.

For me, the vow was a cry sounding from the depths of despair, a wedding song, which weds Rilke—and all of us who sing this song—to the divine. The *Elegies* illumine the essence of the wedding vow. And each individual elegy, like a crystal, lights a different view of the vow. In the *Elegies* the veil of the vow is lifted over and over again for those who take the time to look and listen.

Who, if I cried, would hear me among the angelic
orders? And even if one of them suddenly
pressed me against his heart, I should fade in the strength of his

stronger existence. For Beauty's nothing
but beginning of Terror we're still just able to bear,
and why we adore it so is because it serenely
disdains to destroy us. Each single angel is terrible.
And so I keep down my heart, and swallow the call-note
of depth-dark sobbing. Alas, who is there
we can make use of? Not angels, not men;
and already the knowing brutes are aware that we don't feel very
   securely at home
within our interpreted world.[1]

When I read these first lines of the *Elegies*, I heard my own lament, my own fear and trembling before the terrible paradox in our
existence of beauty and terror, and the "depth-dark sobbing" which
I was swallowing in my silent despair. In sharing through these
poems the anguish of his vulnerability, his agonizing struggles on
the way to the wedding and what it took for him to make the vow
to life and love, Rilke gave me a vision of the vow to transformation.

Rilke's lament over the dreadful alienation of humankind is directed to the Angels, who transform the visible into the invisible
and who seem to be separated from us by an awesome abyss. Their
very being seems not only unreachable but so overwhelming that it
threatens our very existence. Each single angel is terrible, Rilke tells
us, terrible because it is the beauty which mysteriously affirms and
manifests the whole of existence, vouching for a higher degree of
reality in the invisible.[2] Before this higher way we stand in fear and
trembling. The *Elegies* can be seen as an existential expression of this
awesome paradox—the wedding of Beauty and the Beast.

A woman whose thirty-year marriage had been thrown into question by the unexpected discovery of the Beast in her husband asked
me if any poet had expressed the paradoxes in relationship—the
confusing and unpredictable swings between experiencing the relationship at one time as beautiful and inspiring and then as a terrible
trap. She was experiencing the descent in their relationship. Rilke's
affirmation in the *Duino Elegies* of the necessity to accept the paradoxical wedding of the beautiful and the terrible in existence and
the seasonal cycle of descent and ascent in our interior year spoke to
her. As a woman she was aware of the menstrual cycle of descent and

ascent in her body, and as a naturalist she knew the cycles of the earth—that the green meadows, grasslands, and trees were born from ground that once had been swamps and that these areas of dense growth would in time be annihilated through the natural fire of lightning or volcanic eruption, which in turn would renew the ground with nutrients for growth to continue. Rilke, in looking at the most horrific in existence—at the Beast—is able to see the transcendence, the beauty, and finally affirm the whole mysterious paradox of life and death. It is this ultimate affirmation that must be made in a soul relationship.

The lament that Rilke makes is a reaching out, a venture in relationship, a journey out of the dark depths. And, as the elegies proceed, the conditions of our lamenting and of its transformation gradually appear. Expectation and possessiveness, wanting the absolute, are the major obstacles that keep us from making the vow. We have experiences of the enduring: some tree on a slope, yesterday's walk, even a habit which persists. But we reject them, losing the mysteries in the events of everyday life and thus losing the mystery with one another. We long for the Whole all at once, but when we are confronted with it in the form of Night, its cosmic space overwhelms us, leaving us painfully alone. Even lovers merely hide from this fate in each other. If only we could express the emptiness and loneliness, put them out in the open, maybe this way we'd come into the open, into intimate contact.

> Alas, with each other they only conceal their lot!
> Don't you know *yet?*—Fling the emptiness out of your arms
> into the spaces we breathe—maybe that the birds
> will feel the extended air in more intimate flight.[3]

When we look, the stars wait to be seen by us, and violins sounding through open windows wait to be heard. We have this trust of existence, this possible relationship. But, distracted by longing for the absolute, we fail to relate to these offerings and instead expect the personification of the absolute in someone to love. Those of us who expect the Ghostly Lover or Prince Charming or the Special Princess do not see the daily gifts before us, and so we cease to trust in life. Rilke expresses it this way:

Yes, the Springs had need of you. Many a star
was waiting for you to espy it. Many a wave
would rise on the past towards you; or else, perhaps,
as you went by an open window, a violin would be giving
itself to someone. All this was a trust.
But were you equal to it? Were you not always
distracted by expectation, as though all this
were announcing someone to love?[4]

We look to the lovers as a model. But even they are not immortal;
nature takes them back. Perhaps of all, lovers experience this imper-
manence most intensely, for after the first mysteries of meeting have
worn off, eventually they realize that the loved one was only a brief
respite. Rilke addresses the lovers and asks:

Lovers, to you, each satisfied in the other,
I turn with my question about us. You grasp yourselves. Have you
    proofs?
Look, with me it may happen at times that my hands
grow aware of each other, or else that my hard-worn face
seeks refuge within them. That gives me a little
sensation. But who, just for that, could presume to exist?
. . . Yet, when you've once withstood
the startled first encounter, the window-longing,
and that first walk, just once, through the garden together:
Lovers, are you the same? When you lift yourselves
up to each other's lips—drink unto drink:
oh, how strangely the drinker eludes his part![5]

We long for the eternal, but it eludes us. Rilke believed that we
should let the eternal come forth freely rather than try to gain it
through possession, a desire doomed to failure. We must learn to
accept our finitude and live in its measure rather than vanish in
longing for the infinite. The challenge in love is to learn the secret
measure of loving in the human realm. We cannot project all meaning onto the gods or onto each other. We cannot possess another's
soul. But we can share the mystery.

If only we could discover some pure, contained,
narrow, human, own little strip of orchard
in between river and rock! For our heart transcends us

just as it did those others. And we can no longer
gaze after it into figures that soothe it, or godlike
bodies, wherein it achieves a grander restraint.[6]

Perhaps, Rilke suggests, our very conception of the lovers is
wrong. Perhaps instead we should look to the Hero as a model for
human existence, for "the Hero continues, even his fall was a pretext
for further existence, an ultimate birth."[7] Every Hero's battle entails
a fall and a struggle with the powers of darkness, but in the very
falling the Hero continues and is born. Is it not this which we must
learn to accept—that falling is part of human growth, that what
seems to be darkness and defeat is often the very ground from which
fruition springs? The Hero courageously takes on existence: beginning and change, the responsibility of choosing, doing, and moving
on. This is the way we are born, for even within the womb there are
thousands trying to come forth, yet the act of birth is completed
with the one who finally acts and germinates. The Hero is present
within the seed, in the very act of birth, and is symbolic of the
coming-to-be of human beings. The vow to a soul relationship, the
vow to life and love, requires the Hero and the Heroine. For, the
heroic couple does not allow the intrusiveness of the clan or societies'
expectations or the inertial pull of security to destroy their love.

The truly great lovers, those whose love is so great that they free
the loved one from personal possession, heroically accept emptiness,
enter into the open, and loving, eternally grow in the whole of existence. Learning to love is learning to live in the dual realm—in
the tension between life and death, between our wanting and our
giving, between holding on anxiously and letting go of expectations. Rilke gives us the image of the quivering bow and arrow to
express this kind of loving transcendence.

> . . . Is it not time that, in loving,
> we freed ourselves from the loved one, and, quivering, endured:
> as the arrow endures the string, to become, in the gathering
>     out-leap,
> something more than itself? For staying is nowhere.[8]

Such loving transcendence requires listening. Just as the saints
"heard till the giant-call lifted them off the ground; yet they went

impossibly on with their kneeling, in undistracted attention: so inherently hearers,"[9] so, too, must we learn to wait and listen to that which comes in silence, instead of expecting particular messages or absolute answers. If we could do this, we could make our vow to life, instead of grieving over life's injustice.

But not to name and interpret, not to wish for particular things, not to think in terms of a particular human future, is strange for the earthbound. To let go of life, to die, to start anew, to become aware of emptiness and death, and to accept them as part of life are difficult tasks. Yet it is just this to which we must aspire: the terrible secret of the angels, the awesome vow to life and death as one.

The artist, the lover, the saint, the hero, the mother—anyone who has made the vow to life—is the earthly betrothed of the angel, the Orpheus of Rilke's *Sonnets,* the one who is able to descend to the darkest depths to mine the light of life. Though human beings are uniquely capable of this divine activity, our seeming need to particularize, to separate ourselves from the whole, blinds us to the beauty of our heavenly spouse. And so we live a life conditioned by unacknowledged suffering, unable to unite with the angel, the creature who affirms existence and dwells in the whole of being, a dual realm that spirals up and down and overwhelms. Unable to see in ourselves the very divinity that would fulfill our longing to be at home in the world, we look for what we seek in others, attempting to grasp and hold what cannot be possessed. With the enormous effort to possess, we fail to see the meaning in the very sorrows, losses, emptiness, and separation we lament.

The *Duino Elegies* expresses through its poetic vision the path that Jung calls individuation: that process whereby humans differentiate themselves and achieve wholeness. The whole condition of the human journey, both the insufficiencies and the intimations of the way to transformation, is intuitively understood in the *Elegies,* which illuminates our alienation and its ground—that we are open only to part of existence (chiefly the light side), that, still identified with our ego and its wishes, we cling to this narrow possibility, avoiding suffering, pain, and darkness, only to find ourselves frustrated and cut off from our center of meaning. But individuation, the process of becoming a person who is open to the whole of Being, requires a surrender of the wishes which limit one's existence. And part of this surrender is to give up the flight from suffering and turn to face what seems to be dark emptiness.

> The actual process of individuation—the conscious coming-to-terms with one's own center (psychic nucleus) or Self—generally brings with it a wounding of the personality and the suffering that accompanies it. This initial shock amounts to a sort of "call," although it is not often recognized as such. On the contrary, the ego feels hampered in its will or its desire and usually projects the obstruction onto something external. . . . . There is only one thing that seems to work; and that is to turn directly toward the approaching darkness without prejudice and totally naively, and to try to find out what its secret aim is and what it wants from you.[10]

If one can learn to be open to whatever is there, then one can hear the "giant Call," "the uninterrupted news that grows out of silence."[11] For Jung, this is precisely the demand of individuation—to hear the inner voice. But most often the call is originally experienced as dangerous, as something to be avoided. The divine wedding is such a call, as is the wedding of souls, and sometimes throws us into fear, trembling, or even terror before the awesomeness of the union at the altar of the divine. This is why so many couples approaching the outer wedding want to flee at the last moment. And sometimes one person is left at the altar alone. Some never reach the door to the wedding, for fear of losing their identity. The frequent dream of the Missing Bridegroom presents this image. This is why creative people are sometimes afraid to actualize their vision.

If we accept the call and vow with our whole being, then we may hear what Rilke heard: "Someday, emerging at last from this terrifying vision, may I burst into jubilant praise to assenting Angels!"[12]

To enter a soul wedding requires the readiness to accept the call of the creative center. One must be ready to commit oneself to the mystery of the Other, to the I–Thou relationship. Readiness comes from life experience, from having made the journey to discover what is really meaningful and central to who one is. The descent into the underworld brings this knowledge, for down in the depths one is confronted with the essentials of existence. The letting go that happens there enables us to give up our outrageous and overly idealistic expectations. And it teaches us how to sacrifice the inessentials so that we can be free to receive the offerings from the creative center. One of the biggest paradoxes in relationship is how to keep the relationship creative while allowing the partner to live out of his or her individual creative center. As we grow in consciousness and freedom, discarding the unnecessary roles and images that have been hampering our unique development, we change and threaten a relationship that has been built upon convention and collective expectations, upon a narrow ring of identity. The relationship, to endure, must itself enter a transformation process, go through its own descent and letting go, die to its old rigidity so that it moves in wider and wider orbits, allowing each partner to live out of the creative center, which in turn increases the creativity of the relationship. This process presupposes that each partner has questioned his or her own life deeply enough to have a sense of fundamental values and creative needs, so that both have the understanding and willingness to honor and support each other in their creative process. This requires the ability to separate so as to do what each needs individually and the sensitivity to return and share the soul's journey. All this is involved in the wedding vow.

But keeping the vow is a daily struggle because it requires constant transformation. Remember the married couple who kept dreaming they were at their wedding celebration again and again. The opposition in our nature requires this constant renewal of the vow. In Rilke's words, "That's what Destiny means: being opposite, and nothing else, and always opposite."[13]

In contrast to the animals, which, free from the necessity of consciously facing death, exist in open space, we conscious beings, whose death is always before us, never encounter pure space ahead. Even in love we never look purely into the open, for the other is always there, "spoiling the view." For Rilke, the open signified that realm where the distinction between subject and object has been transcended, where separation and limit are experienced no longer, where "timelessness" is achieved. Sometimes children enter into this realm. And sometimes lovers approach it. But the finite human condition always prevents complete entry into the open. Perhaps it is as men and women that we feel this opposition most intensely—wanting to merge with the lover to experience total unity with all existence, yet always shoved back into separateness by our differences.

Lovers—were not the other present, always
spoiling the view!—draw near to it and wonder. . . .
Behind the other, as though through oversight,
the thing's revealed. . . . But no one gets beyond
the other, and so world returns once more.
Always facing Creation, we perceive there
only a mirroring of the free and open,
dimmed by our breath.[14]

Only in the womb did we ever have that sort of unity—the womb-unity for which romantic love longs. This longing is dangerous, for development requires consciousness and separation. Insofar as we lament the romantic love we always lose, consciousness appears as a curse. For once out of the womb we seem to be merely spectators, never wholly in or out of anything. Our being is somehow turned around so that we must forever take leave of what we have just gained.

And we, spectators always, everywhere,
looking at, never out of, everything!
It fills us. We arrange it. It decays.
We re-arrange it, and decay ourselves.
Who's turned us round like this, so that we always,
do what we may, retain the attitude
of someone's who's departing? Just as he,
on the last hill, that shows him all his valley
for the last time, will turn and stop and linger,
we live our lives, for ever taking leave.[15]

If we have only this fleeting existence, always separate, opposite, from what we perceive, never able to stay with anyone or anything, "—oh, why *have* to be human, and, shunning Destiny, long for Destiny?"[16] This is the cry of despair I hear so often from my clients. And it was the silent sobbing in my heart that night I first read Rilke, the night the *Elegies* gave me hope. As one woman who was longing for a soul relationship said to me, "It's very strengthening to have a universal example like the one Rilke gives, so as not to be stuck with my own depression as though that is all there is."

Rilke points to many of the fundamental challenges in the human effort to make the vow of affirmation on our way to the wedding: to sexuality, war, adaptation, our intense dividedness, and our fleeting existence.

In contrast to pure love, which demands no return, passionate love invokes "the Neptune within our blood, oh, his terrible trident!" [17] In the uproar of sexual ecstasy the particular woman or man can become a symbol of all women or men and of ancient terrors exceeding the individual person. Rilke says our love is not bound to this particular time or this particular person. Rather, the whole of our origins comes forth in any particular instance of love. The ecstasies of sexuality in awakening the primeval, archetypal powers can bring forth the ancient terrors of the Sirens, of Medusa, of the Witch, of the Demon Lover, as well as the bliss of Beauty and the Beast.

> Do you really suppose your gentle approach could have so
> convulsed him, you, that wander like morning-breezes?
> You terrified his heart, indeed; but more ancient terrors
> rushed into him in that instant of shattering contact.
> Call him . . . you can't quite call him away from
> those sombre companions. [18]

So Rilke asks the individual man or woman who wants to be the one and only for the loved one to remember that in any deep sexual encounter it is not only he or she but the entire spectrum of the masculine or feminine, indeed the very origins of humanity, that appears. Doing a single earthly task, a loving deed of the daytime, can help to counterbalance and ground these primeval forces so we can enter the divine creative stream.

For despite the uproar it produces in touching the deepest layers of our being and arousing the archetypal dimension, passionate love is a way to the divine. In a letter to a young poet, Rilke writes about the inherent relationship between sexuality and creativity.

In one creative thought a thousand forgotten nights of love revive, filling it with sublimity and exaltation. And those who come together in the night and are entwined in rocking delight do an earnest work and gather sweetnesses, gather depth and strength for the song of some coming poet, who will arise to speak of ecstasies beyond telling. And they call up the future; and though they err and embrace blindly, the future comes all the same, a new human being rises up. . . .[19]

War, whether it is internal or external, emphasizes the absence of the lover and a loss of soul. When we encounter the power drive—in ourselves, in each other, in a nation—love and creativity are threatened. We tend to respond with hostility and try to hold on to the ring of power.

We, though, while we're intent upon one thing,
can feel the cost of conquest of another.
Hostility's our first response. Aren't lovers
forever reaching verges in each other,—
lovers, that looked for spaces, hunting, home?[20]

In contrast to the power drive of war, Rilke appeals to the image of the child whose innocence and spontaneous closeness to both life and death allow openness. To come to the wedding, one needs the pure presence of the child.

Along with the horrors of war and the closed hostility of the power drive, we also have our earthly transience to contend with. Rilke uses the image of wandering circus performers to symbolize the tightrope walk through life. Like the acrobats, pushed by a never-contented will to perform meaningless activities in an external show of pretext and adaptation, we too often juggle and jump on a threadbare carpet while the spectators gaze on until boredom turns them away; we are at once the spectators and the show.

This metaphor can also image the external show of many a wedding performance, which, with its collective moneyed display, can destroy the inner beauty of the quiet joining of souls. A client who was planning a wedding while I was writing this book arrived at her session in a panic. She was beginning to lose her feeling of soul relationship with her fiancé. She was beset with so many demands from her parents—who, while disapproving of the bridegroom, needed to impress friends and relatives with the expected collective idea of the wedding and their own performance—that she almost lost her own relation to the inner wedding. This is a typical story I frequently hear, sometimes before the wedding, and sometimes afterward, when the show is over and the inner relation is left unadorned.

In contrast to all that is inherent in this circus performance, Rilke points to the little girl in Picasso's painting of circus people, *Les Saltimbanques,* symbolizing virginal hope, faith and serenity, a healing affirmation to be preserved. This image of purity and peace amid the performance leads Rilke to ask where in our incomplete existence is the place where the quantitative show and glitter can be transformed into the uncountable golden coins of our souls. Are we merely left with a place like Paris, that "infinite show-place" where death is devalued and fate reduced to appear in the form of cheap winter hats with innumerable frills? Or is there a place we as yet know nothing about, where lovers, those acrobats of the soul, can express and achieve all that here they're unable to show, where the ground is permanent beneath them so they can reveal the pure figure of "heart-flight"?

> Angel: suppose there's a place we know nothing about and there,
> on some indescribable carpet, lovers showed all that here
> they're for ever unable to manage—their daring
> lofty figures of heart-flight,
> their towers of pleasure, their ladders,
> long since, where ground never was, just quiveringly
> propped by each other,—suppose they could manage it
>     there. . . .[21]

In this image Rilke offers the hope of a sacred space for the divine wedding. But that space must be transformed within ourselves. As he writes: "We want to be visibly able to show it, whereas the most visible joy can only reveal itself to us when we've transformed it, within."[22]

First we must find what we seek within ourselves; only then can the divine wedding occur. We must lift the veil to realize that all that we admire and fear in the world, that whole spectrum of life ranging from the most repellent to the most beautiful, from the most fearsome to the most lovable, is also present in ourselves. For Rilke the divine wedding is possible for every human being. So in the *Elegies* there rings forth suddenly the sound of celebration! Now, rather than lament, we can actively make the vow of affirmation. The vow manifests through the expression of form—through the creation of a work of art, as was Rilke's way, or through the birth of a child, through building a city or a culture, or through an act of love. And all these are worthy even to show to the angel.

> . . . Angel,
> I'll show it to you as well—there! In your gaze
> it shall stand redeemed at last, in a final uprightness.
> Pillars, pylons, the Sphinx, all the striving thrust,
> grey, from fading or foreign town, of the spire!
> Wasn't all this a miracle? Angel, gaze, for it's *we*—
> O mightiness, tell them that *we* were capable of it—my breath's
> too short for this celebration. So, after all, we have *not*
> failed to make use of the spaces, these generous spaces, these,
> *our* spaces.²³

With this realization, the lament becomes a song of praise, and the previously unreachable angel is now within the realm of communication. But the angel is not to be wooed, not to be clutched at for help and consolation. When desired or feared, the angel cannot approach, for whatever the angel is, it transcends possessiveness. Hence, Rilke concludes:

> . . . Don't think that I'm wooing!
> Angel, even if I were, you'd never come. For my call
> is always full of "Away!" Against such a powerful
> current you cannot advance. Like an outstretched
> arm is my call. And its clutching, upwardly
> open hand is always before you
> as open for warding and warning,
> aloft there, Inapprehensible.²⁴

Our wanting only repels. To receive, our hands must be open, not grasping. A friend who is a singer told me that when she feels too attached to her goals in singing and begins to lose the joy of the process, she goes back to read the *Elegies* to regain her center and the wisdom of letting go. Then she remembers that she sings not to be "good," but because she loves it!

We are human not to gain happiness, "that premature profit of imminent loss,"[25] for happiness is too elusive and is usually built upon false expectations. Neither is curiosity or feeling sufficient to require this painful destiny. Not for these reasons are we here.

> But because being here amounts to so much, because all
> this Here and Now, so fleeting, seems to require us and strangely
> concerns us. Us the most fleeting of all. Just once,
> everything, only for once. Once and no more. And we, too,
> once. And never again. But this having been once, though only
>    once,
> having been once on earth—can it ever be cancelled?[26]

This is the ecstasy that is ours. As earthly creatures with a conscious relation to the eternal, we are needed to praise existence. This is at once our greatest possibility and our task. The act of constantly praising, offering up, and celebrating the here and now becomes a bridge for others to find a way to the wedding. The dream of the woman I wrote about in the Ghostly Lover chapter illustrates the beauty of being human. In the dream the Holy Mother says to her as she is in the depths of despair:

> I want you to know that *I envy you your physical life.* The way has been cleared for you now to continue on a new path and you must, as my divineness depends on your humanness, on your living out the human life intended for you to its fullest. We cannot do our work without you doing yours. You must go on. There is work intended for you.

Existing on the threshold between the finite and the infinite, between the temporal and the eternal, our task is to praise from the side of the finite, as Rilke's angel praises from the side of the eternal. Our work is to praise the things we have seen.

> For the wanderer doesn't bring from the mountain slope
> a handful of earth to the valley, untellable earth, but only

some word he has won, a pure word, the yellow and blue
gentian. Are we, perhaps, here just for saying: House,
Bridge, Fountain, Gate, Jug, Olive tree, Window,—
possibly: Pillar, Tower? . . . but for saying, remember,
oh, for such saying as never the things themselves
hoped so intensely to be.[27]

We who have the power of speech can praise with the word.

Not to appreciate the finite things of the world is to betray the
trust that existence reposes in us. As Rilke points out over and over
again in the *Elegies,* we often overlook this offering because we expect
more, always wanting the absolute. Perhaps this is also why our task
is not to praise the "untellable," the more absolute experience which
the angel knows far better, but rather to praise the simple things of
the earth.

What we, as adults, must do is relearn the relationship to things
which we once had as children. To "retrieve" things has a double
motion and effect. On the one hand we can transform the external
thing into something inward which remains with us and through
which we learn more about ourselves. And on the other hand we can
express our inwardness in an outer work of art, through which we
share the mystery with others.

When we name a thing, whatever it is, be it a fountain or a tear,
we reveal its form, and thus we show the positive structure even in
what may on first sight seem to be sorrowful. And, in this way, we
can give something to existence too. For, Rilke proclaims, fleeting
things "want" us to transform them and are there for us to do so.
The transitory things of the earth need us to make them permanent
in spirit, through proclaiming their existence in the word. And by
praising their existence, we become part of the whole. Our task is
to show the angel

how even the moaning of grief purely determines on form,
serves as a thing, or dies into a thing,—to escape
to a bliss beyond the fiddle. These things that live on departure
understand when you praise them: fleeting, they look for
rescue through something in us, the most fleeting of all.
Want us to change them entirely, within our invisible hearts,
into—oh, endlessly—into ourselves! Whosoever we are.[28]

If we can show "how even the moaning of grief purely determines on form," as Rilke actually did by writing the *Duino Elegies,* then we will begin to see that turning point where lament turns into praise. Then we will also realize how our very suffering has meaning and enables us to achieve this task of transformation. Rilke once wrote that the *Duino Elegies,* finally achieved out of so much despair, was a testimony to this possibility of transforming despair, and that he hoped it would serve as an encouragement to others.

> That a person who through the wretched harassings of those years had felt himself split to the roots, into an Aforetime and a dying Now not to be united with it: that such a person should experience the grace of perceiving how in yet more mysterious depths, *beneath* this gaping rift, the continuity of his work and his soul re-established itself . . . , seems to me more than just a private event; for with it a gauge is given of the inexhaustible stratification of our nature, and how many, who for one reason or another believe themselves cleft apart, might draw from this example of possible continuation a singular comfort.[29]

Once we realize that all of our experiences, even those dark ones from which we usually flee, aid us on the way to the wedding, we will be able unreservedly to praise existence, recognizing that even the most fearsome, Death, is a friend in this venture. Hence, Rilke celebrates the vow in a song of acceptance and praise.

> Earth, isn't this what you want: an invisible
> re-arising in us? Is it not your dream
> to be one day invisible? Earth! invisible!
> What is your urgent command, if not transformation?
> Earth, you darling, I will. Oh, believe me, you need
> your Springs no longer to win me: a single one,
> just one, is already more than my blood can endure.
> I've now been unspeakably yours for ages and ages.
> You were always right, and your holiest inspiration's
> Death, that friendly Death.
> Look, I am living. On what? Neither childhood nor future
> are growing less. . . . Supernumerous existence
> wells up in my heart.[30]

A woman who had faced her own death and the possible death of her husband, who was suffering from a serious illness, told me that these lines of Rilke expressed the vow of affirmation to life for her. As she said, "The Elegies offer me both a solace and a challenge."

The act of celebrating the earth and transforming the visible into the invisible, of preserving the transitory, is possible for us because we stand on the threshold between the transient and the eternal. As we learn to transform the visible into the invisible, we will experience that our lives really spring from a great unity—the wedding of heaven and earth.

In the symbolic experience, what Rilke would call transforming the visible into the invisible, we return to this experience of unity. This is the wedding! It requires a turning in (the *veil*) and a return (the *vow*). Erich Neumann, in his essay "Creative Man and Transformation," describes this symbolic unitary reality as follows.

> When things, a landscape or a work of art, come alive or "grow transparent," this signifies that they are transformed into what we have called unitary reality. . . . There is nothing mystical about the symbolical unitary reality, and it is not beyond our experience; it is the world that is always experienced when the polarization of inside and outside, resulting from the separation of the psychic systems, has not yet been effected or is no longer in force. It is the authentic, total world of transformation as experienced by the creative man.[31]

The unitary reality can be revealed in a variety of experiences, including nature, things, dreams, love, and art; and when this happens we experience a reality that is deeper than the one we are able to grasp every day. The transformation of the visible into the invisible puts us into this unitary realm where we experience the coming together of the archetypal and the concrete, and hence in this way we enter into unity. But the unity we enter into is not that of the all-protective womb, the unity which devours our uniqueness. Nor is the way we enter into it through regressive longing. Instead, it is the unity of all aspects of existence, a unity which is differentiated and which requires our conscious acceptance of it. In this unity, as conscious and finite, we are the most perishable and yet the place where Being opens up. As Heidegger has said, our being is to "be there" where Being opens up and reveals itself, and our task is to open to the revelation and to try to preserve it through expression. For Heidegger, the fundamental opening-up experience for the human being occurs when one is able to accept and affirm the mystery of death within one's being. For in the acceptance of our "being-unto-death" we surrender our desire to control reality and thus are able to accept whatever offers itself to us. For Rilke, death has the same significance, hence it can really be that "the holiest inspiration's Death, that friendly Death." For death is the ultimate transformation and threshold. As Rilke writes in commenting upon the meaning of the *Elegies:*

> *Affirmation of life-AND-death appears as one in the "Elegies."* To grant one without the other is, so it is here learned and celebrated, a limitation which in the end shuts out all that is infinite. *Death is* the *side of life* averted from us, unshone upon by us: we must try to achieve the greatest consciousness of our existence which is at home in *both unbounded realms, inexhaustibly nourished from both.* . . . The true figure of life extends through *both* spheres, the blood of the mightiest circulation flows through *both: there is neither a here nor a beyond, but the great unity* in which the beings that surpass us, the "angels," are at home.[32]

When Death, that ultimate "dragon" we must face, who is perhaps a "princess" in disguise, is understood to be our innermost possibility, enabling our surrender to and acceptance of the whole of existence, then our lament can be transformed into a song of praise.

> Someday, emerging at last from this terrifying vision,
> may I burst into jubilant praise to assenting Angels!
> May not even one of the clear-struck keys of the heart
> fail to respond through alighting on slack or doubtful
> or rending strings! May a new-found splendour appear
> in my streaming face! May inconspicuous Weeping
> flower! How dear you will be to me then, you Nights
> of Affliction! Oh, why did I not, inconsolable sisters,
> more bendingly kneel to receive you, more loosely surrender
> myself to your loosened hair? We wasters of sorrows!
> How we stare away into sad endurance beyond them,
> trying to foresee their end! Whereas they are nothing else

than our winter foliage, our sombre evergreen, *one*
of the seasons of our interior year,—not only
season—they're also place, settlement, camp, soil, dwelling.[33]

In these verses, Rilke affirms that sorrows themselves are a part of
our growth, a necessary season of our interior year. It is only when
we cannot accept suffering and sorrow as part of our existence that
we are doomed to lament. And, paradoxically, as soon as we are able
to accept sorrow and not "waste it," we find it mysteriously ground-
ing our growth and even our joy, giving us a depth and richness we
had previously not foreseen. Often people are "wasters of sorrows,"
evading them through numerous distractions, seeking a "market of
comfort." Rilke contrasts the bourgeois way of existence, which tries
to evade sorrow, with the way that courageously faces lament. Calling the former the "City of Pain," he describes life there: the vacuity
behind the facade of this superficial carnival of existence, its profit
orientation, always shooting for happiness and hoping for luck, ever
replete with new distractions which keep one from facing death.
Such an existence is superficially novel on the one hand, boring and
nonvital on the other—and always in flight from death.

Just behind this realm, however, lies a more genuine realm, an
instinctual realm in which children play and lovers love. Some of us
get that far and then, looking a bit farther, see the Land of Lament.
Rilke uses the metaphor of a youth who, attracted to a young
maiden from this realm, follows her for a while, but when she shows
him how far he must go, he turns back, not understanding her real
worth. This symbolizes the attitude of those who still are unable to
see the worth of suffering and dying, who still are prisoners of that
artificial separation between joy and sorrow, between life and death.
Only those who have ceased to make this division can follow the
maiden.

Once in the Land of Lament, one finally discovers pure feelings,
mined up from the depths, from the original times when people died
their own death, as contrasted with modern times in the City of
Pain, where death and all other genuine and mysterious experiences
are avoided. And, continuing, one is led through the great range of
archetypal figures, the origins of humankind. Describing this land,
a Lament says:

—We were once,
she says, a great family, we Lamentations. Our fathers
worked the mines in that mountain-range: among men
you'll find a lump, now and then, of polished original pain,
or of drossy petrified rage from some old volcano.
Yes, that came from there. We used to be rich.

And lightly she leads him on through the spacious landscape
of Lamentation, shows him the temple columns, the ruins
of towers from which, long ago, Lords of the House of Lament
wisely governed the land. Shows him the tall
Tear trees, shows him the fields of flowering Sadness
(only as tender foliage known to the living);
shows him the pasturing herds of Grief. . . .[34]

Entry into this Land of Lament, "into the deeps," as Rilke calls it
elsewhere, constellates the deepest layers and configurations of humankind, the various archetypal figures which we all must sooner or
later confront. Rilke names a few of these "Stars of the Land of Pain":
for example, "the Rider," symbolizing the unity of humanity with
its instincts, "the Way," symbolizing the journey we all must take
through life, "the Window," symbolizing that open entry we must
gain with the world, and finally, "the clearly-resplendent M, standing for Mothers," symbolizing the creative origins of all things.[35]

But the way leads ultimately even beyond these particular archetypal constellations, so that eventually all of us must go on to the
source, confronting our very origins, the stream which carries us all.
And then we see that at the very source of sorrow, in the Land of
Lament, the stream is Joy—the uniting stream of humankind.
Seeing this, one can accept all things, even the most mysterious of
fates.

If those who know death were to show us their understanding
through an image that is ours as well, they would point to those
growing things that fall—for example, the catkins—or those falling things that bring growth—for example, the rain.

And yet, were they waking a likeness within us, the endlessly
    dead,
look, they'd be pointing, perhaps to the catkins, hanging
from empty hazels, or else they'd be meaning the rain
that falls on the dark earth in the early Spring.

And we, who have always thought
of happiness climbing, would feel
the emotion that almost startles
when happiness falls.[36]

With these lines which affirm that "falling," too, can be joyous, and
that ultimately to allow ourselves to fall into the depths is our source
of growth and creativity, the *Duino Elegies* closes. With the completion of the *Elegies,* the transformation from Rilke's despair to affirmation was accomplished.[37] Rilke did what Malte had not been able
to do—accept the whole of reality with all of its oppositions and
paradoxes, the horrifying and defeating aspects as well as the pure
and inspiring. He was now able, in his own finite way, to achieve
what Malte had envisioned: "to love is to endure."

The soul's wedding song to the divine is sung out by Rilke in this
ultimate vow to existence. The wedding vow affirms the union of
love and death in a song to life as a whole. Even the darkest destiny,
death, is affirmed as an essential part of life. The elegies end with
the cycle of growth, with the image of rain falling from the tall tear
trees into the deep, dark earth, the ground of Being, the rain that
softens earth hardened by bitterness, the rain that nurtures Being
with tears of receptive fruition, allowing for new growth and the
flowering of our existence. As wanderers on the way to the wedding,
so can we all join hands and dance and sing in the cyclical ring of
the holy wedding.

*I live my life in growing orbits*
*which move out over the things of the world.*
*Perhaps I can never achieve the last,*
*but that will be my attempt.*

*I am circling around God, around the ancient tower,*
*and I have been circling for a thousand years,*
*and I still don't know if I am a falcon, or a storm,*
*or a great song.*

RAINER MARIA RILKE
*The Book of Hours*

# 13

# *The Ring of Love*

To be on the way to the wedding is to honor the great ring of mystery in which we live. It is to praise the circling movement that is ours, the ever-growing orbits of our lives. When I look at my life dancing in the great ring of mystery, I know now that each season will greet me with the energies I need to transform to make my life and love richer. I know that I will come around and around on my personal cycles to all that I have lived before, and no matter how painful or terrible or dark some of that time was, it is now the rich rock from which I mine the crystal visions for my healing. The wounds in my life, I have learned, become the source of the cycle of healing. Just as the vibrating ring of my life moves in its mysterious manner from depths to heights and around again from agony to ecstasy, so does the ring cycle in my soul relationship. The wedding, too, has its descents and its wounds, and they are the source for renewal and for transforming energies so that together the circle of a shared life becomes more open and more giving.

The wedding ring symbolizes the wholeness of each person and the cosmic wholeness in which the lovers dwell. When they give and receive the wedding ring, they honor the vow to affirm this mystery, even unto death. The gift of rings celebrates the divine love that is greater than the two.

If the rings exchanged are rings of power, then the wedding is denied its transcendent ground. Instead we experience all the frustrations of power games and manipulations. It is the tight egos that are married in a union of perpetual discord that can only end in divorce and alienation, or a relationship under the eye of a Witch or a Dracula. Instead of the open generosity of growth one feels in a soul wedding, the ring-of-power exchange narrows existence to a quantitative count (as the giants, the dwarf Alberich, and Wotan related to the ring). Only in the ring of power do we ask another to give up his or her center or give it up ourselves, and this usually happens out of our fears and desires, our dependency, projections, and power needs. As Jung says: "Where love reigns, there is no will to power; and where the will to power is paramount, love is lacking. The one is but the shadow of the other."[1] Jung points out that in the initial meeting and the early part of a relationship, projection provides the major attraction. The projections can be either conscious fantasy ideals we want our partner to have or qualities from the unconscious which we project onto the other but really need to integrate ourselves. When these projections begin to fall from the partner, there is usually a descent in the relationship, in the form of depression, anxiety, or anger that the partner is not what we fantasized. It is then that we are forced inward, to look at the Other in ourselves. As one woman said to me, "It was only after the fantasy of my husband collapsed, when I had to find the inner lover in myself, that I began to feel the possibility of the divine wedding within myself."

When the projections begin to fall off the partner, or when the partner refuses them because they don't correspond to who he or she is, or because they reduce the mystery of the Other to a role or false image, then the power struggle begins. The ring of power becomes threatened. The secure identity of the relationship falters. The breakthrough from the ring of power to the ring of love requires a descent. Just as transformation in an individual life requires descent, a death before rebirth, so it is in relationship. The creative process in both an individual life and in a relationship throws us into a ring of descent and ascent, a ring that pulls us away from our ego projections and plans into a sacrifice of the ordinary way we look at ourselves, the world, and the Other. One of the dangers of breaking through the ring of power by descending into the abyss is that of being torn apart by the wild, chaotic forces which rant and rave down there. But without this risk, one risks losing all creative human potentialities. As Rilke emphasizes, courage before all aspects of existence, even the "unheard-of," is essential for the human journey, for the search for a soul relationship. He writes:

> We must assume our existence as *broadly* as we in any way can: everything, even the unheard-of must be possible in it. That is at bottom the only courage that is demanded of us: to have courage for the most strange, the most singular and the most inexplicable that we may encounter. That mankind has in this sense been cowardly has done life endless harm; the experiences that are called "visions," the whole so-called "spirit-world," death, all those things that are so closely akin to us, have by daily parrying been so crowded out of life that the senses with which we could have grasped them are atrophied. But fear of the inexplicable has not alone impoverished the existence of the individual; the relation between one human being and another has also been cramped by it . . . only someone who is ready for everything, who excludes nothing, not even the most enigmatical, will live the relation to another as something alive and will himself draw exhaustively from his own existence.[2]

Only if we confront the chaotic, irrational powers at the very depths of our being will we be able to transform them into something productive and, perhaps more important, only then will we be able to face them in another. We must be able to face the Dracula and the Witch in ourselves, look at the pull of the Ghostly Lover, see the limitations of Prince Charming and the Special Princess, before we can find the depth of the soul wedding. This was the journey that Rilke took in his life, and out of his ring of descent into the void of the center arose the *Duino Elegies* and the *Sonnets to Orpheus,* which ecstatically praises life. The center that seemed void to his ego wishes was the center of transformation and birth, and the source of their origin was "the relation toward the center of *that* realm whose depth and influence we share, everywhere unboundaried, with the dead and those to come."[3] The sonnets express the entry into that great unity, that "open world," the ring which encompasses the two realms of life and death. What Rilke wrote about the creation of the

*Elegies* and the *Sonnets* describes as well what is necessary to break through the ring of power to the ring of love.

> Two inmost experiences were decisive for their production: the resolve that grew up more and more in my spirit to hold life open to death, and, on the other side, the spiritual need to situate the transformations of life in this wider whole differently than was possible in the narrower orbit of life (which simply shut out death as the Other).[4]

Rilke elaborates on his view of death and love in a letter written after the completion of his two works, in which he maintains that death does not contradict love, but rather is implanted in the nature of love. For love accepts the whole of existence, including death, and the act of love itself is a kind of death insofar as it requires a surrender of control and possessiveness, a death of the ego, a sacrifice of the ring of power. Love requires giving up one's preconceptions and demands on the other and on the universe, accepting whatever comes, the whole. The way from the ring of power to the ring of love is the path of patience, waiting for the possibility to realize the vision, enduring the tension of the opposites within and without, seeking always to unite them. Rilke considered waiting essential to the creative process of love and life, the ultimate sacrifice, the surrender to grace.

> . . . all progress, must come from deep within and cannot be pressed or hurried by anything. *Everything* is gestation and then bringing forth. To let each impression and each germ of a feeling come to completion wholly in itself, in the dark, in the inexpressible, the unconscious, beyond the reach of one's own intelligence, and await with deep humility and patience the birth-hour of a new clarity: that alone is living the artist's life: in understanding as in creating. There is here no measuring with time, no year matters, and ten years are nothing. Being an artist means, not reckoning and counting, but ripening like the tree which does not force its sap and stands confident in the storms of spring without the fear that after them may come no summer. It does come. But it comes only to the patient, who are there as though eternity lay before them, so unconcernedly still and wide. I learn it daily, learn it with pain to which I am grateful: *patience* is everything![5]

And so it is with love—the patience for the Other to transform, the patience for oneself to transform, and the patience for the relationship to become whole.

In a soul wedding, when the lovers give each other their rings, they affirm the open ring of love, they affirm the wholeness of each other and their relationship in the greater cycle of existence. The ecstasy of the gift of the rings is that open giving that so purely lets one stand out of the narrow circle of compulsive ego control into the orgasmic energy that vibrates into ever-wider spheres of Being. This is the ecstatic ring that Marc Chagall expressed in so many of his paintings. Chagall's vision of love, symbolized by the lovers flying in space with the other beings of creation, acknowledges the whole of existence, the terrible as well as the beautiful. But, as he says, love is the central color:

Despite the trouble of our world, I have kept the love of the inner life in which I was raised and man's hope in love. In our life there is a single color, as on an artist's palette, which provides the meaning of life and art. It is the color of love. I see in this color of love all the qualities permitting accomplishment in all fields. I have often used the word chemistry in art. This chemistry can also exist in life itself. I often wonder why in this grandiose nature, man sometimes seems so cruel. I ask myself how that can be when alongside are the Mozarts, Beethovens, Shakespeares, Giottos, Rembrandts and so many others, as well as all the humble and honest workers who built the cathedrals, monuments, and works of art, and those who have invented all the things that improve and facilitate our lives. Is it possible that with all the new means of mastery, man is incapable of mastering himself? That to me is something inadmissible. One must not search outside nature but within oneself where the keys to harmony and happiness lie. They are in our own hands. Everything I have tried to do is a weak response to this challenge. The art I have practiced since my childhood has taught me that man is capable of love and that love can save him. That, to me, is the true color, the true substance of art. It is as natural as a tree or a stone. All my works, here and there, are reflections of all I have seen, as in a sky, and felt every day in my soul. I have tried to keep all that in my heart.[6]

When the lovers jump into the center of the ring of love together, the center space of the open allows them to fly, as we see in so many of Chagall's paintings. Time and space are no longer subject to the clock and the measuring rod; they are cyclic patterns of process, vibrations of energy. Time and space in the open ring of love are the Great Whole of continuous duration—the Tao. In this ring of wholeness, in this ceaseless process of being, descent and ascent are experienced differently. A story told in the ancient revered Taoist book *Chuang-tzu* illustrates this different attitude. An old man was swimming in a turbulent river, playing in the raging water rapids, when suddenly he was swept under. Just then Confucius and his pupils saw him and rushed to save him. But by then the old man was standing up on the bank, vibrant and unharmed. When Confucius asked him how he had been able to survive the raging river and rocks, the old man replied, "Oh, I know how to go in with a descending vortex, and come out with an ascending one."[7] This man had learned to move in the Tao by intuiting with all his senses the currents of energies in the flowing weave of time and change; he had learned to live in harmony with the great ring of mystery. Able to let go, he could flow with the descending as well as the ascending currents. This is the mode of movement that a love relationship requires, and in Taoism it is the lovers who symbolize the harmony between heaven and earth through the union of *yin* and *yang,* the oscillating feminine and masculine energies of the universe which weave the movement of the Tao.

In Taoism human beings are the mediators whose destiny is to harmonize the vibrating energies of heaven and earth. The lovers, in their erotic union, give the energy of their unique sexuality to each other to absorb—each man and woman gives of his or her own and receives from the other the opposite sexual energy to become whole. The gifts that the human lovers exchange in their wedding of the opposite sexual energies reflect the wedding that takes place within each individual through inner meditation and the great cosmic wedding of heaven and earth that brings forth the mysterious movement of the Tao. Since the Tao, the Great Whole, is reflected within each person, the divine wedding of the opposite energies which unite in this majestic moving mystery of Being can occur within each individual, in the relationship of the lovers, and in the cosmic creation. The divine wedding of the Tao is an ecstatic event that can happen in three spheres—the inner wedding, the outer wedding of the lovers, and the wedding of heaven and earth. And it is this divine wedding that is expressed in all great art. The great artists, through their own personal inner divine wedding, attune themselves with the divine wedding of the Tao, revealing and celebrating the wedding in their creative works. Chagall described how his paintings express the wedding of heaven and earth as follows:

> . . . to the best of my ability, in the course of my life—though I sometimes have the impression that I am someone else entirely, that I was born one night say between heaven and earth, that the world for me is a great desert in which my soul wanders like a torch—I have painted these pictures in keeping with that remote dream. I wanted to leave them in this House so that men may try to find here a certain peace, a certain spirituality, a religious feeling, a sense of life. To my mind these paintings do not represent the dream of a single people but of all mankind.[8]

If we look at the movements of nature, we can see a wondrous wedding ring, a tranquilly transcendent ring containing all change. We see nature's ring revealed in the wedding of heaven and earth through the movement of the water cycle. The sun in the heavens draws up the waters of the earth from the oceans, rivers, lakes. As the winds blow the watery air upward toward the sun in whirling clouds and mist, the air cools as it ascends to higher altitudes, and rain is born, falling down into the ground to the forests and the grasses of the earth. Then the great water cycle starts anew as the forest trees breathe moisture in the air, to rise once more to the heavens to be transformed into rain or snow, which flows down on the earth again in a continual cycle. The wedding bursts forth in the tree, the Tree of Life, as heaven and earth make the vow of their union. And sometimes we see the ecstasy of their marriage in the rainbow, the ecstatic ring of color uniting heaven and earth. Whenever we join in the wedding of heaven and earth, we feel life's energy, the élan vital of existence. As in every soul wedding, the vital energy shows itself in many ways—in the joyous, youthful spring sunlight streaming through lacy leaves in the forest or lighting up the enchanting meadow flowers, in the veil of rain, in the angry thunderclaps and tears of summer storms, in the cold winds that blow off the ripened gold-red leaves in autumn, in the peace of the soft snow silently falling on the ground to deepen the seasonal cycle of the ring anew.

As it is in the cycle of nature, so it is in the cycle of our lives and our love relationships. The romance of spring, as in that magic love of Tristan and Isolde, promises the ecstatic union that transcends clock time and measured space. In that love we leap and fly in the wonder of the Whole. We love, we create, we soar with our divine visions. Without spring, without the generous promise of hope, love, faith, and creativity, our lives and our loves would wither in the dull routine of practical affairs. We need the springs, and the springs need us to see them and sing the song of existence. Yet there is in spring already the necessity of death, for spring itself arose from the death of winter. And so it is for Tristan and Isolde. Their readiness to die for each other symbolizes the change to a new season of life and love. The spring glories in its burst of beauty, in its rapture, then suddenly transforms into the mature, rich, flowering fruit of summer, the varied weather of rains and storms and hot, solid sunlight that we experience in the deepening of our lives and loves and that absorb the tears of suffering and separation, the anger of opposition and differences, and the renewed joys of reunion. In summer we feel the ground of our love and creativity, taste its fruits, and come to know that this process requires us to let go for a while, to allow a resting time for underground maturing and nourishment, the deep and silent time of pregnancy. Autumn announces this time to us, showing us life's paradox—the rich red and gold colors of the leaves of our lives, the bliss of Indian summer's deep beauty together with the dying of this fullness into the approaching hibernation, the separation time of solitude we all need for renewal. In relationship, in our individual lives, and in nature, the winter of our Being is that time of silent space of faith and loyalty to the ring, in which miraculously the new Being gathers itself in the dark to appear and surprise us once more in spring, when the whole ring cycle dances its round anew.

# NOTES

*Chapter 1: Through the Woods*

1. "The armored amazon" is a term used in *The Wounded Woman: Healing the Father-Daughter Relationship* to describe an archetypal pattern of existence in which a woman identifies with the masculine mode as a defensive reaction to control life, usually as a compensation for having had a weak father. The opposite pattern is "the eternal girl" (puella), a mode of existence that tends to operate out of weakness and passivity. Four modes of the eternal girl are "The Darling Doll," who adapts to projections to please the partner; "The Girl of Glass," who retreats from life into inner fantasy; "The High Flyer" who is continually on the move from one possibility to another; and "The Misfit," who rebels against convention in a self-destructive way. Four modes of the armored amazon are "The Superstar," who attempts to control life through success and achievement; "The Dutiful Daughter," who controls via obedience and conformity; "The Martyr," who maintains control through excessive self-denial; and "The Warrior Queen," who controls via offensive fighting.

*Chapter 2: Prince Charming and the Special Princess*

1. Martin Buber, *I and Thou* (New York: Scribners, 1958), p. 4.
2. Ibid., p. 34.
3. Rainer Maria Rilke, *Letters to a Young Poet*, trans. M. D. Herter (New York: W. W. Norton, 1963), pp. 53–54.

*Chapter 3: The Ghostly Lover*

1. M. Esther Harding has described the Ghostly Lover in detail in her book *The Way of All Women* (New York: Colophon Books, Harper &

Row, 1975), p. 36ff. She focuses on this archetypal figure as an aspect of the animus, or masculine soul, within the woman, corresponding to the siren aspect of the anima in the man, whereas I see this phenomenon in all humans. In describing the psychic structures of the human being, those universal archetypes which govern the life of every person, Jung found that a major part of the developmental process entailed becoming conscious of the contrasexual aspect within—for the man the feminine and for the woman the masculine. Moreover, this contrasexual aspect seemed to him to be the very image of the soul. As such it is also the link to the unconscious realm, which contains creativity but also danger. Hence integration of this element is essential for every human being and is a link to the person's creativity. In the man, the anima, or feminine soul, reflects every element of femininity, hence to meet her consciously requires of the man that he open himself to the terrors of woman as well as the blisses. Moreover, every individual woman carries for the man all the varied aspects of femininity, reflecting the many-sided facets that belong to his feminine soul. If he never realizes that these very fascinating aspects which he meets in every woman are in fact part of himself, then he will always be both drawn to but also anxious before every woman he meets, projecting what is within upon her. It takes, indeed, much courage and heroism to meet the dark aspects of the woman within, but only if a man responsibly takes on this task will he gain access to his own creativity, to independence, and to the freedom to relate genuinely to the woman without. The same is true for the woman. The inner man must be met and faced in all its dimensions before she is truly free to relate to the outer male partner.

2. Richard Wagner, *The Flying Dutchman* (London: John Calder Publishers, 1982), pp. 60–61.

3. Ibid., p. 63.

4. Ibid., p. 52.

5. Ibid., p. 55.

6. Ibid.

7. Elizabeth Barrett Browning, *Sonnets from the Portuguese and Other Love Poems* (New York: Doubleday & Company, 1954), p. 40.

8. R. Wilhelm, trans., *I Ching: The Book of Changes* (New York: Bollingen Foundation, 1967), pp. 208, 665.

9. Ibid., p. 663.

10. Ibid., pp. 664–665.

11. George Balanchine and Francis Mason, *101 Stories of Ballet* (New York: Doubleday and Company, 1975), p. 468.

### Chapter 5: The Demon Lover

1. Bram Stoker, *Dracula* (New York: New American Library, 1965), p. 30.
2. Ibid., pp. 46–47.
3. Ibid., pp. 196–197.
4. Ibid., p. 243.
5. Ibid., p. 293.
6. Ibid., p. 297.
7. Ibid., p. 382.
8. Program notes, *Dracula,* performed in San Francisco, Calif., January–February 1985.
9. *Dracula,* p. 326.
10. Ibid., p. 236.
11. Adapted from Peter S. Beagle, *The Last Unicorn* (New York: Ballantine Books, 1968), pp. 176–177. The poem was adapted by this woman by reversing all the masculine and feminine gender words.
12. Stephen Crane, "The Heart," in *Modern American Poetry, Modern British Poetry.* Louis Untermeyer, ed. (New York: Harcourt, Brace and Company, 1950), p. 153.
13. Rupert Brooke, "The Hill," ibid., p. 322.
14. D. H. Lawrence, "A Young Wife," ibid., p. 288.
15. Rupert Brooke, "The Busy Heart," ibid., p. 325.

### Chapter 6: The Ring of Power

1. Richard Wagner, *Die Walküre* (New York: G. Schermer, 1960), p. 28.
2. Richard Wagner, *Siegfried* (New York: G. Schermer, 1960), p. 38.
3. Richard Wagner, *Götterdämmerung* (New York: G. Schermer, 1960), p. 13.
4. Ibid., p. 22.
5. Ibid., p. 23.
6. Richard Wagner, *Twilight of the Gods* (London: John Calder Publishers, 1985), pp. 123, 124.

## Chapter 7: Into the Clearing

1. Wendell Berry, *Standing by Words* (San Francisco: Northpoint Press, 1983), p. 205.
2. Ernest Hemingway, *The Snows of Kilimanjaro* (New York: Scribner, 1961), p. 11.
3. Ibid., p. 8.
4. Ibid., p. 27.
5. Ibid., p. 3.
6. Denise Levertov, "An Embroidery," in *News of the Universe: Poems of Twofold Consciousness* (San Francisco: Sierra Club Books, 1980), pp. 148–149.

## Chapter 8: The Missing Bridegroom and the Woman in Black

1. See Sylvia Brinton Perera's insightful and detailed analysis in *Descent to the Goddess: A Way of Initiation for Women* (Toronto: Inner City Books, 1981).
2. Wim Wenders, Sam Shepard, *Paris, Texas* (Berlin: Road Movies/ Greno, 1984), pp. 84–85.
3. Ibid., p. 87.
4. Ibid., p. 95.
5. Ibid., p. 97.
6. Wim Wenders in *Film Quarterly*, Winter 1984–1985, p. 5.
7. Rilke, *Letters to a Young Poet*, p. 59.
8. Ibid., p. 65.

## Chapter 9: Beauty and the Beast

1. Andrew Lang, ed., *The Blue Fairy Book* (New York: Dover Publications, 1965), p. 108.
2. Ibid., p. 109.
3. Ibid., p. 114.
4. Ibid., p. 115.
5. Ibid., p. 118.
6. Ibid.
7. Rilke, *Letters to a Young Poet*, p. 54.

8. Keith Thompson, "What Men Really Want: A New Age Interview with Robert Bly," in *New Age,* May 1982, p. 30ff.

9. Rainer Maria Rilke, *Duino Elegies,* trans. J. B. Leishman and Stephen Spender (New York: W. W. Norton & Co., 1963), pp. 66–69.

10. Ibid., p. 69.

11. Rainer Maria Rilke, "The Panther," in *Selected Poems of Rainer Maria Rilke,* trans. Robert Bly (New York: Harper & Row, 1981), p. 139.

12. Francis Thompson, "The Hound of Heaven," in *Collins Albatross Book of Verse,* ed. Louis Untermeyer (London: William Collins Sons and Co., 1968), pp. 492–493.

*Chapter 10: The Divine Wedding*

1. C. G. Jung, *The Psychology of the Transference* (Princeton, N.J.: Princeton University Press, 1971), p. 34.

2. E. O. James, *Marriage and Society* (London: Hutchinson's University Library, 1952), pp. 67, 68, 109, 110.

3. Jung, *The Psychology of the Transference,* pp. 82–83.

4. Martin Heidegger, *Poetry, Language, Thought* (New York: Harper & Row, 1971), pp. 96–97.

5. Wendell Berry, *Standing by Words,* p. 205.

*Chapter 11: The Veil*

1. Rainer Maria Rilke, *The Notebooks of Malte Laurids Brigge,* trans. M. D. Herter Norton (New York: W. W. Norton, 1964), pp. 14–15.

2. Ibid., p. 18.

3. Ibid., pp. 26–27.

4. Ibid., p. 51.

5. Ibid., pp. 61–66.

6. Ibid., pp. 61–62.

7. Rainer Maria Rilke, *Selected Letters,* trans. R. F. C. Hull (London: MacMillan & Co., 1946), pp. 156–158.

8. *The Notebooks of Malte Laurids Brigge,* p. 68.

9. Ibid., p. 208.

10. Ibid., p. 209.

11. Rilke, *Selected Letters*, pp. 265–266.
12. *The Notebooks of Malte Laurids Brigge*, pp. 214–215.
13. Rilke, *Selected Letters*, p. 264.
14. Ibid., pp. 184–185.
15. Rainer Maria Rilke, *Requiem, and Other Poems*, trans. J. B. Leishman (London: Hogarth Press, 1957), p. 140.
16. Ibid., p. 141.
17. *The Notebooks of Malte Laurids Brigge*, p. 7.
18. Quoted in Eudo C. Mason, *Rilke* (London: Oliver and Boyd, 1963), p. 72.
19. C. G. Jung, *Symbols of Transformation* (New York: Harper Torchbooks, 1962), pp. 292–293.
20. Rilke, *Selected Letters*, p. 264.
21. Jeláluddin Rumi, *The Ruins of the Heart*, trans. Edmund Helminski (Putney, Vt.: Threshold Books, 1981), p. 25.

*Chapter 12: The Vow*

1. Rainer Maria Rilke, *Duino Elegies*, p. 21.
2. Ibid., pp. 129–130. The angel of the Elegies is not to be confused with the angel of Christianity. Rilke clarifies the meaning of the angel in a letter to his Polish translator, Witold von Hulewicz, as follows: "The Angel of the Elegies is the creature in whom the transformation of the visible into the invisible we are performing already appears complete. . . . The Angel of the Elegies is the being who vouches for the recognition of a higher degree of reality in the invisible.—Therefore "terrible" to us, because we, its lovers and transformers, still depend on the visible.
3. Ibid.
4. Ibid., p. 23.
5. Ibid., pp. 31, 33.
6. Ibid., p. 33.
7. Ibid., p. 23.
8. Ibid.
9. Ibid., pp. 23, 25.
10. Marie Louise von Franz, "The Process of Individuation," in *Man and His Symbols* (New York: Dell Publishing Co., 1971), p. 169.
11. *Duino Elegies*, p. 25.
12. Ibid., p. 79.

13. Ibid., p. 69.
14. Ibid.
15. Ibid., p. 71.
16. Ibid., p. 73.
17. Ibid., p. 35.
18. Ibid.
19. Rilke, *Letters to a Young Poet*, p. 37.
20. *Duino Elegies*, p. 41.
21. Ibid., p. 53.
22. Ibid., p. 61.
23. Ibid., p. 63.
24. Ibid., pp. 63, 65.
25. Ibid., p. 73.
26. Ibid.
27. Ibid., p. 75.
28. Ibid., p. 77.
29. Rainer Maria Rilke, *Letters (1910–26)*, trans. Jane Bannard Greene and M. D. Herter Norton (New York: W. W. Norton and Co., 1969), p. 382.
30. *Duino Elegies*, p. 77.
31. Eric Neumann, *Art and the Creative Unconscious* (New York: Bollingen Series, 1959), pp. 175–177.
32. *Letters (1910–26)*, p. 373.
33. *Duino Elegies*, p. 79.
34. Ibid., p. 83.
35. Ibid., p. 85.
36. Ibid.
37. *Letters (1910–26)*, p. 290. Having endured many periods of emptiness when poetic inspiration was lacking, Rilke was finally graced with the sudden inspiration through which the *Duino Elegies* was completed. According to Rilke, the *Elegies* came "All in a few days, it was a nameless storm, a hurricane in the spirit (like that time in Duino), all that was fibre in me and fabric cracked,—eating was not to be thought of, God knows who fed me." And along with the *Elegies* came, as a complete surprise, another cycle of poems, the *Sonnets to Orpheus*, fifty-five in number, jubilant in mood—indeed, songs of praise.

*Chapter 13: The Ring of Love*

1. C. G. Jung, *Psychological Reflections* (Princeton, N.J.: Princeton University Press, 1973), p. 99.
2. Rilke, *Letters to a Young Poet,* pp. 67–68.
3. Rilke, *Letters (1910–26),* p. 376.
4. Ibid., p. 330.
5. *Letters to a Young Poet,* pp. 29–30.
6. Marc Chagall, *Chagall by Chagall* (New York: Harrison House, 1982), p. 195.
7. Philip Rawson and Laszlo Legeza, *Tao: The Eastern Philosophy of Time and Change* (London: Thames & Hudson, 1973), p. 11.
8. *Chagall by Chagall,* p. 189.

# CREDITS

The author thanks the following publishers for permission to reprint material copyrighted or controlled by them: Beacon Press for permission to quote Poem 44 from *The Kabir Book: Forty-four of the Ecstatic Poems of Kabir,* versions by Robert Bly, © 1971, 1977 by Robert Bly, © 1977 by The Seventies Press; Dodd, Mead & Company, Inc., for permission to quote "The Hill" and "The Busy Heart" from *The Collected Works of Rupert Brooke,* © 1915 by Dodd, Mead & Company, copyright renewed 1943 by Edward Marsh; E. P. Dutton, Inc., for permission to quote from *The Ring of the Nibelung* by Richard Wagner, translated by Stewart Robb, © 1960 by Stewart Robb; Harper & Row, Publishers, Inc., for permission to quote from *Selected Poems of Rainer Maria Rilke:* A Translation from the German and Commentary by Robert Bly, © 1981 by Robert Bly, and for permission to quote "The Moon and the Yew Tree" from *The Collected Poems of Sylvia Plath* edited by Ted Hughes, © 1963 by Ted Hughes; New Directions Publishing, Inc., for permission to quote from *Relearning the Alphabet* by Denise Levertov, © 1967 by Denise Levertov Goodman, first published in *The Partisan Review,* 1967, and by Black Sparrow Press, 1969, and for permission to quote from "Requiem" in *Possibility of Being* by Rainer Maria Rilke, translated by J. B. Leishman, © 1957, 1977 by New Directions Publishing, Inc.; W. W. Norton & Company, Inc., for permission to quote from *Duino Elegies* by Rainer Maria Rilke, translated by J. B. Leishman and Stephen Spender, © 1939 by W. W. Norton & Company, Inc., copyright renewed 1967 by Stephen Spender and J. B. Leishman, and for permission to quote from *Letters to a Young Poet* by Rainer Maria Rilke, translated by M. D. Herter Norton, © 1934 by W. W. Norton & Company, Inc., copyright renewed 1962 by M. D. Herter Norton, revised edition © 1954 by W. W. Norton & Company, Inc., and for permission to quote from *The Notebooks of Malte Laurids Brigge* by Rainer Maria Rilke, translated by M. D. Herter Norton, © 1949 by W. W. Norton & Company, Inc., copyright renewed 1977 by M. D. Herter Norton, and for permission to quote from *Sonnets to Orpheus* by Rainer Maria Rilke, translated by M. D. Herter Norton, © 1942 by W. W. Norton & Company, Inc., copyright renewed 1970 by M. D. Herter Norton; David Pountney for permission to quote from his translation of *The Flying Dutchman* by Richard Wagner; Threshold Books for permission to quote from *Open Secret* by Jelaluddin Rumi, translated by John Mayne, © 1984, and for permission to quote from *The Ruins of the Heart* by Jelaluddin Rumi, translated by Edmund Helminski, © 1981; the University Press of Virginia for permission to quote from Volume X of the University of Virginia Edition of *The Works of Stephen Crane,* edited by Fredson Bowers, © 1975 by the Rector & Visitors of the University of Virginia; Viking Penguin for the permission to quote from *The Last Unicorn* by Peter S. Beagle, © 1968 by Peter S. Beagle; and Viking Penguin, Laurence Pollinger Ltd., and the Estate of Mrs. Frieda Lawrence Ravagli for permission to quote "A Young Wife" from *The Complete Poems* by D. H. Lawrence, © 1971. Thanks also to M. Mercedes Girón-Cerna for permission to print the unpublished poem "Dracula" on page 75.